Photoshop 6
Primer

ISBN 0-13-027018-0

90000

9 780130 270184

Photoshop 6
Primer

JASON I. MILETSKY

Prentice Hall PTR
Upper Saddle River, NJ 07458
www.phptr.com

Library of Congress Cataoging-in-Publication Data

Miletsky, Jason I.
    Photoshop 6 primer / Jason Miletsky.
        p. cm.
    Includes index.
    ISBN 0-13-027018-0
        1. Computer graphics. 2. Adobe Photoshop. I. Title.

    T385 .M5356 2001
    006.6'869--dc21   2001033847

Production Editor: Nick Radhuber
Acquisitions Editor: Tim Moore
Technical Reviewer: Craig Little
Editorial Assistant: Allyson Kloss
Marketing Manager: Debby vanDijk
Manufacturing Manager: Alexis R. Heydt
Buyer: Maura Zaldivar
Cover Designer: Anthony Gemmellaro
Cover Design Direction: Jerry Votta
Art Director: Gail Cocker-Bogusz
Composition: Ronnie Bucci

© 2002 Prentice Hall PTR
Prentice-Hall, Inc.
Upper Saddle River, NJ 07458

The publisher offers discounts on this book when ordered in bulk quantities. For more information contact: Corporate Sales Department, Prentice Hall PTR, One Lake Street, Upper Saddle River, NJ 07458. Phone: 800-382-3419; Fax: 201-236-7141; E-mail: corpsales@prenhall.com

Printed in the United States of America

10 9 8 7 6 5 4 3 2 1

ISBN 0-13-027018-0

Pearson Education LTD.
Pearson Education Australia PTY, Limited
Pearson Education Singapore, Pte. Ltd.
Pearson Education North Asia Ltd.
Pearson Education Canada, Ltd.
Pearson Educación de Mexico, S.A. de C.V.
Pearson Education--Japan
Pearson Education Malaysia, Pte. Ltd.
Pearson Education, Upper Saddle River, New Jersey

Dedicated to

Jackie Kajzer

One of the best people to come into my life in a long, long time.

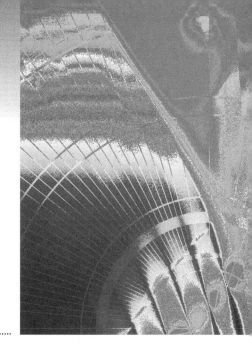

CONTENTS

CHAPTER 2

CHAPTER 3

CHAPTER 6

COLOR CORRECTION AND IMAGE ENHANCEMENT . . .197

CHAPTER 7

CHAPTER 8

AUTOMATION, FILTERS AND ADVANCED IMAGERY . .287

APPENDIX A

ACKNOWLEDGMENTS

As usual, I never want to forget the people who helped me get this book written.

First, all the guys down at Prentice Hall. Tim and Jim, Nick, and the girl who copy-edited my stuff who I never met but who did a damn good job, Allyson, the salespeople (I don't know them, but they were still a part of it!), and everyone else who was part of the mix.

My parents, as always, not because I'm supposed to thank them, but because I want and need to thank them.

I've also got to thank Rob, Dean, and Bobby Vitalo, who got me started on Photoshop to begin with, so many years ago. And on that note, to Henry VanderPlaat, who gave me my first real job to work on.

My friends, as always—finding friends who don't give up on you even when you're too busy to spend time with them is not very easy. I've been lucky that way. Jackie (the best DJ ever!), Chris and Ida (even though you moved off to Geneva, I don't consider that abandonment), Chris Senft (who should have given up on me considering how often I cancel plans), Jason Violetti, Lydia, Tara, Vineeth, and Shireen and Julia. Thank you.

Everyone at my office deserves a huge amount of thanks, especially Dennis and Deirdre, who have been awesome partners, and have made the struggle that much more fun!

I'd like to thank whoever was the original poet of the Nibelungenlied, an awesome German epic that is way better than either the Iliad or the Odyssey. It's the book that I escaped to night after night when I couldn't take graphic design anymore.

And, finally, I want to thank Lisa. It's hard to believe that it's been almost eight years already. Eight years, and I still think about you every day.

PREFACE

GOING OVERBOARD

I distinctly remember the week when I realized that I had been spending way too much time working in Photoshop. It started one particularly early morning, around 5:00 a.m. I usually never wake up that early—I'm much more of a nighttime kinda guy—but I think I had a meeting or something so I had to be at the office earlier than usual. So, still half asleep, I drag myself out of bed and stumble into the bathroom, banging into a few walls on my way. I remember standing in front of my mirror to brush my teeth, and being confused for a second as I looked around my countertop. Where had I put that Magic Wand, so I could make a selection of my teeth? And then how would I be able to access the Level command so that I could make them whiter? Oh, right. This is the *real* world, not Photoshop. And in the real world, we use brushes and toothpaste to whiten our teeth, not selection tools and color adjustment devices.

Twenty minutes later, when I cut myself shaving and immediately looked up and to my left to see if I could find the Undo command, I knew that I needed a break from designing.

That break never came, of course. I could have forced myself to take one, I suppose, but I really didn't want to. Photoshop is just one of those programs that is too much fun to play with to ever really put away. Unlike your average Sega game that you eventually conquer, pass on to a friend, or just toss in a closet, Photoshop never gets boring. It turns work time into playtime, and makes hours fly by faster than Ben Johnson before the drug test. And the best part about it is that for as much fun as it is, and as much of a game as it can be to try to figure out the best way to do certain things…you can never really win. Any piece that you do can always be improved, any amount of talent can always be heightened. Photoshop gives the design world—print, Web, CD interface, etc.—to you, and say "do what you can." It's your job to figure out what to do with it.

It's my job to help show you how to get it done.

WHO SHOULD READ THIS BOOK

Considering I earn a commission on each book sold, my natural belief is that this book should be read by *everybody*. Twice. We should have missionaries wandering to the most remote parts of the jungles, teaching even the gorillas the principals of good Photoshop technique. And each one should buy a book.

That's the way the world works in my personal fantasy land (the same land where I win the Pulitzer for my outstanding work in *Photoshop 6 Primer*—but that's another fantasy altogether). In the real world, not everyone needs to read this book. And not everyone *should* read this book. Basically, this book is for you if you fall into one of the following categories:

- Your Photoshop ability falls somewhere between "basic working knowledge of" and "strong control over" the program
- You've been using Photoshop mostly for color correction and need or want to know what else it does
- You've been working with an older version of Photoshop, and need to see what's going on in this latest version

If you fall into one of those categories, then this book is for you. I tried to start each chapter with some basic info to get beginning users up to speed quickly, and enough advanced information to ensure that experienced users learn new things as well.

HOW THIS BOOK HAS BEEN WRITTEN

For everything that this book is, it is certainly not the "everything you never really wanted to know about Photoshop" book that you might expect. Instead, it's a clear, to-the-point text that that doesn't bother with the boring stuff that you don't really need to know. For example, the section about file types gives you what you need to choose a proper file type for your images, but stops short of explaining how a JPEG image is built or how color palettes are indexed. I know you want to get into the creation process as quickly as possible, so aside from my witty interjections, most of the fluff, or "fat" if you will, has been trimmed out.

It is not necessary for you to read this book in a linear fashion—in fact, I'd recommend jumping around from section to section. If possible, try to read this book at your computer. There are a lot of follow-along examples for each topic, and practicing while you read is the best way to learn.

Throughout each chapter, you'll be confronted with a few symbols to help you better understand what you're reading. The symbols are—

Note icon gives a more detailed explanation of the topic.

The Warning icon tells you when there is a potential for a problem. You'll see very few of these—in my opinion, as long as you end up in your bed at the end of the day, there are a few problems worth stressing about.

The Tip icon provides additional information of the topic.

Another thing that you may notice as you read is that most all references, including screen shots, are taken off the Macintosh version of Photoshop. When I give an example and include a keyboard command, the command configuration will be for Macintosh, and the equivalent Windows command will follow in parentheses.

WHAT YOU WILL NEED

In Web Photoshop 5 To Go, I recommended having at least 32 megs of RAM in your computer. Good luck with that.

Photoshop 6 has pushed the term "RAM hog" to new heights. Because of some of the additions and changes, you'll need far more than 32 megs to get anywhere with this program. On my Mac, I allocate 80 megs just to Photoshop alone, and sometimes that wasn't enough.

I recommend you have at least 128 megs installed and either a G3 or Pentium II system at the very least. I'm not going to tell you whether to use a Mac or a PC. I'm not that suicidal, and I've written this book for fans of both.

Of course, you should also have a copy of Photoshop 6 lying around, but it's not crucial. You can read this book on a plane or in a waiting room and still get a lot out of it. But, because of some of the radical changes that were made in version 6.0, you probably won't do too well if you are still working on version 5.5, so go and get the upgrade.

You also need a browser. I'd recommend IE 4.0 or higher, but for the purposes of this book any browser will be fine.

CONTACTING ME

I am an everyday person, and although proper etiquette and political correctness mandates that I say something like, "I really look forward to all of you contacting me, and I've been simply overjoyed with all the people who called me and sent me letters from my last books," I can't say that with a straight face. The truth is, I don't mind when someone contacts me—it's kind of cool, especially when I get a letter telling me how much you've learned from my books. That's awesome. Even if you write to tell me that you didn't like my books, and you make your case for why you didn't like it, that's cool too. And I'll always respond. So if you have any questions, or comments, or want to show me some of the work that you've done using some of the techniques that I've written, then please, contact away! My e-mail address is jmiletsky@pfsmarketwyse.com.

However, that is not an open invitation to contact me regularly (like the guy in Canada who called here once a week for months at a time), or to write in telling me about the typo on page 92. And it's definitely, definitely, definitely not an invitation for anyone to come up to me in an airport, invade the "stranger space" (what I typically refer to as the two-foot radius of space around me that strangers should keep outside of), and feel that because I've written Photoshop books, I must want nothing more than to talk about graphic design and stuff during the five-hour trip from Newark to Paris. I don't care if your son *did* get a lot out of my book, sir, I just want to sleep.

Ah, fame. Tiger and I have often been caught talking about the price of it.

Lastly, it's time for me to make my standard plea, which has become a tradition in my books: my printed serenade to Katie Couric. To recap recent history (I've also recapped this in *Web Photoshop 6 Primer*), my very first book had a brief mention of how I had an "enormous crush" on said newscaster. To which she replied, "get in line," when a friend of a friend had her sign my book.

But it hasn't deterred me. So, Katie, if you're reading this book (and why wouldn't you be? There's nothing like a good passage about Layer Masking to put you to sleep at night), I'm a nice, cute, single guy (who's really not obsessed or insane—I'm just having fun writing). But if it's not meant to be, then I guess I'll have no choice but to take extreme measures: give up on you completely, and pursue my other enormous crush, Linda Carter.

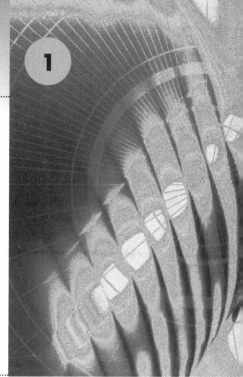

chapter 1

AND SO IT BEGINS

One of the best things about working with Photoshop on a day-to-day basis is that it makes work fun. This is not accounting, folks (no offense to the CPAs in the audience), this is graphic design—the new art, so to speak. And nothing but your imagination (and lack of RAM) can hold you back. So stop thinking of this as work—this is all fun!

Well, actually the *real* fun doesn't start until next chapter. This one is a bit dull.

But that's okay—it can't all be a trip to Disney World. Everything that's worth doing is worth spending some time to learn about first. And to really understand what you'll be doing on this graphic adventure, there are a few basics that you should understand. So here's the deal: You try to get through this chapter, and I'll try to keep it as short and to the point as possible.

WHAT IS PHOTOSHOP, ANYWAY?

In short, Photoshop is the industry's most powerful and widely used image-editing program. Adobe, dubbed the Microsoft of graphic design, has developed this program and, watched as it literally transformed the entire design industry while traditional mechanical artists watched with gaping mouths as their jobs were given to 17-year-old computer prodigies.

On a bit more technical level, Photoshop is a bitmap program. This means that images are created out of a series of pixels. Each pixel, or small square, contains a color, and, when viewed at a normal, 1:1 aspect ratio (100% or less), these colored squares combine to create a continuous-tone image, or photograph.

The benefit of working with a bitmap program like Photoshop is that you can preserve integrity and realism of colors and objects. However, as you increase the physical size or magnification of an image, the picture begins to pixelate. Figure 1–1 shows an image with the magnification increased to 400%. As you can see, each of the pixels in the image is quite clear, and the image itself is blurred.

This is in contrast to using a vector program, such as Adobe Illustrator. Vector programs use a complex mathematical formula to create images, instead of using pixels. Because of this, the image will look clear as a bell, regardless of the size or magnification, as shown in Figure 1–2. Although size may not be an issue to a vector program, realism is. Continuous tone photography is not really an option, and much of the work done in these programs tends to be either cartoonish or illustrative (hence the name, *Illustrator*).

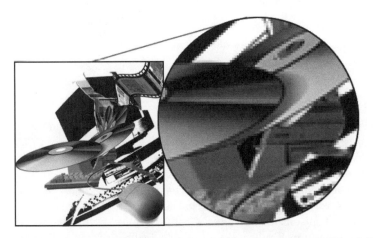

Figure 1–1: The image on the left is clear, whereas the magnification of 400% on the right is pixilated.

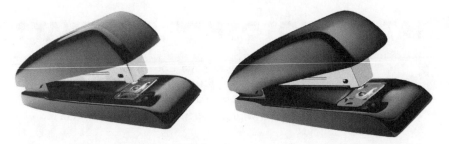

Figure 1–2: Unlike the bitmap Photoshop image that we saw in the previous figure, this image created in Illustrator won't lose any resolution, regardless of how much we magnify it.

Photoshop 6, however, has started the migration of vector images into its traditional bitmap territory. Although Photoshop is still far from being confused with Illustrator, Photoshop does allow for vector shapes and text, which helps in more interesting manipulations.

WHEN TO USE PHOTOSHOP

Knowing when to use Photoshop is an important part of graphic design. Especially if you are working at a company where neither time nor quality can be compromised, you don't want to find yourself developing content in one program, when it could be done quicker and better in another program. Table 1–1 lists a comparison of when to use Photoshop.

Table 1–1: When To and When Not To Use Photoshop

When To Use Photoshop	When Not To Use Photoshop
You need to manipulate color or fix problems in a scanned photograph.	Your need calls for you to create a cartoonish image that utilizes mostly flat colors.
You want your custom-created image to have a photographic realism.	The images you intend to create are detailed line drawings, such as technical plans of complex machinery.
You intend to use, create or manipulate a lot of shadows and highlights in your imagery.	You are laying pages and pages of copy (layout programs such as QuarkXPress are best for this).
You want to take advantage of lighting effects and multiple other filters, discussed in Chapter 7.	You want to accomplish cool text effects such as following text along a path, which Photoshop can't do.
You just don't like illustrations very much.	You plan to create diagrams, charts or other such information-related graphics.
You really want to buy this book, but would like a legit reason to expense it.	Your images will be crisp, sharp logos.

Of course, that's not to suggest that any one program needs to be used to accomplish a given project. Often, you'll need to use a combination of programs to achieve your ultimate creative goal. The three programs that I require designers at my agency, PFS New Media, to be proficient in are Photoshop, Illustrator, and QuarkXPress. (The new Adobe product, InDesign, is supposed to be the big "Quark killer," but I haven't heard or seen much of it yet, so the verdict is still out.)

By using a combination of those three programs, I know that we can accomplish a print-related project that our clients call for. Obviously, there is little or no need for that specific combination to be used when creating graphics for Web, video or multimedia, but those are the big three that most design firms will insist that you know.

WHAT'S NEW IN THIS VERSION?

At first glance, the changes may seem a bit radical, but many of the changes are just aesthetic window dressing. In fact, without sounding like a grouch, many of the changes that have been between 5.5 and 6.0 really aren't all that great.

How much you'll really need to learn will depend on which version you were previously using. Many of you will be coming from 5.5, so the change will be startling, but nothing too radical. But many other readers will be coming from 5.0, having skipped 5.5 altogether (even though it wasn't a full upgrade, it had a lot of changes in it), so the new features in 6.0 could be overwhelming.

Because there is a pretty radical difference between 5.0 and 6.0, I'll start by reviewing the upgrades that were made in 5.5, then discuss the new improvements and changes from 5.5 to 6.0. The rest of this book, however, will use the Photoshop 6.0 interface in any screen shots. Color Figure 1 provides you with an illustrated example of some of the more important upgrades to Photoshop 6.0.

The Upgrade from 5.0 to 5.5

If your only reason for using Photoshop is to create images for print, very few of the changes in the 5.5 upgrade will interest you. Nearly all of the changes in this version are Web-related, as Adobe aptly responded to Web master requests that the Photoshop become a more Web-friendly program. However, although the Web improvements are abundant and superexciting, there are few features than non-Web users will appreciate, as well. The following reviews all of the major improvements and additions:

The ImageReady Addition

Photoshop's ImageReady, a specifically Web-based program, now comes bundled with the Photoshop software. The nearly identical (to Photoshop) interface and crowd of great features make ImageReady an easy-to-use "no brainer" for Web professionals. Plus, the new Jump button at the bottom of the Photoshop toolbar makes working between the two programs a seamless process (watch out— shameless plug coming); you might want to pick up my other book, *Web Photoshop 5 Primer*.

Easier Optimization

Not only does Photoshop 5.5 make optimizing your JPEG and GIF files more convenient, but with true brilliance they did in it an incredible new dialog box. The Save for Web dialog box lets you compare and contrast the image quality, file sizes and download times of your original image against up to three previews of that image with customized settings. This should be a huge time saver, but it's so much fun to play with that you might end up spending more hours than you planned!

New Masking Tools

Photoshop designers always get giddy about new masking tools, but these are especially worth the hype. The two new Eraser Tools and the Extract function make creating transparencies so easy that the GIF 89a format has become obsolete.

Enhanced Color Picker

Finally, getting both a hexadecimal value and a Web-safe color are convenient and easy in the new Color Picker.

Better Text Features

Nothing earth-shattering here, but the improvements are good enough to make text easier to work with.

History…Monet Style

Eh. I'm not too excited about this, but if you're into water color paintings, you might like this feature.

Picture Package

Photographers and grandparents will appreciate this one. With just the click on a few buttons, Photoshop will lay out one image in various sizes on an 8.5" x 11" page. If you have a quality color printer, go nuts printing endless pages of you, your family, the goldfish, in 5" x 7", 4" x 6" and wallet size.

The Upgrade from 5.5 to 6.0

Well, this is a whole different ball game now. On first glance, Photoshop 6.0 looks and acts differently than it ever has before. In a way, Adobe's star product is beginning to integrate certain qualities from Illustrator and ImageReady, making me wonder how much longer before it just becomes one, really large, all-encompassing program? When you start using it for a while, though, you realize that the changes are really awesome, but, except for a few distinct areas, not terribly dramatic.

But this newest version is not without its faults. I have more than a slight concern that the saturation point is being reached, and we'll soon be in an area of overkill. The Liquify dialog box, for example, is cute and a lot of fun, and may by itself be worth the upgrade purchase price just to tool around with, but I'm not too sure it has an real practical value. It almost like watching a great TV show that, after years of success, feels the need to add an adorable 4-year-old to the cast—a sure indication that a downward slope is inevitable. This new version is also a complete RAM hog and forces even the hobbyists to go out and purchase state-of-the-art computers, or at least increase their current stock of RAM to get any use out of the program. Plus, it doesn't work for any Macintosh version below 8.5 or with any version of Windows older than Windows 98. Although I

believe that there is always room for improvement, there is also a train of thought that
if it ain't broke, don't fix it. I like this upgrade, but, based on what I see here, I worry
about what future upgrades will do to a once and still great design program.

The following are just some of the major changes, or at least the more interesting
ones, made to Photoshop in the new 6.0 version. Other new features will be more
prevalent throughout the rest of the book.

The Options Palette

Although this might not be the most important upgrade, it's probably the most
immediately visible. The Options Palette, which used to look like any other
palette in Photoshop, now has a different layout, expanding across the width of
the monitor. In addition, some of the tools have new options included in their
respective palettes.

The Layers Palette

The Layers Palette has made some dramatic changes—and all for the better. Some
of the changes are fairly modest—Layer Effects are now where they belong, conveniently at the bottom of the Layers Palette, along with the Adjustment Layers.
Both also have far more options than they ever did before. More significantly, you
can now lock Layers from being edited or moved and preserve the image, as well
as the transparent portions of a Layer. Probably best of all, you can easily organize
Layers in sets, making life for designers such as me (who use an inordinate amount
of Layers in practically any image) far, far easier.

The Text Editor

The Text Editor as you knew it is gone. Hitting its peak in version 5.5, the new
Type Tool in 6.0 is a step in the wrong direction. The cumbersome Editor may be
gone in favor of placing copy directly onto a canvas, but this new method brings
with it more problems than it's worth. Options are spread out over three separate
palettes, placing new copy sometimes interferes with editing old copy and the very
usage of the new tool goes against the grain of what seasoned Photoshop users
have gotten used to. The only small plus is the ability to create wild text effects
that you couldn't do outside of Illustrator before this version.

Liquify

Okay, this is probably not really one of the most *important* new features, but it's
surely the most fun! This is the one that will make you sit down to play with
Photoshop, look up at the clock and suddenly notice that 3 hours have passed!
Liquify makes your image a little less solid, allowing you full control of contor-
tions, distortions and just all-out craziness. Unfortunately, once you've had your
fun with it, you come to realize that it holds very little practical value and it's one
of the reasons why you suddenly need about a million megs of RAM to keep

Photoshop open for more than 5 minutes. Besides, Liquify doesn't do anything that Kai's Power Goo didn't do better over 3 years ago, and with a killer interface.

The Slice and Slice Selection Tools

An addition to Photoshop that could be predicted since day one of version 5.5, the Slice and Slice Selection Tools have migrated over to Photoshop. It's not bad to have these tools in Photoshop, too, I guess, but for Web designers, slicing an image is really best done in ImageReady anyway.

Other New Tools

Other tools make their debut in version 6.0, including (finally) an easy way to make polygons and fill shapes in with color upon creation, and two useful "notes" tools to leave notes in certain places, either for yourself, or as instructions for someone else who may be working on the same piece at another time.

Saving Files

The Save a Copy command is gone as a stand-alone option in the File menu. It's now incorporated into the Save As dialog box, along with some other interesting changes.

Easier Color Management

This is about as easy at it ever has been, because setting color profiles within Photoshop now practically holds your hand in deciding how to set up your profile and when to include the profile in with a saved file.

Increased User-Friendliness

Photoshop seems to have recognized how difficult the program can be and that too many "designers" never actually get past the color correction functionalities. Although it's not "in your face," the program has provided small descriptions here and there for tools, dialog boxes, and select other things that designers typically have trouble understanding, to make life just a little bit easier.

There are certainly plenty of other upgrades that we'll review in more detail at the appropriate time.

SETTING UP PHOTOSHOP BEFORE WORK BEGINS

There are many steps that you can take before you even open an image that will make your time in Photoshop a more pleasant and efficient one.

Calibrating Your Monitor

As a professional designer and a teacher of students, I am *supposed* to tell you that calibrating your monitor is vastly important and shouldn't be overlooked.

That's what I'm supposed to say. My own truth, though, is that calibrating your monitor isn't that big a deal. True, calibrating your monitor might improve the colors a bit on screen, but because of the differences between how monitors and computers present graphics, you'll never rely on the monitor version, anyway. The best you can do is get to know the differences as best you can to anticipate any changes when the image goes to print.

On the flip side, calibrating is pretty easy and rather quick, so if it will put your mind at ease, it can't hurt to do it. At worst, it will be a waste of a few minutes and, at best it could help reduce the color gap a bit between monitor and paper.

Calibrating will bring your monitor closer to the printed page, but it will never be exact, so if your client likes what they see on-screen, be wary of promises you can't keep. Even if you're working in CMYK mode, you're still seeing those colors through an RGB monitor, and the colors will be different when they come off the press.

The best part about calibrating your monitor is that, since Photoshop 5.0, Adobe has made it easy. Gone are the days when we had to hold up a piece of paper to match paper white with monitor white. Now all you have to do is the following:

1. Leave your monitor off for at least a half an hour before you calibrate.

2. Turn off your desktop pattern and set the background color to a light shade of gray.

3. Set the lighting in the room to the lighting that you'll most often use when working.

4. Find the Photoshop 6 folder in your local drive and open it. Open the subfolder named *Goodies* and find a folder within it called *Adobe Photoshop Only*. Open this folder and, in the folder called *Calibration*, double-click on the item marked *Adobe Gamma.cpl*.

5. The dialog box that appears is shown in Figure 1–3. The first choice you'll have to make is which version of the calibration you want to run. Step by Step is essentially the same as Control Panel, but is generally easier and will walk you through each step of the process. Make your selection and press the Next button.

6. Follow the instructions on each screen and continue to click Next when through. Most instructions will be fairly straightforward, although there may be a few questions that could stump you. If you find yourself in a position in which you don't know the answer to a question, look in the manual that came with your monitor or call the manufacturer.

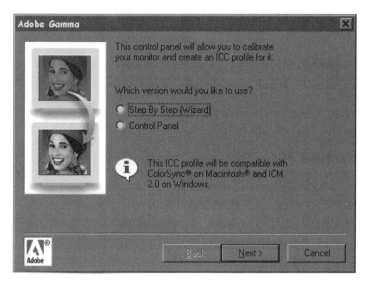

Figure 1–3: The opening dialog box for calibrating your monitor.

Establishing Color Space

Establishing color space is not glamorous, but if you intend to use Photoshop in conjunction with any other program, such as Quark XPress or Adobe Illustrator, or even on a different monitor, you really should do it. At the very least, establishing color space has never been easier than it is in Photoshop 6.0. Establishing color space will help to keep colors consistent, regardless of where you view them (this doesn't go for lessening the differentials between computer and paper—you still can't count on a monitor for accuracy. But it does count for cross-application and cross-platform color considerations).

Setting Up RGB Color Space Version 5.5

RGB has a very wide range of colors to choose from. However, the monitor that you're working on can't display all of the RGB colors—it can show only some of them. Photoshop allows you to work in larger RGB spaces that are beyond your monitor's color space, so that your images can utilize colors that may be able to be displayed on other monitors.

To manipulate the RGB color space:

1. Choose File -> Color Settings -> RGB Setup. Your monitor profile is displayed at the bottom of the dialog box, shown in Figure 1–4.

2. In the RGB pull-down menu, choose SMPTE-C from the list provided. This is generally considered to be the best option for images that will go to print, because it includes more of the CMYK color gamut that you'll work in for printing. The Gamma, White Point and Properties will change, depending on your chosen color space.

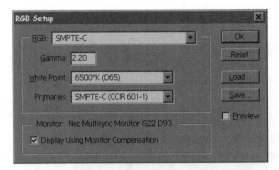

Figure 1–4: The RGB Setup dialog box.

 If you're going to be doing Internet-based work, like building a Web site, choose sRGB for for your color space, because it is used more widely as the default for many monitors, scanners and desktop printers.

3. Click the Display Using Monitor Compensation checkbox on. This will display the images in your selected RGB color space in real time.

4. Click OK when through.

Setting Up CMYK Color Space in Version 5.5

You'll set up the CMYK color space in Photoshop to establish the way that RGB images will convert to the CMYK color mode. This is especially important if you plan on doing most of your work in RGB to save RAM and hard disk space but will eventually convert to CMYK for printing and desire a close on-screen representation of what the printed image will look like.

Establishing the CMYK color space is similar to the way you established the RGB color space:

1. Choose File -> Color Settings -> CMYK Setup. You will access the dialog box shown in Figure 1–5.

2. The dialog box will let you determine your own choices for how inks, printers and paper combine to compose the final image. Unless you're really versed in color management, though, I would recommend using one of the pre-established ICC profiles instead. Do this by choosing ICC from the CMYK Model radio buttons.

3. Figure 1–6 shows the new dialog box, with significantly fewer options. From the Profile pull-down menu, make your selection based on which printer you will be using.

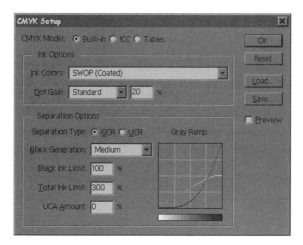

Figure 1–5: The CMYK Setup dialog box.

4. Choose Built-in from the Engine pull-down menu to access the ICC profile inter-
   preter that is native to Photoshop.

5. Select Perceptual (Images) from the Intent pull-down menu to maintain the way
   each color works together.

6. Make sure that the Black Point Compensation checkbox is checked to maintain
   equilibrium in neutral color value when converting from RGB to CMYK. Click
   OK when through.

Setting Up RGB and CMYK Color Space in Version 6.0

One of the nicest changes about the 6.0 upgrade is that establishing color space went
from complex and boring to really easy and…well, still boring. But at least it's really
easy! Figure 1–7 shows the new dialog box, which incorporates RGB and CMYK color

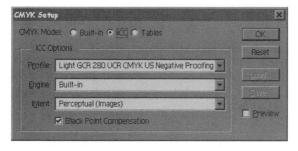

*Figure 1–6: The CMYK Setup dialog box condenses after you choose ICC for your desired
CMYK Model.*

in one area. Even better—roll over anything in the dialog box, and an explanation will pop up at the bottom of the dialog box to tell you what to do. It's so simple that you really don't need me to help out with much here, so, moving on....

Setting Up Scratch Disks

Because Photoshop needs so much in terms of memory, you're going to want to have as much RAM as you can loaded into your machine. This is especially true of Photoshop 6, which is a particularly heavy program. But what do you do when all of your RAM is used? You can "trick" Photoshop into thinking that you have more RAM than you actually do by setting up free disk space to act as RAM.

Choose Edit -> Preferences -> Scratch Disks. The dialog box will give you four drop-down menus to select an alternative source for memory. If you can, purchase an external 4- or 8-gig hard drive and hook this to your computer—don't use it to save information, use it for scratch disk purposes instead. This will help let you work faster and longer.

You'll need to close Photoshop and launch it again for the changes to take effect.

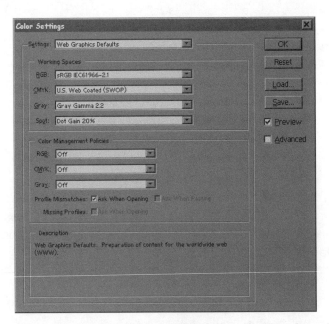

Figure 1–7: Setting up RGB and CMYK color space has changed in Photoshop 6.0.

Purge—What To Do If You Run Out of Memory Anyway

One of the more annoying roadblocks that you'll come across if you don't have enough RAM or scratch disk support is a pop-up message telling you that Photoshop is unable to process your last command because it is low on RAM. As much as it'll make your blood boil when that happens, don't go throwing your computer out the window just yet. You can always quit out of Photoshop and restart the program, which will also reset the RAM, or you can use the Purge feature.

Purging means that you will be erasing certain things from memory, thereby freeing up necessary RAM. You can access the Purge menu by selecting Edit -> Purge. Of all the available options, choosing Histories or All ("All" includes Undo, Clipboard, and Patterns) will free up the most amount of RAM.

 Be careful—once you choose to purge something, you can't undo it. Any information that you purge will be lost forever.

Typically, even if you choose to Purge All, it won't be super long before you'll run short on RAM again. So after purging, I would recommend that you use your newly freed memory to accomplish one or two more tasks, save your work, then quit out of Photoshop and restart it again.

Changing Tool Icons

By default, the icon for each of the tools that you'll work with will look like the tool itself. It's cute at first, but they'll almost always get in your way eventually (it's kind of hard to see what you're doing when there is this, too, in your way!).

To change them, choose Edit -> Preferences -> Display and Cursors. In the area marked Painting Cursors, select Brush Size (this will allow you to see an outline of the brush size you are painting with, which is really convenient). For the area marked Other Cursors, choose Precise to turn the cursors for nonpainting tools into small crosshairs.

Ditching the Mouse

A traditional mouse is fine for everyday computer use and maneuvering from program to program or using a word processor, etc. But Photoshop is a highly sophisticated art program. You'll be working with individual pixels in some instances—close detail in color, shadows, and other subtleties that make your work stand out. You need your fingers for that—not your wrist. The traditional mouse makes you use your wrist for movement. That's not too helpful.

Try buying an electronic tablet. I prefer the Wacom Stylus tablets—they're functional, smooth, and relatively inexpensive. When buying one, keep in mind that, although the larger tablets look more appealing, they take up a lot of desk space. Plus, they really don't hold any huge advantage over the smaller versions—in fact, I find the larger tablets more tiring, as my hand has further to travel to get to any one area.

Tablets can take a bit of getting used to, but believe me, they're worthwhile.

Believe It or Not...

Even though using a mouse or an electronic tablet is a necessary part of using Photoshop, the really surprising aspect of this art program is that it is highly keyboard-driven. The more keyboard shortcuts you know and memorize, the better you'll do. Table 1-2 includes a list of the most useful keyboard shortcuts that I use on an everyday basis. There are others, but not all of them are worth memorizing.

Table 1–2: Keyboard Shortcuts

Command	Macintosh Shortcut	Windows Shortcut
The Tool Bar		
Rectangular and Elliptical Marquee	M	M
Crop	C	C
Move	V	V
All Lasso Tools	L	L
Magic Wand	W	W
Airbrush	J	J
Paintbrush	B	B
History Brush	Y	Y
Rubber Stamp	S	S
All Eraser Tools	E	E
Pencil and Line	N	N
Blur, Smudge and Sharpen	R	R
Dodge, Burn and Sponge	O	O
All Pen Tools	P	P
Add Anchor Point	+	+
Delete Anchor Point	-	-
Arrow	A	A

(continued)

Table 1–2: (continued)

Command	Macintosh Shortcut	Windows Shortcut
All Type Tools	T	T
Measure	U	U
All Gradient Tools	G	G
All Eyedropper Tools	I	I
Paint Bucket	K	K
Hand	H	H
Zoom	Z	Z
To Scroll through Underlying Tools	Shift + [Letter]	Shift + [Letter]
Switch Foreground and Background Color	X	X
Revert to Black & White Foreground and Background	D	D
All Edit Modes	Q	Q
All Screen Modes	F	F
The Palettes		
Brushes Palette	F5	F5
Scroll Right through Brushes	]	]
Scroll Left through Brushes	[	[
Color Palette	F6	F6
Layers Palette	F7	F7
Info Palette	F8	F8
Actions Palette	F9	F9
Any Options Palette	Enter	Enter
Change Opacity (by tens)	1, 2, 3…0	1, 2, 3…0

(continued)

Table 1–2: (continued)

Command	Macintosh Shortcut	Windows Shortcut
Menu Commands		
New File	Cmd + N	Ctrl + N
Open File	Cmd + O	Ctrl + O
Open As	Not Available	Ctrl + Alt + O
Save	Cmd + S	Ctrl + S
Save As	Cmd + Shift + S	Ctrl + Shift + S
Save A Copy	Cmd + Option + S	Ctrl + Alt + S
Close File	Cmd + W	Ctrl + W
Quit	Cmd + Q	Ctrl + Q
Copy	Cmd + C	Ctrl + C
Cut	Cmd + X	Ctrl + X
Paste	Cmd + V	Ctrl + V
Paste Into	Cmd + Shift + V	Ctrl + Shift + V
Undo/Redo Last Command	Cmd + Z	Ctrl + Z
Delete	Delete	Backspace
Print	Cmd + P	Ctrl + P
Show or Hide Rulers	Cmd + R	Ctrl + R
Show or Hide Guides	Cmd + H	Ctrl + H
Nudge One Space	Arrow Keys	Arrow Keys
Nudge Ten Spaces	Shift + Arrow Keys	Shift + Arrow Keys
Free Transform	Cmd + T	Ctrl + T
Exit Transform	Esc Key	Esc Key
Preview in CMYK	Cmd + Y	Ctrl + Y
Color Manipulations		
Levels	Cmd + L	Ctrl + L
Curves	Cmd + M	Ctrl + M
Color Balance	Cmd + B	Ctrl + B
Hue/Saturation	Cmd + U	Ctrl + U
Desaturate	Cmd + Shift + U	Ctrl + Shift + U
Fill Selection or Layer with Foreground Color	Option + Delete	Alt + Backspace
Fill Selection or Layer with Background Color	Cmd + Delete	Ctrl + Backspace

(continued)

Table 1–2: (continued)

Command	Macintosh Shortcut	Windows Shortcut
Selections		
Select All	Cmd + A	Ctrl + A
Deselect All	Cmd + D	Ctrl + D
Hide/Show Edges (marching ants)	Cmd + H	Ctrl + H
Feather Selection	Cmd + Option + D	Ctrl + Alt + D
Reverse Selection	Cmd + Shift + I	Ctrl + Shift + I
Constrain Marquee to Square or Circle	Shift while Dragging	Shift while Dragging
Create Marquee From Center	Opt while Dragging	Alt while Dragging
Move Marquee while Creating It	Spacebar	Spacebar
Add to Selection	Shift	Shift
Subtract from Selection	Option	Alt
Intersect Selection	Shift + Option	Shift + Alt
Constrain Movement Horizontally/Vertically	Shift while Moving	Shift while Moving
Temporarily Access the Move Tool	Cmd	Ctrl
Clone Selection with Move Tool Active	Opt while Dragging	Alt while Dragging
Clone Selection with Any Other Tool Active	Cmd + Opt Drag	Ctrl + Alt while Dragging
Navigation		
Fit on Screen	Cmd + 0	Ctrl + 0
Zoom In	Cmd + Plus (+)	Ctrl + Plus (+)
Zoom Out	Cmd + Minus (-)	Ctrl + Minus (-)
Temporarily Access Hand Tool	Spacebar	Spacebar
Layers		
Create New Layer and Set Layer Options	Cmd + Shift + N	Ctrl + Shift + N
Create New Layer and Bypass Layer Options	Cmd + Opt + Shift + N	Ctrl + Alt + Shift + N
View Single Layers (Make Others Invisible)	Option + Click Eyeball	Ctrl + Click Eyeball
Move Up One Layer	Option +]	Alt +]
Move Down One Layer	Option + [	Alt + [
Move Directly to Top Layer	Option + Shift +]	Alt + Shift +]
Move Directly to Background Layer	Option + Shift + [	Alt + Shift + [
Move Layer Up One Level	Cmd +]	Ctrl +]
Move Layer Down One Level	Cmd + [	Ctrl +]
Move Layer Directly to Top	Cmd + Shift +]	Ctrl + Shift +]

(continued)

Table 1–2: (continued)

Command	Macintosh Shortcut	Windows Shortcut
Move Layer Directly to Bottom (Just over Background)	Cmd + Shift + [	Ctrl + Shift + [
Layer Via Copy	Cmd + J	Ctrl + J
Layer Via Cut	Cmd + Shift + J	Ctrl + Shift + J
Select Everything on Layer	Cmd + Click on Layer	Ctrl + Click on Layer
Go to Layer Containing Element	Cmd + Click on Element	Ctrl + Click on Element
Merge Layer with Underlying Layer	Cmd + E	Ctrl + E
Merge All Linked Layers	Cmd + E	Ctrl + E
Merge All Visible Layers	Cmd + Shift + E	Ctrl + Shift + E

A key guide to the toolbar is provided in Figure 1–8.

SOME RESOLUTIONS ARE WORTH KEEPING

I once heard a joke that made me laugh, and for the life of me, I can't remember where I heard it.

Question: What is Kai Kruise's New Year's resolution?
Answer: 300 pixels per inch.

If you understand that joke, this chapter is probably running a bit slow for you, and you can move on to the fun stuff. If you don't get it at all, then you haven't become a complete graphics nerd yet. There's still time to save yourself and choose another industry.

If you understood it and, like me, thought it was *really* funny, then all hope is lost. I'll be seeing you at the next support group meeting.

Anyway, having a clear understanding of image size and resolution is a vital part of ensuring the highest quality detail and color for your work. Because Photoshop is primarily a bitmap program, images are made up of pixels (as opposed to *vector* programs, like Illustrator, in which images are made up of mathematical formulas). The term *resolution* is a reference to the number of pixels that make up an image, usually measured in linear (straight) inches. Basically, the higher the resolution, the more pixels there are in an image. Higher resolutions are better for most print pieces, while lower resolutions are fine for digital projects, such as Web design and CD-ROM interface design.

Depending on the type of project you're working on, there are many different types of resolutions that you'll need to know:

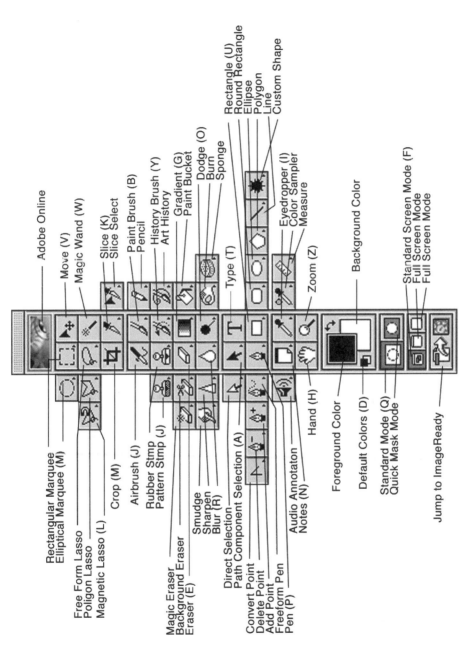

Figure 1–8: Key Guide: The Toolbar. The letters pointing to each tool are the keyboard shortcuts for simplified activation. Shift + letter will scroll through underlying tools.

◆ **Image Size:** The Image Size describes an image's physical size, such as 3" x 5", if you printed the image out on a piece of paper.

◆ **Pixels Per Inch (ppi):** Also referred to as the *image resolution*, this measures the number of ppi in your image. Pixels can be added to or subtracted from each inch of your image without changing the Image Size. For example, your 3" x 5" picture can have 72 ppi, or it can have 300 ppi. Because each pixel contains color information, there will be more detail and clarity in print work if you have more pixels within each inch. Figure 1–9 shows the difference between two versions of the same image, each set to a different resolution. Each version is displayed at 300%. Notice that, in the low-res version, there are so few pixels that it becomes blurry, or pixilated, when you zoom in on it.

Having more pixels means having a higher resolution, although the extra color detail will also increase the file size for your image. To understand why, take a look at how many pixels exist in a 1" x 1" image with different resolutions. At 72 ppi, there are 5,184 pixels (72 x 72). At 300 ppi, however, there are 90,000 pixels (300 x 300). This is a huge difference that not only explains why there is a difference in the amount of detail, but also why there is a difference in file size.

◆ **Dots Per Inch (dpi):** also known as monitor resolution, the dpi is the number of pixels or dots that appear per inch on a monitor. You can expect that a monitor displays 72 dpi. Therefore, if your image is 72 ppi, it will appear as its actual size when viewed at 100%—one monitor pixel for each image pixel.

Figure 1–10 shows two versions of the same image, as they might appear on a computer monitor. In each version, the image is 6" x 4" and displayed at 100%. However, the low-res version easily fits within the confines of the monitor screen, whereas the high-res version is so big that you can see only a portion of it on the monitor. Why is that?

Since the monitor can only display 72 ppi, the image on the left can fit comfortably in the monitor because at 100% view, it provides one image pixel for every monitor pixel. The higher resolution image provides too many ppi for the monitor to handle

Figure 1–9: Although both of these images have retained identical physical sizes, the lower-res version (right) is obviously blurrier.

Figure 1–10: If the black outline represents the edge of the computer screen, you can see how the low-res version of the image has plenty of room, whereas the high-res version runs past the edges, even though both are the same physical size.

at the same 1:1 ratio. Therefore, the image will appear larger on screen than it would on paper. In this case, the image resolution is 288 ppi. That's four times larger than the 72 ppi that the monitor displays. The image will appear on screen to be four times its actual size, or 24" x 16", in this case. The monitor needs 24 inches to show all 432 horizontal pixels (6" x 72 = 432) properly.

To understand the pixel dimensions of an image, simply multiply the pixel width by the pixel height. In the previous example, the 6" x 4" image at 72 ppi would have a total of 124,416 pixels ([72 ppi x 6"] x [72 ppi x 4"] = 124,416). This is an important concept to understand when you review a later section, which discusses changing the resolution of an existing image.

The only setting that you have to worry about when it comes to dpi is the resolution settings of your monitor itself. Most standard monitors are set to display 800 x 600 pixels, though many of them can be changed (other common settings are 640 x 480 or 1072 x 740). Besides that, understanding dpi is really just a matter of under-standing why images will appear certain ways in Photoshop.

◆ **Lines Per Inch (lpi):** Strictly a concern for print designers, the lpi (also known as the *screen frequency*) is a measurement of the lines per linear inch of halftone screens used to produce images. If you are sending something to a commercial printer, you'll need to know what line screen they are printing at and pass this information along to the service bureau that outputs your film. There will be more on creating film seps and working with service bureaus and commercial printers in Chapter 8.

Specific resolutions for various types of projects and work environments can be found in Chapter 9, which discusses more detail on how to use Photoshop for either print or Web needs.

Setting and Changing Image Resolution

Typically, you'll determine the image resolution when you digitize your pictures. Later in this chapter, we'll review some of the popular ways to get an image into Photoshop. If you are starting a new document from scratch (choose File -> New), you'll have the opportunity to set the ppi in the dialog box shown in Figure 1–11.

The top of the dialog box displays the file size of your document. Notice that, as you increase the ppi, the file size of the document will also increase, because there is more information in the new document.

The rule of thumb here is pretty simple: Decreasing an image resolution is fine. Increasing an image resolution is…well, not fine. (Sorry, I couldn't think of anything more catchy for my rule of thumb). That's because, as you reduce the resolution of an image, Photoshop will simply remove any unnecessary pixel. As you increase the resolution, however, say from 72 ppi to 300 ppi, you are asking Photoshop to create pixels of information where none exist—an extra 228 pixels for every inch! Photoshop has no idea what to put in these pixels, so it chooses colors from neighboring pixels. The result is usually nothing more than a blurry mess.

When it comes to changing the size of your image, you'll typically be confronted with two options: resizing or resampling. (I'm talking about changing the size of an entire image, so that you can save the nasty e-mails telling me that cropping or altering the canvas size are other options.)

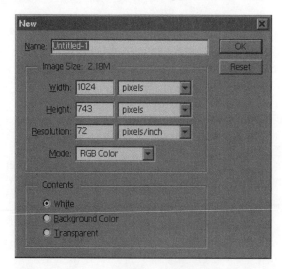

Figure 1–11: The New Image dialog box.

To change the size of an image using either of these methods (both will be explained in their respective place):

1. With an open image, choose Image -> Image Size to access the dialog box shown in Figure 1–12. The dialog box on the left is for *resizing* images—notice that the Resample Image checkbox is left unchecked. The dialog box on the right is for *resampling* images. The dialog box changes subtly, depending on whether that checkbox is checked on or off. In both, though, the top portion displays the pixel dimensions, as well as the file size. The lower portion allows you to view and change the physical size of the image in any number of measurements, including inches, percent, points and picas.

2. Decide how you want to change your image:

   Resizing your image generally implies changing its physical size without changing the number of pixels. To do this, make sure that the Resample Image checkbox is left unchecked. As shown earlier, you'll notice that you cannot change any of the information in the upper portion of the dialog box. You'll also notice that the Constrain Proportions checkbox is grayed out, and there is a chain link icon linking all of the variables in the lower, Print Size info area.

   As you change any of the Print Size values, the other values will change accordingly. As we saw in the previous section, when we were deriving the mathematics behind resolution and pixels, there were 124,416 pixels in our 6" x 4", 72-ppi image. By leaving the Resample Image checkbox unchecked, we are, in essence, saying that, no matter what, we want there to always be 124,416 pixels in this image. Therefore, if we decrease the resolution in the Print Size area, the Width and Height values have to go up. If we decrease the Height, the Width will also decrease, but the Resolution will decrease.

   In the end, the following mathematical equations will always hold true:

   Width (Print Size) x Resolution = Width (Pixel Dimensions)
   Height (Print Size) x Resolution = Height (Pixel Dimensions)

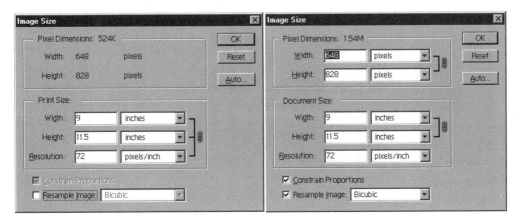

Figure 1–12: The Image Size dialog box.

Because there will always be the same amount of pixels in your image, the file size will also remain unchanged. Figure 1–13 shows an example of a resized image and its file size, before and after.

Resampling will actually change the number of pixels in your image and can be done by checking the Resample Image checkbox. As was shown in Figure 1–11, when Resampling an image, the dialog box changes in a few distinct ways:

◆ The Pixel Size Width and Height can be changed.

◆ A chain link icon links the Width and Height in the Pixel Size area together (provided that the Constrain Proportions checkbox is checked on).

◆ The chain link icon only links the Width and Height values together (provided that the Constrain Proportions checkbox is checked on).

◆ The Constrain Proportions checkbox is made active (when checked off, the chain link icons disappear).

◆ A pull-down menu for how you want to resample your image is made active.

Regardless of how you resample your image (whether through the Resolution, Width or Height), the file size and pixel dimensions will change. The same formulas that we used when resizing hold true for resampling, also. So, if you increase the Resolution and the Print Size Width and Height remain the same, it holds that the pixel dimensions would have to increase, as well. With this change also comes a change in the file size.

In terms of how to use Resample an Image, the pull-down menu will offer you three choices:

◆ *Bicubic* is the smoothest but also the slowest

◆ *Bilinear* is faste, but not quite as smooth

◆ *Nearest Neighbor* will cause Photoshop to throw away (if Resampling down) or duplicate (if resampling up) pixels, as necessary.

Figure 1–13: You won't see any difference between these two images on screen, but there's a huge difference on paper. The picture on the left is 7" x 4.685" with a standard 33-ppi resolution. The image on the right has been resized, though, and has a print size of only 4" x 2.67". Because the number of pixels can't change when we resize an image, the resolution of this small image has increased to almost 600 ppi.

You'll most often want to use the Bicubic option, even if it takes a few seconds longer. The quality increase is worth the minimal wait. Figure 1–14 shows an image that has been resampled up from 72 to 300 ppi. The image on the left is the picture at 72 ppi, whereas the image on the right is the result after being resampled up to 300, shown at 100%. Only a portion of the image is shown, because the image has become too large to fit on the monitor. You can see that the edges, although not as pixilated as what we saw in Figure 1–3, have still lost a lot of the detail and crispness, especially along the edges.

Resampling up is usually not a good idea and rarely has a useable effect, as has been described briefly. When you increase either the physical size or the resolution, independent of each other, Photoshop is forced to add pixels to the image where there were none. Because Photoshop does not have any information as to what to put into these new pixels, an image that is resampled up usually looks blurry, or pixilated. Resampling down, though, is a good idea. This is especially true when creating Web sites or other low-res imagery. To make sure that scanned images have the maximum quality, scan each image in at 300 ppi (or even 600 ppi, depending on the details in your image). Then resample down to the 72-ppi resolution level. The number of pixels and the file size will both be smaller, but your image will have the best chance of retaining high detail and color quality.

FILE SIZES

I remember my first computer. I was 13 years old, and I had an Apple IIe. It had one of those headache-inducing green screens, and I spent weeks writing an if/then program inevitably to make a dot bounce from one side of the screen to the other. The best part, though, was that it had a full 256-k memory!

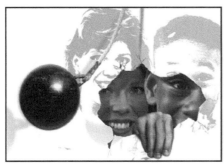

Figure 1–14: The image on the left has sharper edges at 72 ppi than it does on the right after being Resampled up to 300 ppi.

Now it's tough to find a computer that has less than 4 gigs.

When you manipulate the size or resolution of an image, you may also be manipulating the file size of that image. As you could see in Figure 1–12, when you resample an image, the file size (labeled *Pixel Dimensions*) at the top of the dialog box, can change, depending on the changes that you make (notice that the Width and Height values can be manipulated, as well). When an image is being resized, however (when the Resample box is *not* checked), the physical size and the resolution compensate for each other, so that the file size does not change at all.

File sizes will vary from project to project, depending on a lot of factors. If you plan on working in print, however, you should be ready to work with images that have very large file sizes attached to them. There are many reasons, though, that file size could be large or increase, including the following:

- A larger canvas size
- An increase in the resolution
- A change from Grayscale Mode to RGB Mode
- A change from RGB Mode to CMYK Mode
- The addition of more Layers
- The addition of more Channels

If you're serious about graphic design, you're going to want to get yourself a lot of RAM in your computer. One of the hazards of large file sizes is that images not only take longer to open, but it'll take longer to process each command, and it'll be tougher to open many images at once. Having more RAM will help to overcome these problems.

COLOR MODES

I don't want to write about how color works in nature any more than you want to read about it. We all want to get on to the fun, creative stuff. Suffice it to say, then, that the colors you see in nature aren't emanating from the objects at all—leaves, sky, water, Santa's coat and the marshmallows in Lucky Charms are all shades of gray. The reason we see them in color is due to the light that reflects off of them. Our eyes use red, green and blue *cones* to interpret this light and filter out various colors (depending on the chemicals or elements that are in the object). Various amounts of red, green and blue values combine to create millions of colors in nature. When there is a maximum intensity of red, green and blue, our eyes see white.

Your computer monitor works much the same way. It shoots red, green and blue light into your eyes to create an image on the screen. However, this does not mean that the red, green and blue (RGB) color model is the only one available. It is also not the only one you need to work with, and other models are available in Photoshop, depending on what type of project you are working on. You can change your image to any of the following color modes by choosing Image -> Mode -> (desired color mode):

RGB

The particular model just described is used most often when you are creating graphics that will be seen primarily on a monitor. This includes images used for Web sites, videos, or CD-ROM/DVD applications. Because you will be using the monitor as your primary (or only) display source, keeping your images in RGB is desirable, because it remains consistent with the display source.

Typically, your images will look best in RGB and will leave you the freedom to manipulate it more widely than, say, when working in CMYK mode (covered next). This is especially true when it comes to using filters on your images, many of which can't be done in CMYK mode.

CMYK

You'll most often use this mode when your images are destined for the printing press. As we discussed earlier in this section, colors in nature appear to us through combinations of red, green and blue light. Full intensities of each of these create white. Therefore, the RGB color mode is said to be *additive*. When you print, the color of the paper in its original form is white. To see an image, we need to subtract color. We do this by using standard printing inks, cyan, (kind of like an aqua blue) magenta and yellow, which, in theory, are the opposite of red, green and blue. When each is placed on a white page at its full intensity, the theory says that we will subtract the RGB elements from the page and achieve a pure black. This is called the *subtractive* color mode.

Theory and practice don't always mix, however. Because of impurities in printing inks, a full mixture of cyan, magenta and yellow actually gives us a muddy brown. To compensate for this lack, printers add one more element, which is blacK, (the *K* in CMYK). By adding the black component, we can create a nice black on a printed page.

The CMYK color model does not have as many colors as its RGB counterpart, because certain colors, such as some neons and metallics, can't be achieved through CMYK combinations. These combinations of CMYK, the range of print colors you can achieve, is called the *gamut*. When you are working with a color that cannot be printed with a CMYK mixture, that color is considered to be *out of* gamut. Therefore, if you are developing images for print, be careful not to rely on images that you see in RGB color mode—they will probably look more dull and flat on paper.

Grayscale

Grayscale images lack color completely, instead representing images in black, white and shades of gray. One of the immediate benefits of this color mode is that the file size will be significantly reduced, making your images a bit easier to handle. Grayscale images are often used when budgetary constraints (or just personal taste), calls for just one color to be printed, instead of the four colors in a typical CMYK piece.

Duotone

Another color mode that is often used when budgets are tight, duotones display images by combining two colors. Photoshop gives you complete control over which two colors you will use and how much of each is mixed. The Duotone color mode option will not be available until you first change your image to Grayscale.

Lab

Most designers tend to not work in Lab mode, opting for either RGB or CMYK. However, lab Mode is the best format to work in if you intend to transfer files and work on your images on different monitors or computer systems. Its designed to maintain the integrity of colors, regardless of the display device, and is the internal mode which Photoshop uses to convert images between CMYK and RGB.

Although it's safe to work in this mode, don't forget to change the mode to CMYK before sending the image to a printer or to RGB before saving it for the Web.

Indexed Color

With the addition of the Save for Web dialog box (discussed in detail in *Web Photoshop 6 Primer*), the Indexed Color color mode is almost obsolete—at least when it comes to choosing it manually. Indexing the colors in your image, which will basically eliminate all but 256 colors, is necessary for saving your image in the GIF format (covered later in this chapter). Although this will typically reduce the file size, you will obviously lose image quality—especially in photographs which rely on many different colors and shades.

Bitmap

Chances are that you won't be using this one very often. However, working in this mode will likely save you a lot of time—you won't be able to transform anything, use any filters, color correct different parts…you're really kind of limited. All images in Bitmap Mode are strictly black and white—no color, no grays. Each pixel is either on (white) or off (black). And that's all there is to it. So, you ask, why would I ever work in this mode? Well, as soon as I figure it out, you'll be the first to know.

Keep in mind that, when you change from one color mode to another, information may be lost. For example, if your image is in RGB mode and you change it to CMYK, you'll lose all of the color information that is out of gamut. You can change it back to RGB all day long, but you won't regain those colors. Change any color image to Grayscale and the color information will be permanently gone—even changing it back to a color mode won't bring the color back.

Don't panic. When I say permanently I don't mean to imply that it's irreconcilable. You can always use the Undo feature, the History palette, or just close the image without saving it and reopen it again.

The chart in Table 1–3 gives you an at-a-glance rundown of what each color mode (and file format, covered in the next section) is typically used for.

Table 1–3: Color Mode Usage Chart

Color Mode	Description
CMYK	Used for print pieces. Desktop and commercial printers use Cyan, Magenta, Yellow and BlacK to create color images on paper. CMYK has a smaller range of color than RGB.
RGB	Used mostly for images that will be viewed only on a monitor, such as a Web site or CD-ROM interface. Red, Green and Blue light is used to create a wider spectrum than CMYK.
Grayscale	Will represent images in black, white and shades of gray. Most often used in print pieces, either for effect or to save money.
Duotone	Used mostly for print pieces, again either for effect or to save money. Duotone will mix two colors together to create an image.
Lab	Good mode if you are going to be switching monitors often. It's designed to maintain the integrity of colors, regardless of the display device.
Index	Indexed colors are used for creating GIF images used on Web sites. Designers will likely never have to choose it again, because new features, such as Save for Web, have made Web designing easier and made this particular mode obsolete.
Bitmap	This will change all the pixels to be either black or white. If you use it at all, it would be for doing some really precise print work for noncolor images, but chances are you won't really have a need for it.
Format	**Description**
Photoshop (.psd)	The generic Photoshop file format; you'll most often use this if you're saving images with layers.
CompuServe GIF (.gif)	Used primarily for Web images with flat colors. GIFs are not only used for their ability to make certain images lower in file size, but also due to their ability to animate images and allow transparency.
EPS (.eps)	Encapsulated PostScript, most often used for print projects. Retains detail and color well but can be heavy in file size.

(continued)

Table 1–3: (continued)

Color Mode	Description
JPEG (.jpg)	The other commonly used Web format, JPEG, is more often used for images with continuous tone color.
Photoshop PDF (.pdf)	Retains layouts as is, as read by Adobe Acrobat.
PICT (.pct)	A handy format if you need to retain alpha channels. I've found them useful when importing images to video.
	Mac only.
PNG (.png)	A new format for Web images; as of now, it hasn't caught on much, since older browsers don't recognize it.
RAW (.raw)	Just like the name indicates, these files are strictly no-frills-added. No compression, no color mode—not even a file size. You won't ever want to save an image as raw, but if you have an image that you want to open and there is no file type associated with it, opening it as a raw document might be your only choice.
TIFF (.tif)	The other important format for print images. TIFFs, like EPSs, can retain color and detail well, but a compression options helps to reduce file size significantly.

A FORMAT FOR ALL OCCASIONS

Photoshop allows you to save your images in any number of formats. Not all formats will be available every time you save an image—the color mode you choose may make certain formats unavailable, as will the existence of channels or layers (both covered in detail later in this book). Beyond that, it's up to you to decide which format to save your images as, depending on the type of project.

The following is a list of all the available file formats in Photoshop and a description of what they are and when to use them. Not all of the formats that you can choose from have made the following list: In the spirit of keeping this chapter short and to the point, I've excluded those formats which, in my 5 years of designing, I have never, ever needed to use. The lowercase letters in parentheses are the file extensions.

Photoshop (.psd)

This is the only file format you can choose when your image has multiple layers. It will retain all layers and channels for you to work on at a later date. It won't, however, save the History (Chapter 2), so don't expect to be able to close an image, reopen it, then go back to an earlier stage. You can't import Photoshop files into Quark XPress for page layouts or Web browsers, but I would recommend that, even when you are done with an image, if it has multiple layers, you save it as a Photoshop file and archive it someplace. That will make life easier on you if you need to make changes later.

It what seems like a massive and unveiled coup to dominate completely all areas of design, Adobe has started to marry many of their programs closer together. InDesign, their newish answer to QuarkXPress, allows users to import images with the layers still intact. With this kind of benefit, a similar feature in QuarkXPress can't be far behind.

Compuserve GIF (.gif)

Your image will need to be in Indexed color mode before you can save it as a GIF. GIFs are used in Web sites and typically will result in smaller file sizes if your image is line art or has large fields of flat color. GIFs can be animated and transparent, but you probably won't have to worry about choosing this option from the Save As dialog box—you'll be saving your GIF images through the incredible Save for Web dialog box.

The Save for Web dialog box, (file -> Save for Web) shown in Figure 1–15 has made saving Web images far easier then in older versions of the program. Introduced in version 5.5, the Save for Web dialog box not only allows you to compare and contrast up to three compression qualities of your image against each other and against the original, but it also calculates how long each image would take to download at various speed modems. It's a huge help for saving Web images that has not only helped to improve the quality and download time of Web pics, but has also made them easier to create.

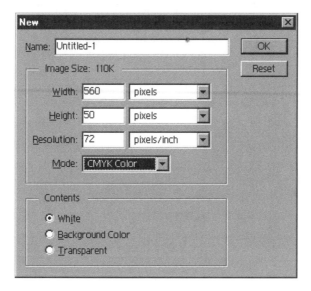

Figure 1–15: The Save for Web dialog box.

Photoshop EPS (.eps)

The Encapsulated PostScript (EPS) file format is a favorite among those who are sending their images to print. Not only does the format translate your images into PostScript (which allows you to print faster and more accurately), but it will save clipping paths. Paths, which will be covered in Chapter 4, allow you to isolate a portion of an image and extract it from the background when you import the graphic to a page layout program (such as Quark XPress).

The downside to EPS is that the images tend to be very large in terms of file size. Depending on how big the file is that you're creating, this could cost you in both time (for opening, placing and outputting) and hard disk space. For an alternative to the EPS format when you plan on going to print, read up on the TIFF format later in this section.

JPEG (.jpg)

Another file format used primarily for Web sites, the JPEG file format does a good job of reducing file size (a key ingredient to creating quality Web graphics) when your image is a continuous-tone photograph. A small warning though: JPEG is a *lossy* format, which means that, when you save it, Photoshop will eliminate color information it doesn't find relevant. Each time you resave your image, the quality will reduce just a bit.

Photoshop PDF (.pdf)

The ever-popular Adobe Acrobat now has a home in Photoshop. The PDF format, which opens in Acrobat Reader, is used for saving entire pages of information in their original layout. This not only includes the layout of the page, but also the font types and sizes, colors and anything else. Chances are that you've seen a lot of PDF files on Web sites, offering newsletters, technical drawings or catalog pages. Because of the relatively low file size, you can create PDF files containing multiple pages of a publication for easy distribution. The Acrobat program itself allows the user to zoom in and out of a page, search for a topic based on a keyword and a lot of other cool features.

For really good quality PDFs, though, especially for print, you're best off using PostScript and Distiller, instead.

PICT (.pct)

PICT is typically a low-res file format, often used for on-screen displays (such as when an image is need for video, CD-ROM or PowerPoint). Note, however, that even though PICT is used for on-screen purposes, as opposed to printing purposes, it is not one of the formats that you can use for creating Web graphics.

When you take a screen shot on a Macintosh, the image is automatically saved as a PICT (even though this can be very annoying, especially when you need a lot of screen shots for, say, a book…).

PNG (.png)

The new kid on the Web block, PNG is supposed to combine all things great about GIF and JPEG; however, many browsers don't currently support the PNG format, so it is, for now, rendered temporarily useless, pending wider support.

RAW (.raw)

RAW files are more for opening than they are for saving. This format is about as no-frills as you get. These files contain no more information than is vitally necessary for creating an image. They aren't compressed, have no concept of image size, no clue as to color modes and offer no information on bit depth. You have to provide all that information yourself when you open a Raw file.

Um…you must be trying to figure out why you would ever even bother. Usually, you won't, unless for some reason you're dealing with a file whose format is unknown to you. In that case, Windows users have the advantage of a cool feature, Open As, found in the File menu. Open As allows you to choose what file type you would like to open your file as. However, if it's not a TIFF file, and you try to open it *as* a TIFF file, for example, it just won't open. In these cases, opening the file as RAW is usually your best bet.

TIFF (.tif)

TIFF is arguably the best format available for printing. I use the word *arguably* because, although I tend to use it most often for my own work, there are those who prefer to use the EPS format instead. TIFF can not only retain excellent image quality, but it utilizes the LZW compression system. This keeps the file size very small without compromising the image's quality, color or detail. In addition, the TIFF format allows you to save an alpha channel to be used in much the same way that EPS files use clipping paths. Import a TIFF image with an alpha channel into QuarkXPress for page layouts, and everything outside the Alpha Channel (the *mask*—see Chapter 5 for more detail) will be removed from the image.

TIFF is also a good format for transferring an image from Macintosh to PC. Not only will it retain all the detail in your image, but it will allow you to specify which operating system it is destined for.

If you're not sure, choose the IBM PC option. Macs typically do a better job with cross-platform issues than PCs do.

CREATING NEW IMAGES AND OPENING EXISTING ONES

Creating a new image from scratch is a fairly simple process. Figure 1–15 shows the New Image dialog box that can be opened by selecting File -> New.

The name area at the top allows you to name your image if you'd like (if you plan on saving your work, you're going to have to name it eventually, either now or when you save it). The Image Size selections allow you to set the measurements for your canvas (the drop-down menus let you select how you want this measured—pixels or inches are the most common), as well as the resolution of the image.

The file size of the canvas is displayed at the top of this section. Watch how it changes, based on the values that you input for any of these areas.

The Mode option allows you to select which color mode you want to open your canvas in, although the color mode is easy enough to change later if you have to (by choosing Image -> Mode -> your desired color mode).

The bottom area of the dialog box allows you to select whether you want your canvas to have a black, white or transparent background.

Open and Open As

The easiest thing you'll do in Photoshop is open an image. Choose File -> Open, and locate the desired image on your computer.

But what if you can't open an image or the image won't even be recognized by Photoshop? One of the more convenient features for opening files whose format is unknown is the Open As command, and it's available only for Windows (sometimes being a Mac purist isn't easy). If you have an image with an unknown format, choose File -> Open As and try various format options to open your image. Typically, PICT is a good bet. If that doesn't work, try JPEG. When you've exhausted all other options, try opening your file as RAW.

If you know that your file was saved as a certain format, such as TIFF, for example, but it still won't open, it can probably be assumed that it was saved on a Macintosh without a file extension. In this case, just add the appropriate extension yourself. You can do this even from the Open As dialog box by right-clicking on the file and choosing Rename. Add the .tif extension in this example, and you should be good to go.

MOMMY, WHERE DO IMAGES COME FROM?

Once Photoshop is open, you probably don't want to spend hours looking at the interface. As exciting as that may be, the real fun comes when you actually have an image that you can manipulate.

Of course, you don't necessarily need images at all. Many areas throughout this book will show how to create graphics from scratch, without the benefit of having a photograph or drawing to start from.

There are many ways in which you can get images to work on. Stock photo CDs are an increasingly popular method of obtaining all sorts of pictures taken by professional photographers that you can use in your work. Or, if you're intent on using your own photography or drawings, you can either digitize them yourself with a desktop scanner or have them professionally scanned onto disk or CD.

Stock Photo CDs

Let's say that you're working on a brochure for a travel agency and they would really like a picture of Greece on the front cover. Unfortunately, they don't have photography to give you. Well, chances are, flying to Greece for a photo shoot is not in their budget. So what do you do? It's easy—you use someone else's photograph. No, you don't steal it—you buy it. From Corell, Comstock, Eyewire, or any one of a million companies that provide you with a river of images on practically any topic you can think of.

How the images work depends on the company that you buy from. Some companies sell you a CD that has anywhere between 50 and 150 images on it for one set price. These images are typically royalty free, meaning that you (and anyone else) can use them for nearly any purpose.

Make sure you read the royalty-free agreement. Typically, you are not allowed to use an image in a derogatory way or to have as a direct endorsement of a product (like putting the words "I love Pepsi" in a speech bubble over a stock image of a person).

Usually, all of the images on the CD are high-resolution, and the price per CD will depend on both how many images are on the CD and the subject matter of the images. For example, titles that have to do with business and industry tend to be more expensive than titles that have to do farm animals.

Other stock photo companies will sell you individual images, either on a CD or by providing a slide or transparency, which you will have to pay to have professionally scanned. These are usually rather expensive, and price is typically determined by how the image will be used and how many units of the piece will be distributed. For example, the same image of a man at a drafting table will be more expensive if it is going to be run in an ad in *Time* magazine than if that same image is going to be used for an interoffice flyer.

The upside to this method of stock photography is that, for a set amount of time, nobody else can use that image. This is in contrast to the royalty-free method, in which the same image can appear in a number of places, even for competing companies! As you enter deeper into the Web, printing and/or advertising industry, you'll recognize a lot of popular stock photography appearing all over the place.

The following provides a list of both mainstream and off-the-beaten-trail stock photo companies

1. Photodisc   www.photodisc.com
2. Eyewire   www.eyewire.com
3. Corel   www.corel.com
4. Comstock   www.comstock.com
5. Digital Stock   www.digitalstock.com

Custom CD Scans

If you have a bunch of your own pictures that you would like to put onto a CD, it can be done fairly easily. Many shops provide the service of scanning imagery to a CD. Your local one-hour photo-developing shop typically will advertise this service, although with the exception of a relatively few cases, most of these don't do the work in house. Instead, they send out the jobs to a central Kodak scanning center. This can cause a delay in the return of your CD for a number of days. In addition, they are typically more accustomed to working with families and individuals whose scan demands run pretty low.

For truly professional, high-end projects or projects that have an impending deadline, you'll want to find a local service bureau. These shops do most all work on location and are in the business of scanning for businesses and professional projects.

For the best results, try to provide them with transparencies of your images, slides or chromes. If you don't have any of these available or don't have the resources to get them, a positive will usually be good enough as a last resort.

You'll usually be given a number of scan resolution choices. For a minimal price difference, you can usually get five resolutions, ranging from 18-meg files for an 8.5" x 11" image to a 72-meg file. If your service bureau's prices are reasonable, get the highest resolution possible. As we discussed earlier in this chapter, it's very easy to go down in resolution but difficult to impossible to go up without losing significant quality.

Prices for scanning images to a CD will typically run anywhere from $2 to $15, depending on the number of scans and the resolution. The CD itself constitutes another $20 to $25. The hidden secret, though, is that CDs hold 650 meg. You can keep using the same one for new projects until it gets filled and not have to keep paying the extra money for the CD.

Desktop Scanning

Desktop scanners are a convenient means of digitizing photography, illustrations or other images into Photoshop for on-demand use. As of the writing of this book, most scanners are a relatively affordable cog in the computer setup, capable of scanning in four colors in just one pass.

The benefit of desktop scanning depends on what type of project you will be working on. Web projects or other projects that require a low resolution (such as graphics for video, or Director applications) are prime candidates for desktop scanning images. A little bit of color correction, some selective cropping and you're good to go. High-res projects, such as brochures, print ads or annual reports, would probably require better quality scans than you can expect from most desktop scanners. Even though most desktop systems allow the ability to scan up to 600 ppi or even 1,200 ppi, they still won't give you the sharpness and color integrity that more upscale scanning methods will provide (see "Drum Scanning," below and "Custom CD-Scans," above). However, you can scan an image at high-resolution for use in your print project for comping purposes or for projects that don't have the budget to support more sophisticated methods.

 When scanning images for Web or other low-res destinations, you'd be wise to scan in at a higher resolution. Try a minimum of 150 ppi. Do any color corrections or manipulations at this size, then resize the image down. This way, you begin with a higher quality image and color detail to work with.

 When scanning a picture into Photoshop, the image will scan in as an RGB image. This is important to remember if you're working on a print project (assuming that you are not outsourcing for a drum scan). As mentioned earlier in this chapter, you'll want to work in CMYK color mode for print projects. The colors that you capture in your scan will likely be different than what will end up on paper.

Other hazards of scanning include the inclusion of a grayish film over your images or dust speckles on the scan bed scanning. Chapter 6 will discuss in greater detail the methods you can use to fix these problems.

Most scanners will have tools and buttons to help you change the contrast or color issues of an image before your scan. Although each model of scanner is different, on the whole, you'd do better to avoid these. They're not as strong or as useful as the same tools provided in Photoshop. Leave the tools or settings at some neutral level and do any manipulations or color enhancements in Photoshop instead.

To begin scanning once you have installed your scanner and the Photoshop plug-in:

1. Launch Photoshop.
2. Choose File -> Import -> Select Twain Source.
3. From the selection box that appears, click on the newly installed scanner. Click OK. (You do not need to do this every time you want to scan—just the first time.)
4. Choose File -> Import -> Twain Acquire to access the scan bed interface. Because so many scanners are on the market, I will not show one here, to keep from confusing anybody.

You may wonder where the word *Twain* comes from. I wondered that for years. Maybe it didn't keep me up at night, but I wondered. Anyway, thanks to my editor, Craig Little, I now know that TWAIN stands for *Technology without an Interesting Name*. Thank you, Craig, you get a lollipop!

Drum Scanning

Drum scanning typically requires the paid assistance of an outside service bureau. Pictures are put onto a cylindrical drum, which spins around very quickly. The scan that results is usually a very high-quality digital image with exacting colors and intensely accurate details.

Drum scans can run around $100 per high-res scan. The quality is great, and some service bureaus will even do the RGB-to-CMYK conversion for you (like *that's* a tough thing to do), as well as any necessary color correction. In my opinion, unless you are working on a job which really requires exacting colors, such as a car brochure, you'd be better off having the images scanned to CD-ROM. It tends to be faster, cheaper, and, besides, do you really want to trust a stranger with color correcting your image for you?

Digital Cameras

Digital cameras have been all the craze in the digital publishing world the last few years, because models have been quickly coming down in price while improving in quality. Most of the affordable ones, however (affordable meaning anything under $1,000), still aren't good enough to use for print jobs. But they are great for capturing imagery for Web sites and other low-res destinations.

Digital cameras make life as simple as snapping a shot, saving the ones you like and downloading them directly into your computer.

SUMMARY

As designers, you're probably anxious to get to the artistic parts—enough with the dpi's and the ppi's—this is art, not science! But unfortunately, with art—especially computer art—there is a lot of science that needs to go along with it. Resolution, color, and some of the specific features that make Photoshop such a unique program are a necessary component to making the fun stuff not only more fun, but more successful in terms of how your work will be viewed.

chapter 2

PAINTING IN PHOTOSHOP

If you've seen any computer art program at all, there's probably not too much in terms of painting in Photoshop that will surprise you. You have standard airbrushes, paintbrushes, pencils, lines, erasers, etc. These are, frankly, items more of sheer necessity for Photoshop than they are features that make it stand out over other programs. But Photoshop does handle them nicely and has added just enough of something extra to make them more entertaining and useful than many other paint programs do. So, let's uncharacteristically skip the long-winded intro and get right into the mandatory drill about how to paint.

BEFORE WE PAINT: UNDERSTANDING ASSOCIATED PAINTING PALETTES

Before we actually start painting or exploring technique, there are a few supporting features of Photoshop paint tools that we should review.

Choosing a Color

Color is one of the most important aspects of Photoshop and can be a deciding aspect in terms of the overall success of any piece you design. Color (and working with it properly) is so important to Photoshop that I've given an entire chapter to it, and will continue to bring it up time and again throughout this book. This section won't necessarily show you how to work with color but will instead guide you in how to properly select and manage colors that you'll be working with.

The Color Picker

This is Central Station for Photoshop color selection methods. The Color Picker (Figure 2–1) is accessed primarily by clicking on either the Foreground color or Background color in the toolbar. The color you click on appears toward the top right of your palette as the "old" color. The new color you select while you are within the Color Picker appears in a box just above it, as the "new" color.

To select colors, you'll usually want to have the Hue (H) radio button selected, as it is by default. Try the other radio buttons to see how they each display colors, but by and large, the Hue will be the easiest and most efficient to use.

Obviously, the Photoshop guys didn't put the radio buttons next to all the other letters in the Color Picker just because they had a couple of hours to spare. They're all useful. Each group of letters represents the four color modes: HSB, CMYK, LAB and RGB. The H is the most useful because it lets you scroll through all of the Hue values, giving you an easy way to access the most amount of colors. But if you need to add a blue component to your image, you can click on the B button, and the slider will let you scroll through all the blue values.

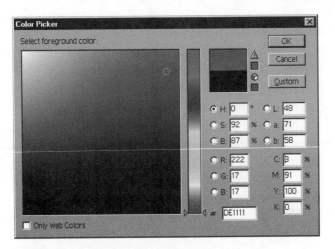

Figure 2–1: The Color Picker dialog box.

1. Open the Color Picker by clicking on either the Foreground or Background color swatch in the Toolbar.

2. In the Color Picker, drag the color slider up and down to decide which area of the spectrum you wish to extract your color from.

3. From within the color field, move the Color Marker to select a color. Moving it horizontally will change the saturation, while moving it vertically will make it lighter or darker. If you simply click in a new area, instead of dragging the marker, the marker will automatically "jump" to the place where you have clicked. As you drag or click through the color field, you'll see that the number in each of the value areas will change. Which set of values you pay closest attention to will depend on what type of project you're working on. For the extent that this book will explore various color modes, you'll mostly be looking at RGB for your monitor-based work and the CMYK values for print images.

4. If you know the values that you need to create a specific color, you can enter them in yourself. For example, let's say that a client tells you that a corporate color is made up of 27% cyan, 14% magenta, 58% yellow and 9% black. Just type those values into their appropriate field and the color will be mixed.

5. When you have selected your desired color, click OK. The swatch that you originally clicked on to access the color Picker will have changed to the color you just chose.

In numerous places throughout this book, as I discuss using Photoshop either for print or Web design, I'll mention small warnings that the Color Picker will send to you. As you can see in Figure 2–1, both such warnings are present for my newly selected color. The "out-of-gamut" warning tells me that this color falls outside the range of printable colors, while the "Web-safe" color warning lets me know that this new color does not lie within the Web-safe color palette.

If your selected color is out of gamut, click on the small box next to the warning to automatically select the closest possible color that will print. Similarly, if your selected color is not Web-safe and you wish to find the closest one that is, click on the small swatch next to the "Web-safe" warning to be taken to the closest possible Web-safe color. If Web-safe colors are really a concern, click on the small box at the bottom of the palette marked "Only Web Colors." The color field within the Picker will show only Web-safe colors, as shown in Figure 2–2.

Two last features include an odd box at the bottom with what seems to be a random configuration of letter and numbers and a small button on the right side of the Picker called *Custom*. Both of these issues are covered later in enough depth that I won't repeat them here. The box of random numbers gives you the hexadecimal values for creating Web color, and the Custom button gives you access to selecting Pantone and other manufactured colors, which can't be exactly replicated with CMYK mixtures, and is covered in Chapter 6.

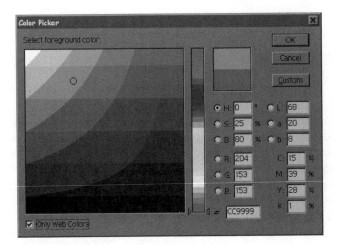

Figure 2–2: Click the Only Web Colors checkbox to restrict the colors shown in the Color Picker to those that are safe to use on the Web.

The Color Palette

I might be the only one in the world who doesn't really get the usefulness of this palette, shown in Figure 2–3. Accessed by choosing Windows -> Show Colors, it works in a similar fashion as the Color Picker but it allows to you to mix colors more visually to achieve a desired result. You can drag any of the sliders left or right to mix that particular color into the existing color, and the gradient along any of the side bars gives you a preview of what that color will look after the mix has occurred.

I guess that's a fairly neat feature, but to tell you the truth, when I'm sitting in front of a monitor all day and night, the last thing I want to do is try to discern any particular color from a box that's smaller than a postage stamp. Give me the big, loud Color Picker any day, and I'll survive without the preview.

Figure 2–3: The Color Palette.

The Swatches Palette

Ugh! More small boxes! But these are useful enough to suffer through the minuteness of them all. The Swatches Palette is shown in Figure 2–4 and is accessible by choosing Windows -> Show Swatches. The Swatches Palette allows you to save colors for later use. If you have color in your foreground that you like and want to use again some other time, move your cursor to the vacant area in the Swatches Palette. Your cursor will turn into a Paint Bucket icon. Click to create a new swatch of your desired color.

To use one of the saved colors, simply move your cursor over the swatch of your choice. It will turn into an Eyedropper icon. Click on the color, and it will become your Foreground color.

To remove a color from the Swatches Palette, push the <Command> button (<Ctrl> in Windows). Move your cursor over the color you wish to delete, and it will change to a Scissors icon. Click to delete the color.

Another nice feature of this palette is that you can save your colors, so you can use them at any point in the future, even after you've shut Photoshop down. From the palette menu (accessed by clicking the small triangular arrow in the top right of the palette), choose Save Colors. This will open a dialog box, which will allow you to give your palette a name and save it any place on your computer. Load any set of colors again by choosing Load Colors from the same palette menu.

The Options Palette

Well, actually, it's a lot of palettes. Each of the tools that you'll be using to paint has its own Options Palette (the same is true of all the nonpainting tools, as well). In previous versions of Photoshop, there wasn't a tremendous difference between most of the Options Palettes. But with version 6.0, there are new tools involved and enough new changes and additions to previously existing tools and the way the palettes work that it makes more sense to deal with each Options Palette as we discuss each tool individually.

However, there are a couple of features that are common to many of the Options Palette for each of the tools, and it makes sense to review them here, rather than individually.

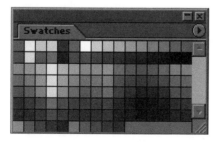

Figure 2–4: The Swatches Palette.

In version 6.0, the Options palette has a different look than Photoshop's other palettes and is typically meant to stay visible at all times. The options within the palette will change, depending on which tool you are using, simply by activating a new tool. If the palette does get closed, however, and you wish to open in again, simply activate a tool and either choose Windows -> Show Options, double-click on the desired tool, or simply push <Return> (<Enter> in Windows) when the tool is activated in the toolbar.

Figure 2–5 shows the Options Palette for the Paintbrush Tool, which we'll use as the example. To the far left of each palette is a quick visual reminder of what tool you're using, followed by access to the Brushes Palette, which we'll discuss in greater detail later in this chapter.

Not all tools use brushes. The Line Tool, Gradient Tool and Shape Tools don't use brushes at all.

At some point in most paint tools, Options Palettes will be a pull-down menu called *Mode*. By default, the pull-down menu is set to Normal. Opening the menu shows a long list of different words, including *Screen*, *Multiply*, *Darken* and *Hue*. These are *Blend Modes*, and they affect how the color you paint *with* will interact with the color you paint *on*. With the exception of the Behind Blend Mode option, these will all be covered in greater detail in Chapter 5. We'll take a look at how the Behind option works when we discuss the Paintbrush Tool.

The other similarity that all of the painting tools share is the Opacity slider in the Options Palettes. This is fairly obvious in nature. As you can see in Figure 2–6, using the Paintbrush with a lower opacity means that it will be more transparent (the lower the opacity, the higher the transparency).

For the majority of painting tools, this slider is called *Opacity*. For some tools, though, such as the Airbrush Tool, this slider is called *Pressure*. Although there is a slight difference between the two, it's really nothing you need to be overly concerned with.

To adjust either the Pressure or Opacity settings, click on the small arrow next to the value input area to open the slider or fill in the Opacity/Pressure amounts manually. You can quickly change the values by increments of 10, just by clicking on a number. Pushing the number 4 on your keyboard will change the Opacity/Pressure value to 40%, 6 will change it to 60%, and so on.

Figure 2–5: The Options Palette for the Paintbrush Tool.

Figure 2–6: Lowering the opacity on the Paintbrush Tool means making the paint more transparent.

To change the values in increments of 1 instead of 10, type out the full number quickly. For example, if you want your Opacity/Pressure to be 54%, push the 5 and 4 buttons quickly. If you wait too long in between, you'll change your values first to 50%, then to 40%.

BRUSHES SIZES:
MORE THAN WHAT YOU SEE

For many of the painting tools that we'll be reviewing later in this chapter, you'll need to decide on a brush size to use. In version 5.5, the Brushes Palette was accessible at all times—even if you were using a tool (such as the Marquee Selection Tool) that didn't need brushes. Version 6.0, however, places the Brushes Palette only as a component of a tool that would require you to choose a brush (such as the painting tools that you'll learn about in this chapter). Personally, I kind of liked having the Brushes Palette accessible at all times, even if I wasn't painting something. But of all the things in the upgrade that I am uncomfortable with, this is one of the lesser evils.

To access the Brushes Palette in version 6.0, simply select the tool that you wish to paint with and open the Brushes pull-down menu (click on the small, downward-pointing arrow). The palette, shown in Figure 2–7, allows you to select a size and shape for the brush you'll be using. As you can see, a number of standard circular brushes are already loaded into your Brushes Palette. The hard-edged circles are hard-edged brushed, while the circles that fade out have softer edges. The numbers underneath some of the circles indicate their diameter in pixels (the numbers appear only if the brush is too big to fit in the iconic display of the Brushes Palette). Figure 2–8 provides examples of the difference between painting with a hard-edged and a soft-edged brush, at different size diameters.

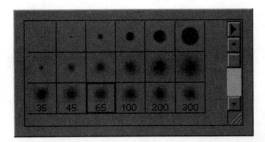

Figure 2–7: The Brushes Palette allows you to choose any one of a number of brushes that are provided for you or allow you to create you own brushes.

Figure 2–8: Painting with different edges and different-diameter brushes changes the result of your strokes.

To select a brush for use in painting, simply click on one. You'll see that the cursor changes to a circle that reflects the diameter of your brush.

Creating New Brushes

The brushes that Photoshop provides you by default in the brushes palette are good for a start. But they definitely won't fill all of your needs. Photoshop gives you plenty of options for creating new brushes, so that you'll always have a brush to paint absolutely anything.

Creating More of the Same

The circular shape might get you through for awhile, but you'll likely need to create some custom sizes, at least. Especially if you will be working on high-resolution pieces—a 45-pixel-diameter brush is barely discernible when working with 300 pixels in every inch.

To create a new standard brush, select New Brush from the Brushes Palette menu; click on a vacant area within the palette itself; or click the brush icon in the Options Palette (to the immediate left of the drop-down menu arrow) to access the New Brush dialog box, as shown in Figure 2–9.

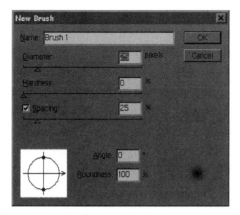

Figure 2–9: Creating a new brush is useful and pretty easy.

 You can access this same dialog box to change any of the settings on an existing brush by double-clicking on it from the drop-down Brushes Palette.

A fairly straightforward command center, you can use sliders or enter custom values manually to adjust the diameter and hardness of any given brush. The Spacing slider that appears last allows you decide how often the brush mark will repeat as you paint. The default, 25%, means that a new circle will appear as you paint at 25% of the size of the previous circle that you painted. At 25% or less, this pretty much gives you a straight line.

Increase the percentage to 150%, and you'll get a much different effect when you paint. A new circle will appear on your canvas at 150% of the size of the previous circle, causing a dotted-line effect, as shown in Figure 2–10.

Figure 2–10: Change the Spacing of your brush to create dotted or dashed lines.

You can change the angle and roundness of the brush by filling in the values manually in their respective value areas. For an easier way of manipulating the brush, change the roundness by dragging one of the handle bars on the wire frame circle at the bottom left of the dialog box. To adjust the angle, drag one of lines in the central crosshair. The preview window shows you the size, shape and angle of your brush as you manipulate it. Figure 2–11 gives a simple example of how I would use a skewed brush to create a shadow effect.

Loading Brushes

Photoshop comes with more brushes than just the circular ones that appear in the Brushes Palette by default. To load more brushes into your palette, open the pull-down menu within the Brushes Palette and select one of the four options provided at the bottom of the menu. Figure 2–12 shows the Brushes Palette with the Assorted Brushes file appended.

Even though the brushes in the Assorted Brushes are really cool, including deer, ducks, eyes and others, they really work only for low-res files. You can't make them bigger for use on high-res print images.

Figure 2–11: I can create a more realistic shadow effect by using a brush on an angle.

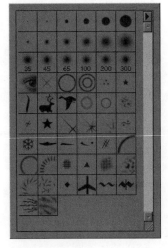

Figure 2–12: Some of the brush shapes that you can load into your palette can be pretty interesting.

Other types of brushes that Photoshop provides in this folder include square brushes, brushes with their own drop shadows and calligraphic brushes—everyone's favorite.

Creating Your Own, Custom Brush

You don't have to settle for either the circular-shaped brushes or any of the other brushes that Photoshop provides. Instead, you can create your own brush from practically anything that you have on your canvas. Take the photograph in Figure 2–13, for example. Let's say that you wanted to turn the center clock into a brush. To do this, take the following steps:

1. With the Rectangular Marquee Tool (for more info on selection tools, check out Chapter 3), make a selection around the center clock.

2. Choose Edit -> Define Brush. In the dialog box that appears, you may enter a name for your brush if you wish.

3. You can now use this new brush to paint with. Figure 2–14 shows the new brush in my Brushes Palette and the result when I use the Paintbrush Tool to paint with that brush on a new, blank canvas.

If the object or design that you want to make into a brush resides in its own layer (Layers and the Layers Palette are examined in detail in Chapter 5), your brush will be defined as anything that is visible within your selected area. That means that, even if an image resides on an underlying, nonactive layer, it will be picked up in the brush you create. To make a brush only from your desired object, without background designs interfering, make all underlying layers invisible, including the Background (<Command-Tab> or <Ctrl-Tab>).

Figure 2–13: I'll make the center clock in this image into its own brush.

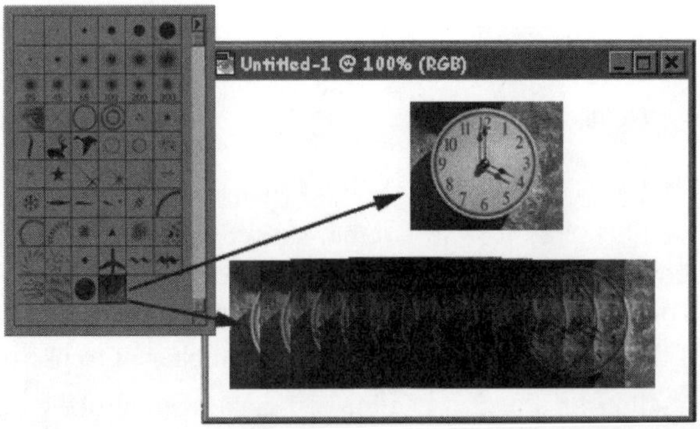
Untitled-1 @ 100% (RGB)

Figure 2–14: The new brush appears in your Brushes Palette, creating a nice effect when used for painting on your canvas.

Brush Dynamics

At the far right of any tool that uses a brush is a button marked with the Paint Brush icon (regardless of which tool you have chosen) and a small arrow indicating the existence of a pull-down menu.

Pushing this button in any Options Palctte rcveals the Brush Dynamics dialog boxes shown in Figure 2–15. As you can see in the figure, each one has a different combination of features available, depending on which tool you're using. For all options, you can choose one of three settings from a pull-down menu: None, Fade and Stylus. "Off" obviously disengages the feature, while "Stylus" applies only if you are using an clcctronic pen instead of a more standard mouse. Choosing "Fade" however, turns that particular feature on and activates the "Steps" value area. A "Step" is the number of times the brush will repeat itself (as established in the Spacing area of the New Brush dialog box, described earlier in this chapter).

Figure 2–16 provides an example of how this feature might be used.

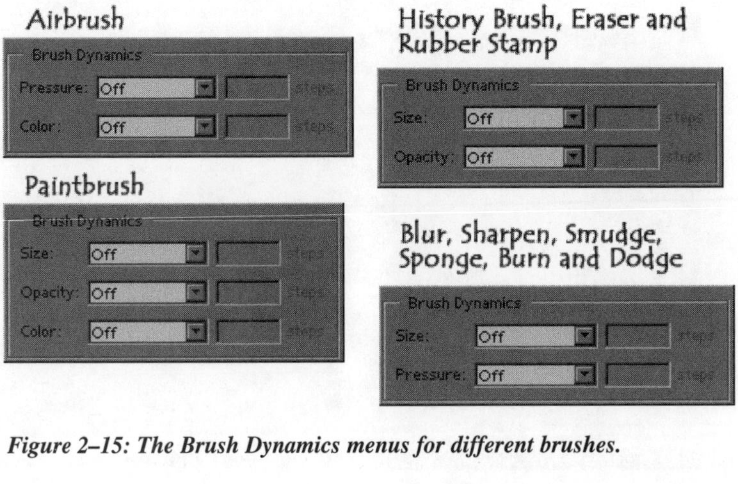
Airbrush
Brush Dynamics
Pressure: Off
Color: Off
Paintbrush
Brush Dynamics
Size: Off
Opacity: Off
Color: Off
History Brush, Eraser and Rubber Stamp
Brush Dynamics
Size: Off
Opacity: Off
Blur, Sharpen, Smudge, Sponge, Burn and Dodge
Brush Dynamics
Size: Off
Pressure: Off

Figure 2–15: The Brush Dynamics menus for different brushes.

Table 2–1 provides an explanation of how the Fade option works for each feature, as well as a list of which tools it is available with.

Table 2–1: Fade Features for Various Brushes

Feature	Tools	Description
Color	Airbrush	This will cause the color on your brush to fade out smoothly and gradually over the course of the number of steps you set.
Paintbrush	Fading Pencil	Color will make your stroke fade into the Background color.
Pressure/Opacity	All Brush Tools	Although these two options go by different names, they're basically the same thing. Choosing to fade the Opacity or Pressure of any brush will, over the established steps, fade the color of the brush to transparency.
Size	All Brush Tools except the Airbrush	This is a new feature in Photoshop that should have been offered three versions ago. Choosing to fade the Size of a brush causes it to reduce the size of the brush over the period of steps that you set for it. It will reduce in size until there is no brush and your paint stroke eventually disappears.

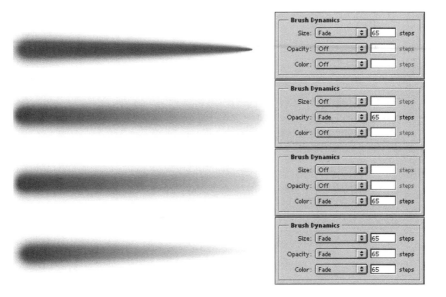

Figure 2–16: Using the Fade feature helps to accentuate an image.

Some tools that use a brush have options that are not listed here, such as the Magic Eraser or Background Eraser. That's because those tools are not used for painting but are used for other things instead. Those options will be reviewed in the appropriate chapters.

NOW WE CAN START TO PAINT

Without further interruption, we can move on to actually putting something on our canvas. This next section will review some of the painting tools in Photoshop, pointed out in Color Figure 1–1. Certain tools overlap each other in functionality, such as the Rubber Stamp Tool, which could be used for painting but is left out of this chapter. Instead, it's reviewed in Chapter 6, which highlights a more likely case for its use. The same goes for the Dodge, Burn and Saturation Tools, which I've lumped into Chapter 6, which deals specifically with color.

Painting with the Airbrush Tool and the Paintbrush Tool

Painting with either the Airbrush Tool or the Paintbrush Tool is as simple as activating the tool, selecting a brush size and holding the mouse button down as you drag. Holding the <Shift> key while you drag will force Photoshop to paint in a straight line.

 The <Shift> key is universally used for constraint, and you'll see it used for this purposes often throughout this book.

 If you want to paint a straight line at an odd angle but don't have a very steady hand, hold the <Shift> key and click and release in the area that you want to start painting. Continue holding the <Shift> key and click and release once more in the spot that you want to stop painting. A straight line will be created between your start and stop points.

When you paint, you do not have to lay your color on at 100%. Both the Paintbrush Tool and Airbrush Tool have sliders in their Options Palette that allow for varying amounts of color in each stroke. Each slider has a different name, even though the general idea is the same. As Figure 2–17 shows, there is a minor difference in how the Opacity valve (Paintbrush) and Pressure values (Airbrush) will affect a brush stroke from each tool, because Pressure has really nothing to do with transparency, as Opacity does. The top line in the figure was done with the Airbrush Tool, while the lower line was done with the Paintbrush Tool. Both used dark black at 50% (Pressure and Opacity, respectively).

Figure 2–17: There is a difference, though, when it comes to the effect of either Pressure or Opacity.

Painting Behind

Earlier in this section, I mentioned that the Blend Mode choices, found in the upper left of all painting tool Option Palettes, will be discussed in greater detail in Chapter 5, which discusses Layers and the Layer Palette (except for the Behind Blend Mode option, which is unique to Painting, and does not apply to Layers at all).

It might be worth mentioning why I've decided to discuss Blend Modes in Chapter 5, rather than here. My rationale is that I would never advise anyone to paint with any Blend Mode other than Normal, with the exception of Behind (and maybe Dissolve). That's because, once you paint in a Blend Mode, say Multiply, it's doomed to stay like that for the life of your project—there is no going back without unraveling other things you have done in the meantime. Instead, I would recommend that if you want to apply a Blend Mode to a color, create a new layer and paint with the Normal Blend Mode option. Then change the Blend Mode of the layer itself. This ensures that you can always go back to that layer and change the Blend Mode at any point in the future. This will become clearer to you after you read Chapter 5.

To use the Behind option:

1. Activate any layer other than the Background. Layers are discussed in detail in Chapter 5.

2. Choose an image that sits in its own layer with transparency around it, much like the duck I am using in Figure 2–18. In the canvas on the left of the figure, my duck resides on its own Layer.

3. To paint behind your image (in this example, I'll paint water behind and below the duck), activate your desired tool, such as the Paintbrush, and select Behind from the Blend Mode options in the Paintbrush Options Palette. As you paint, the color will paint only on the transparent area of the layer and will not paint over any existing colored pixel. The canvas on the right of Figure 2–18 illustrates how this has affected my duck picture.

Figure 2–18: The effect of using the Paint Behind Blend Mode.

 Again, I want to stress that I would rather see you use Layers as much a possible. Even though the Behind Blend Mode is not available on the Layers Palette, I would recommend staying away from it for instances like the previous example and, instead, just applying normal paint to an underlying Layer. This gives you the most freedom to make changes later.

Painting with Wet Edges

One feature that you'll find in the Paintbrush Options Palette that you won't see in the Airbrush Options Palette is a small box marked *Wet Edges*. This creates a pretty cool aesthetic effect when you paint, as though your paintbrush were dipped in water before it picked up any color. The result as you apply the paint to your canvas is that more of the color gets pushed to the edges, which become more saturated, and less color is retained in the center area of your brush stroke. Figure 2–19 provides examples of single strokes with Wet Edges applied, as well at the cool effect you can achieve with multiple wet edge strokes placed on top of one another.

You can use Wet Edge Paintbrush strokes to really add to an image. In Figure 2–20, I've used Wet Edges with black paint along the tear in paper image. Because the color was pushed to the edge and made lighter inside, it created the effect that the edge of the paper had been burnt by a small flame. Because this particular effect takes steps that include knowing layers and selections (which we haven't covered yet), you can see the full step-by-step for creating burnt paper in Chapter 11.

Figure 2–19: Painting with Wet Edges. The strokes were painted with black. Notice how the color gets pushed to the edges. When strokes are overlapped, as they are in the X, the overlapped areas becomes darker.

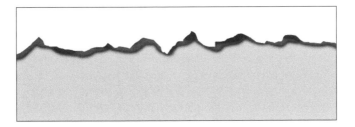

Figure 2–20: Paint with Wet Edges to create a burnt paper effect.

The Pencil Tool

The Pencil Tool, for the most part, is very similar in use to the Paintbrush Tool and Airbrush Tool, at least in terms of how to use it. As with those tools, you can draw free-hand with the Pencil by clicking on a starting point and moving your cursor to create a free form line until you're through. Or you can create straight lines at any angle by <Shift> + clicking a start point, then <Shift> + clicking an end point, and a straight line will be created between both points.

There is one area in which the Pencil tool dramatically differs from its other painting counterparts—the effect it has on the Brushes Palette. As soon as you activate the Pencil Tool, the Brushes Palette changes, as shown in Figure 2–21. As you can see, any "soft" edge that a brush may have had has disappeared, and all the brushes are now hard-edged. Don't worry, though—you didn't lose the soft-edged quality permanently. Once you select another Paint tool that utilizes the brushes, the soft edges will reappear.

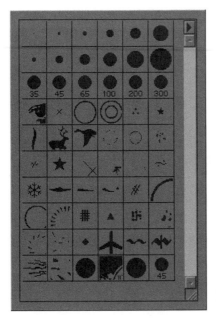

Figure 2–21: Soft-edged brushes do not exist when using the Pencil Tool.

The Eraser Tool

The Eraser Tool is as easy to use as any of the other painting tools that we've covered so far. Simply choose a brush from the Brushes Palette and click and drag over your canvas until you are done erasing. Also, like the other tools, you can erase in a straight line by <Shift> + clicking on one spot, then <Shift> + clicking in another spot.

The difference is in the result that the Eraser has. And that result is dependent on where you erase. As you'll see in Chapter 5 when we discuss Layers, the Background Layer has different properties than other Layers do. When you erase something from a non-Background Layer, it will erase to transparency, simply removing whatever it is that you're erasing, allowing objects, images and designs from underlying Layers to show through.

If you erase something from the Background Layer, however, it will not erase to transparency. Instead, it will fill the area that you are erasing with your Background color.

If you are erasing from a non-Background Layer that has Preserve Transparency checked to the On position, it will act like the Background Layer, and the area that you erase will be filled with your Background color.

One of the nice features of the Eraser Tool is that you can choose which painting tool to emulate as you erase. The pull-down menu in the upper left of the Eraser Options Palette, which usually contains the Blend Mode options, instead provides choices for brush types. You can choose from Airbrush, Paintbrush, Pencil or Block. If you choose Block, your eraser will become a small white square—you won't have to choose a brush size from the Brushes Palette—the size of the block will be set for you.

The Wet Edges options work the same way that they did in the Airbrush and Paintbrush Options Palette.

You can't choose to fade if you've selected Block as your brush type, and the Wet Edges option is available only if you select Paintbrush as your desired brush type.

LINES AND SHAPES

Creating simple solid shapes in pre-6.0 versions of Photoshop was never that difficult—to make a solid square, create a selection with the Rectangular Marquee Tool, and fill it in with a color. The same went for circles. Where it became tedious, if not downright difficult, was in creating polygons. Photoshop 6.0 has added a number of Shape Tools which make the creation of polygons quick and easy, as well as save steps by filling in with color upon creation.

But while the Shape Tools are a great addition to Photoshop, they come with a complex maze of options on the Options Palette that change somewhat radically, depending on which state you create in or which Shape Tool you want to use. Figure 2–22 shows the portions of the Options Palettes that are universal for all of the Shape and Line Tools.

As you can see, there are three creation states for Lines and Shapes: Fill Region, Create Shape Layer and Create Work Path. Before we review what each Shape and Line Tool does, we need to understand the difference between each state (all the states are the same for each of the Shape and Line Tools).

Creation State One: Fill Region

Choosing this option for any of the Shape or Line Tools will change the Options Palette to look like it does in Figure 2–23. The Mode and Opacity are as they were described previously in this chapter, and the Anti-aliased option ensures that the lines and edges around your shapes will be smooth. As you create any of your shapes or lines, they will be created on the active Layer (see Chapter 5 for more about Layers) in the Foreground color. Figure 2–24 provides an example, with the associated Layers Palette.

Figure 2–22: The Options Palette for the Shape Tools.

Figure 2–23: The Palette changes when you select the Fill Region option.

Figure 2–24: Various shapes you can make.

Creation State Two: Create Shape Layer

This option will change your Options Palette twice: The top portion of Figure 2–25 shows the Options Palette as it appears for any of the Shape or Line Tools. Again, the Mode and Opacity areas appear, but this time are accompanied by a new area, called *Layer Style*. A cool addition that allows you to instantly create shades with pre-developed bevels, embosses, drop shadows, and other attributes.

The real difference with this creation state is that the line or shape that you create will appear on its own layer, with a clipping path around it, as Figure 2–26 shows. (Paths are discussed in more detail in Chapter 4.) In addition, once your place you line or shape, the Options Palette will change, as shown in the bottom portion of Figure 2–25. This new area allows you to very easily add to the path area, subtract from the path area, restrict or invert the path area.

You can change the color of any shape that you place on a Shape Layer without having to change your Foreground or Background color, just by clicking on the left-hand thumbnail of the Shape Layer. This will bring up the Color Picker, and you can quickly change the color of your shapes.

Figure 2–25: The Options Palette in its various states.

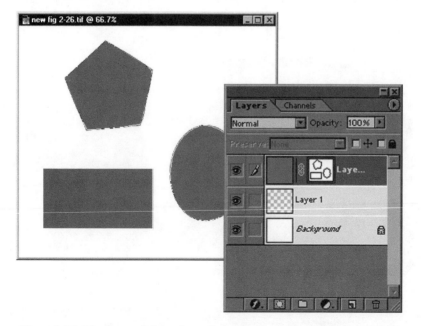

Figure 2–26: The Layers Palette shows the paths that are created around the shapes.

To return to the original Options Palette, you must first activate a layer that does not contain shape paths.

Creation State Three: Create Work Path

The third creation state has to do with making and working with instant paths for the shape you create. I'll review it further in Chapter 4.

Creating Lines

This is a pretty straightforward tool (Ha!! Get it? Lines...*straightforward*! Sometimes I make myself laugh). The Line Tool is used for creating straight and diagonal lines and arrows, at various thicknesses, a collection of which is displayed in Figure 2–27.

To create a line, simply click any place on your canvas where you want your line to start and drag to the point that you want your line to end. Pretty simple.

Line Options and Arrowheads

On the far right of the Shape Tool selection bar in the Line Tool Options Palette is a small arrow, indicating a drop-down menu. Clicking on this with the Line Tool activated accesses the Line Options dialog box shown in Figure 2–28.

 If you're not confused enough already, I agree that naming this dialog box *Line Options* when we're already in the Line Options Palette is confusing. Like having two sons and naming them both *John*.

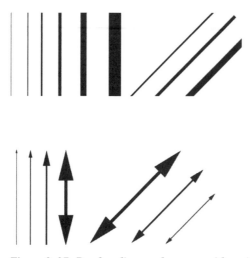

Figure 2–27: Random lines and arrows, with various lengths and thicknesses.

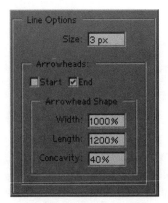

Figure 2–28: The Line Options dialog box.

The first value area at the top of the Line Options dialog box allows you to adjust the width of the line you create. The underlying portion is for creating arrowheads. To activate this area, you must first check a box to have an arrowhead created at either the start or end of your line, or both. This will allow you to adjust the arrowhead shape further.

The Width and Length are measured in percent of the line itself and, by default, are set to 500% and 1000%, respectively. These tend to be okay, although they result in a pretty obvious and large arrowhead. I usually reduce both values a bit but always leave the Length a higher percentage than the Width. The Concavity, which is set to 0% by default, affects how the arrowhead connects to the line itself and is limited to a minimum value of –50% and a maximum value of 50%.

Once you set variables for your lines and arrowheads, those variables will be retained until the next time you decide to change them, even if you close Photoshop and open it again later. Unfortunately, there is no way to save line and arrowhead styles in any sort of palette for library purposes.

Creating Rectangle and Ellipse Shapes

The Circle and Square Shape Tools don't do much more than save you a step (instead of creating a selection and filling it with a color, the Shape Tools fill it in automatically). The color that your shape will fill with is your Foreground color. Creating a rectangle or ellipse is as simple as creating a line—click an area of your canvas in which you would like to create your shape, and drag until you have created your shape the size that you want. If you read Chapter 3 or are familiar with making circular or rectangular selections using the Marquee Tools, this will be a snap for you: The same rules apply with shapes as they do with selections. Shapes will, by default, be created from the corner. Hold the <Option> (<Alt> in Windows) key while dragging to create your shape from the center instead, and the <Shift> key while dragging to constrain the proportions.

If you know the exact size of the rectangle or ellipse that you wish to create, open the Options dialog box from the Palette pull-down menu, as shown in Figure 2–29. From here, you can set the exact dimensions for your shape to be created.

Figure 2–29: The Ellipse Options dialog box lets you fill in the dimensions for precision.

Creating Polygons

Access the Polygon Options Palette's pull-down menu to access the dialog box shown in Figure 2–30. From this dialog box, you'll be able to set the parameter for how your polygon will be created. Although this seems *very* simple, it's a vastly important improvement to Photoshop, because polygons of any complexity used to be very tedious and time-consuming to create.

Enter the number of sides you would like in the Sides value area. Entering the number 8, for example, creates a standard octagon. Check the Star box to change the number from "sides" to "points" (although the word won't actually change from "sides" to "points" in the dialog box). The percentage you set will be the slope of each line for a point in the star.

Figure 2–31 provides a few examples of different polygons, as well as the values and options associated with each.

Figure 2–30: The Polygon Options dialog box lets you be more specific with your polygons.

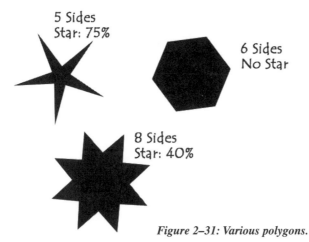

Figure 2–31: Various polygons.

Creating Custom Shapes

Another new tool allows you to customize your shapes for use again in the future. There are already a few shapes ready for you to use that come with Photoshop, such as hearts, stars, moons, diamonds (apparently, the Photoshop guys have a bowl or two of Lucky Charms).

Using the shapes provided is quite easy—from the Shape Tool Options Palette, just click the button for Custom Shape, and select any shape from the Shape menu. Simply drag on your canvas, and the shape is created in your Foreground color. Hold the <Shift> key as usual for constraint.

For more control, click the small arrow next to the Custom Shape button in the Options Palette. The menu that appears will allow you to set the size and proportions of your shape, if you need them to be a certain dimension.

But the real value in this tool is that you can create your own custom shapes to save and use later. Although having your own shapes is helpful, creating them is just weird—a convoluted process that begs the question "Why?" I'm pretty sure that there could have been an easier way...oh, well.

So, if you want to make your own shape, here's the ugly details of how to go about it:

1. Create something on its own layer. Anything, really. Paint a line, put two selections together and fill them with a color. Whatever you'd like.

2. If the object that you want to make into a custom shape is not currently selected, make a selection from it by <Command> + clicking (<Ctrl> + clicking in Windows) the layer that it's in.

3. Choose Windows -> Show Paths to open the Paths Palette (for some reason, Photoshop 6 seems to REALLY want you to use paths...I'm not sure exactly why...). From the Paths Palette pull-down menu, select Make Work Path, and set a Tolerance of .5 (the lowest Tolerance value you can choose). I'll go more into this in Chapter 4. Click OK, and you'll see a path created around your selection.

4. Choose Edit -> Define Custom Shape, and provide a name for your shape in the dialog box. Click OK and your new shape will appear in the Shape menu.

5. To use the custom shape, choose it from the Shape menu, click and drag on your canvas. This is illustrated in Figure 2–32.

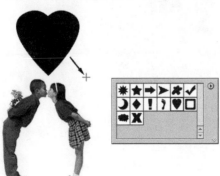

Figure 2–32: Placing a shape from the Custom Shape menu.

You can do this with any path that you have, not just a Work Path that you've made from a selection. You can also create a custom shape from paths found in Shape Layers or Saved Paths, as well.

APPLYING COLOR

Although all of the tools we've seen so far have dealt with color in one way or another—whether painting it on or erasing it off—the following two tools are more immersed in the direct application of color than they are in the artistic rendition of that color.

Using the Gradient Tool

The Gradient Tool has gone through some evolutions in Photoshop, and with each version it continues to get better. You would use the Gradient Tool when you wish to fill an area with a color blend—from one color into another, multiple colors or even transparency. The various Gradient Tools you can choose from allow you to set your gradients in a linear fashion, radial, diamond, angle or even reflective.

To use the Gradient Tool, simply select it from the toolbar, and click and drag through your canvas or selection. The longer you drag, the smoother your gradient will be. Shorter drags will create harsher gradients, as Figure 2–33 illustrates.

By default, your gradient will be created from your Foreground to your Background color and is previewed in the Gradient Tool's Options Palette, shown in Figure 2–34. You can change the gradient to any one of a number of preset gradients provided to you on the pull-down menu, or you can customize your own gradient by clicking on the gradient preview to access the Gradient Editor dialog box, shown in Figure 2–35.

Figure 2–33: Longer drags create smoother gradients, like the one on the left. Shorter drags create sharper gradients, like the one on the right.

Figure 2–34: The Gradient Tool's Options Palette.

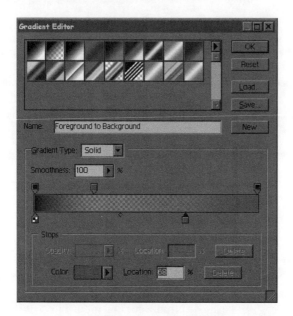

Figure 2–35: The Gradient Editor dialog box.

To use the Gradient Editor:

1. With an open canvas, activate the Gradient Tool from the toolbar.
2. To create a standard gradient with two or more colors fading one into the other, Leave the Gradient Type set at its default of Solid to create a standard gradient, with two or more colors fading one into the other. We'll review the alternate option later in this section.
3. Set the Smoothness value to its desired level. As you reduce the Smoothness, you'll increase the graininess and banding that will occur in your gradient.
4. The Gradient Bar within the dialog box is where you will do your creation work. The top of the bar controls the Opacity and Transparency of your gradient. The two markers on the extreme sides of the bar are solid black, indicating that they are 100% opaque. You can adjust this by clicking on one of the markers and changing the Opacity value. As you reduce the opacity, the marker is represented in shades of gray, with pure white indicating that it is at 0% opacity, or 100% transparency.

5. You can move the transparency markers to another location along the bar by dragging them. Add new markers simply by clicking in the spot along the top of the bar where you wish to add a marker. By doing this, you can create a gradient that has multiple points of transparency and opacity. To remove a marker, simply drag the marker up off the bar.

You need to have at least two markers existing on the gradient bar so that, after you remove so many markers, only two remain; those two will not be able to be dragged off.

6. The bottom of the gradient bar controls the color. By default, the color marker on the extreme left will represent the Foreground color, and the color marker on the extreme right will represent the Background color. To change the color, click on a marker, and use the Color field pull-down menu, or click the color swatch to access the dialog box.

7. Like the Transparency markers, you can add markers anywhere along the bottom of the bar to add a new color. Remove these markers by dragging them downward, away from the bar. You can move the markers anywhere along the bar to create a good array of colors and gradients.

8. In between any of the markers, for both transparency and color, are small diamonds that are made visible when a marker is clicked on. These diamond icons indicate the central point of the gradient between any two markers. Drag it to change the gradient midpoint.

Chapter 11 provides an example in which the Gradient Tool is used.

Choosing Noise from the Gradient Type pull-down menu changes the dialog to look like the one shown in Figure 2–36. With the Noise gradient, you are working with multiple thin bands of color to create a really dynamic, highly colorful gradient. With this one, however, there are no color or transparency markers to adjust—the bands are pretty firm, take them or leave them. You can adjust the way in which they work together, though, by adjusting the Roughness value. A lower value will increase the blur between each color band, while a higher value will increase the stark edges between each color band.

Use the sliders in the Color Model portion to add red, green or blue tints to the color bands, and click the Transparency checkbox on to add transparency to the gradient (oddly enough, you can't control the amount of transparency that is included into the gradient). To radically change the colors of the gradient, click the Randomize button.

The Paint Bucket Tool

The Paint Bucket Tool is nothing unique to Photoshop. If you've seen it in one painting program you've seen it in all of them. But Photoshop does give you wider control over the Paint Bucket than most other programs do.

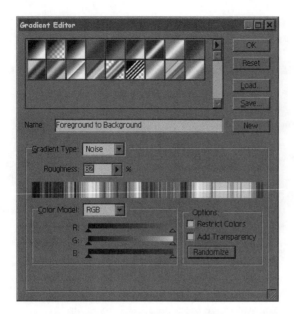

Figure 2–36: The Gradient Editor changes when you choose Noise from the Type drop-down menu.

Basically, the Paint Bucket is used for filling in an area with a color. With the Paint Bucket Tool selected, click on an area that you would like to fill with your Foreground color. The extent of the fill will rely on the Tolerance that you set in the Paint Bucket Options Palette, shown in Figure 2–37. By default, the Tolerance will be set to 32. This means that when you click on a pixel to fill and area with your Foreground color, the fill will encompass all of the contiguous pixels that are within 32 shades of the color you clicked on. Raise the Tolerance value to cause your fill to cover a larger area, or reduce the Tolerance value to ensure that a smaller area will be filled.

You can also limit your fill by making a selection of an area first. Making selections is covered in Chapter 3.

As a quickie editorial to the Paint Bucket Tool, I've never actually figured out why a designer would want to apply a fill to any area if the result was only going to be partial and seemingly random in nature. I have, however, had the displeasure of watching designers use the Paint Bucket to try to fill a large selection by playing with the Tolerance and continuously clicking on different pixels with the Paint Bucket. Depending on the selection, this method could take forever.

Instead, try applying a fill by making a selection first (selections are discussed in Chapter 3) and using the keyboard shortcuts to fill your selection completely with one keystroke. To fill with the Foreground color, push <Option> + <Delete> (<Alt> + <Backspace> in Windows), or <Command> + <Delete> (<Ctrl> + <Backspace> in Windows).

Figure 2–37: The Paint Bucket Option Palette.

The one area where the Paint Bucket Tool is useful, though, is in filling with a pattern. Choose Pattern from the pull-down menu in the Paint Bucket Option's menu, then select a pattern to choose from the choices provided. You can create your own pattern by selecting any design, image or portion of an image, and choosing Edit -> Define Pattern.

THE "MANIPULATION" PAINTING TOOLS

In an about-face from the other tools that apply color to the canvas, the following tools don't apply color at all. Instead, the following tools manipulate color or images that have already been applied or already exist in your canvas.

Smudge Tool

This one can actually be kind of fun. Figure 2–38 (Color Figure 2) shows a planet on fire—the flames were made using the help of the Smudge Tool on a white circle.

As with the other tools, you use the Smudge Tool by selecting a brush size, clicking a point on your image and dragging your cursor until you are through. The other options that are found in the Smudge Tool Options Palette work in pretty much the same way as they do in other brushes that we've already reviewed.

Figure 2–38: The flames of the fire were made with the Smudge Tool.

To experience one of the most frustrating things that you can do in Photoshop, try to open a large image at a high resolution on a computer with a relatively slow processor or insufficient amount of RAM. Then take a large brush and try to use the Smudge Tool over a large area of your image. Wow, does that suck. You'll be forced to wait it out, as Photoshop slowly tries to fingerpaint your image, little by little. On second thought, don't try this after all—take my word for it that you really don't want that kind of stress.

Blur Tool

Another neat tool, the Blur Tool, will cause an image to become blurry in specific areas. It works exactly the same as all of the other tools, in that you choose a brush from the Brushes Palette and click and drag the areas that you want to blur. Obviously, the larger the brush, the more area you'll blur. Figure 2–39 shows a sample of the results of using the Blur Tool.

For particularly useful results, use the Blur Tool sparingly, especially for hard edges that need just minor blending. This is where this tool works the best. For larger areas, use the Gaussian Blur Filter, which is faster and more evenly distributed.

The Hopelessly Pointless Sharpen Tool

Actually, this tool is such a hopelessly pointless tool that I really don't want to waste any time or ink writing about it. It takes a lot of effort to write one of these sections, and I refuse to get carpal tunnel syndrome for a tool that doesn't work.

It's supposed to sharpen blurry images, but a glance at Figure 2–40 shows you how successfully this is usually pulled off. Instead, try to use the Unsharp Mask Filter, described in Chapter 7.

Figure 2–39: Results from using the Blur Tool.

Figure 2–40: Don't even bother with the Sharpen Tool—at least not for sharpening anything.

Liquify

When Photoshop 5.5 came out, I could pretty much predict what changes would be made to version 6.0. The Shape Tools and better text editing features aren't anything new, really—they're just preexisting qualities that already existed in ImageReady and were integrated into Photoshop. But the Liquify feature was kind of out of left field. As I've said in Chapter 1, as well as in other books and numerous magazine articles, the Liquify is part of the reason why Photoshop is such a RAM hog these days (at least a bigger RAM hog than it used to be). While it might do some neat stuff, designers who need to work with this type of feature (and I doubt that it really holds much practical value) should just spend the extra hundred bucks and buy Kai's Power Goo. It does what Liquify does, only far better and with far more options. Plus, it's got what I consider to be the hands-down coolest interface I've seen on a mass-marketed commercial design program.

To use the Liquify command, have an image open and choose Image -> Liquify to open the dialog box shown and described in Figure 2–41. Within this dialog box, your image becomes malleable, in some cases acting as a Smudge tool to the extreme degree.

The Liquify Toolbar

The toolbar at the left of the Liquify dialog box is divided into three areas. The upper portion of the toolbar allows you to choose any one of a number of manipulation tools, including those that warp, twirl or make a portion of your image infinitely bigger or smaller.

To use the Warp, Shift Pixel or Reflection Tools, use your brush as you would any other brush-oriented painting tool that we've reviewed in this chapter: Drag your cursor over the areas that you want to manipulate.

To use either of the Twirl Tools, the Pucker or Bloat Tools, don't move your cursor at all. Instead, place the cursor over the area that you want to affect, and hold the mouse button down. Release the button when you're through.

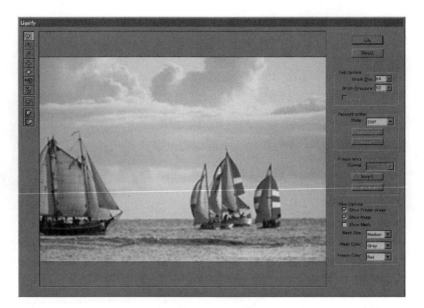

Figure 2–41: The Liquify dialog box.

The center area of the toolbar only has one tool—the Reconstruct Tool, which is really pretty cool. As you drag over an area that you have previously affected with one of the manipulation tools, the Reconstruction Tool will rebuild and undo any of the changes that you've made. It's pretty amazing to watch in action.

The Freeze Tool in the lower portion of the toolbar allows you to preserve any portion of your image that you don't want to be affected by any of the manipulation or reconstruction tools. Simply drag your cursor over the area that you wish to preserve. To unpreserve this area or a portion of this area, do the same with the Thaw Tool.

Figure 2–42 provides an example of an image that has gone through some Liquify manipulations, with each distinct manipulation labeled for convenience.

The Command Areas

On the right side of the Liquify dialog box are the command areas. These are, for the most part, issues of practicality and necessity, with the exception of the Reconstruction area, which is also just kind of graphically fun.

The first command area, called *Tool Options*, allows you to change the pixel diameter of the brush size you will use, either by filling in a numeric value manually or by using the pull-down slider. A subsequent area also allows you to adjust the pressure of your brush—the higher the value, the more effect your strokes will have in manipulating your image.

Figure 2–42: This image has gone through some interesting liquifications.

The Reconstruction area is what controls how your image gets put back together, if you decide that you went a little overboard in your manipulation of your image. The Reconstruction command area can work alone or in conjunction with the Reconstruction Tool in the toolbar. Different options in the Mode pull-down menu change the way that the Reconstruction Tool will rebuild your image. Because some of these choices are so dynamic, the Reconstruction Tool can also manipulate your image just as effectively as any other tool in the dialog box.

The Reconstruct button will rebuild your image from its manipulated state back to its original form over a period of steps. It's fun to watch, but kind of a shame that you can't stop its process when it hits a state in rebuilding that you like.

The Revert button at the bottom of this area simply removes all changes to the image, regardless of what you have done to it. This includes changing any area that you have frozen back to what it was originally.

You can still undo your last step, even if that last step was pushing the Revert button, by pushing <Command> (<Ctrl> in Windows) + <Z> (the keyboard command for Undo). You can also revert by holding the <Option> (<Alt> in Windows) key. As with any dialog box, this will change the Cancel button to a Reset button. Pushing the Reset button will not only bring your image back to original form, but will also reset any value or setting that you have made since you opened the Liquify dialog box.

The main difference between the Reconstruct button and the Revert button is the Revert button will bring your image back to its original state, regardless of what you have done to it. The Reconstruct button, though, will rebuild your image, bringing it back to its original form, but leave any manipulated areas that you have frozen with the Freeze Tool untouched in the reconstruction.

As with the Reconstruction Tool, there really isn't much use for the Reconstruction area or any of the associated buttons, unless you have first made some manipulation to your image.

A HISTORICAL PERSPECTIVE

The History Palette, introduced in Photoshop 5.0, is one of the all-time better additions to the program in recent years. Aside from some creative effects that you can do with it, the History Palette allows for multiple undos, so that there is plenty of room for error and experimentation. But maybe one of the nicest things is that, for the most part, Adobe actually left the History Palette alone in version 6.0. Hint: some things don't need upgrading.

The Palette Figure 2–43 shows and describes the History Palette. Above the solid black line is a picture of the original image, as it was before any manipulations. By double-clicking on it, your picture will revert back to its original state.

In the palette, each state of manipulation is given its own title, such as *Paste* or *Opacity Change*, and are stacked downward in the order that they are completed. By clicking on any title in the palette, your image will go back to the way it looked before you applied that state's command. The History Palette will hold 20 states as its default—any states after that will be added at the expense of the oldest states.

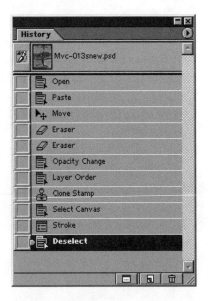

Figure 2–43: The History Palette.

Once you revert to an older state, all of the states that came afterward will disappear. This is by default, which we will learn to change coming up.

Many times when you're working, your image will be at a point that you'd like to be able to revert back to, even though you're going to continue to work on it. As we'll see in the next section, the more states you have in your History Palette, the more memory Photoshop will eat up. If you want to revert back to a state later in your work, regardless of how many commands you go through, you can take a snapshot of your image. To do this, choose New Snapshot from the History Palette menu. A dialog box will appear, giving you the opportunity to name your snapshot if you'd like. Click OK, and your image in its current form will be saved in the History Palette above the black line at the top, right below the image's original state, as shown in Figure 2–44. To revert back to this state at any time, just click on it.

Settings

Choosing History Options from the Palette menu brings up the dialog box shown in Figure 2–45. Most of the options in this check boxed dialog box are pretty straightforward, with the exception of the most important one. The third one down says *Allow Non-Linear History*. I usually keep this one checked, unless I'm really low on memory. As I explained earlier, once you revert to a state, all of the states that had come afterward will gray out. By checking this button, you will be able to revert to one state but keep all subsequent states intact. This is a great feature, but it also consumes memory.

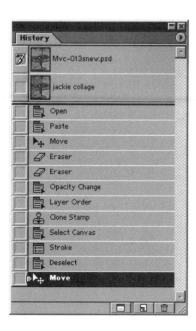

Figure 2–44: The small icon named **Jackie Collage** *is a snapshot of a state that I can go back to at any time.*

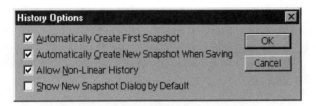

Figure 2–45: The History Options dialog box.

A Few Negatives

There are some negatives that are associated with the History Palette, the two most prominent of which are:

◆   Megatonage: The History Palette takes up a lot of memory. You're likely to run into a lot more "out of memory" type errors than you did in previous versions of Photoshop. To reduce the possibility of running out of memory, or to regain lost memory take one of the following steps:

   1. Open the History Options dialog box (as described above) and uncheck the box marked *Allow Non-Linear History*.

   2. Choose Edit -> Purge -> Histories (you cannot undo this option, so make sure that you really want to do it before making this choice).

   3. You can reduce the maximum number of History states that are allowed. In the past, you could adjust this through a value area provided in the History Options dialog box. But that probably made too much sense, so the boys at Adobe cleverly moved it to the the Preferences area. To change the maximum number of History States, choose Edit -> Preferences -> General. Look off to the right side of the dialog box—it's hiding in there someplace. Nothing like playing a good game of "hide and seek" with an important option.

◆   Too Much of a Good Thing: Don't get too used to the History Palette saving you from mistakes. I've fallen into the trap of continuing to make corrections to my image without saving, thinking that I can always go back to a previous state if I want to. But when I unhappily crash (yes, I use a Macintosh), my History Palette is completely clear when I reopen my image. The information in this palette does not remain between uses of Photoshop.

The History Brushes

The History Brushes feature works in conjunction with the History Palette. Clicking on one of the titles in the History Palette will bring your image back to that entire state, and the History Brush will do the same but only for the portions of your image that you paint over. Each manipulation title in your image has a small empty box next to it on the left. Clicking in one of those boxes will cause an icon of the History Brush to appear. That icon marks the state on the History Palette that you will revert to. As you use the History Brush to paint over your image, it will revert back to the marked state in the areas that you brush over. Figure 2–46 and Color Figure 3 illustrate this.

There is another History Brush, called the *Art History Brush* that works much the same way but with a watercolor style to it. It works exactly the same as the regular History Brush, but the results make your image look more like a watercolor painting.

Figure 2–46: Effects created with the History Palette.

SUMMARY

Would Bob Ross have had as much appeal painting "happy little trees" if he was on a computer instead of a canvas? Who knows—with Photoshop, he could have painted his way into any landscape he wanted, without the mess of acrylics! Photoshop allows you to replicate the painting process with a wide selection of brushes and tools that work together in various ways to provide a strong range of artistic effects. As we'll see in upcoming chapters, when these tools combine with layers, channels, and other Photoshop capabilities, the results you can achieve would even make Picasso get excited!

chapter 3

MAKING

AND USING

SELECTIONS

Selections allow you to isolate a specific part of your image, so that any changes or manipulations, copies or pastes can be made strictly to that area. The fact that you'll need to make selections in Photoshop to accomplish certain tasks is a given. How you'll go about creating them is the real question. Perhaps more than any other function, Photoshop provides a seemingly limitless list of tools and techniques for making selections from an image.

Remember, Photoshop is like a mountain; a completed project acts as the peak. The trick is to realize that there is more than one way to climb the mountain, and each path requires different tools. But whether the challenge at hand is capturing a simple geometric shape, the silhouette of a person or all the green leaves in an October forest, Photoshop provides you the tools you'll need to get the job done. It's up to you which tools you'll use—as long as you reach the top of the mountain, it all works.

GETTING UP TO SPEED: MAKING SIMPLE SELECTIONS

As with in other chapters in this book, I don't want anyone to feel left behind. So I'll use these next few pages quickly to illustrate some of the more basic features of making selections, then move onto the more complex issues.

Making Shape Selections:
The Marquee and Lasso Tools

Color Figure 1 shows the icons for making simple shapes and selections. The icons shown, in order, are the Rectangular Marquee Tool, the Elliptical Marquee Tool, the Free Form Lasso Tool and the Polygonal Lasso Tool. Although these will be described in examples using an empty white canvas, they can obviously be used for selecting similarly shaped objects from within an image.

To make a selection with either of the Marquee selection tools:

1. Open a new canvas. Any size will be fine (just make it big enough to have room to play).

2. With the Rectangular or Elliptical Marquee Tool, click anywhere on the canvas and hold the mouse button down. Drag in the direction that you want to create your shape, and release the mouse button when through. The "Marching Ants" will appear as an outline to show you your selection.

The term *Marching Ants* refers to the dashed lines that surround your selection and seem to flicker on and off, or march, so to speak. These are temporary and will go away when you deselect your selection (discussed later in this chapter).

3. You'll notice that each of the shapes is created from the corner, as illustrated in the left part of Figure 3–1. This can be helpful in certain instances and can make life tougher in other instances. The alternative to creating a shape from the corner would be creating it from the middle, as illustrated in the right part of Figure 3–1. To create your shape from the middle, simply hold the <Option> key (<Alt> in Windows) as you drag your mouse.

4. When you create your shape, you'll also notice that you have free reign over the aspect ratio. To constrain the proportions and create either a perfect circle or perfect square, hold the <Shift> key down as you drag.

Make sure you release the mouse *before* you let the <Shift> key go. If you do it the other way around, you'll end up frustrated, and you'll lose the proportion constraints of your shape.

Holding the <Shift> key down works to constrain a lot of things in Photoshop. You'll start seeing this a lot as you read through this book.

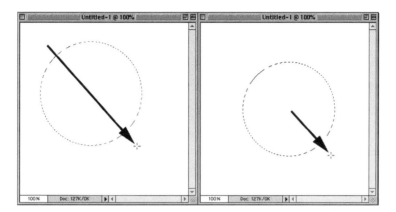

Figure 3–1: The selection on the left is created from the corner, while the selection on the right is created from the middle.

To make a selection with the Free Form Lasso Tool:

1. Open a new canvas. Any size will be fine (just make it big enough to have room to play).
2. Click and drag. Make sure you're holding down the mouse button the whole time. Feel free to go in any direction that you would like—the selection you are making is completely up to you.
3. Your selection will close at the same spot in which it was started. To close your selection, either let go of the mouse button at any time (a straight line will be made from the point at which you stop to the point at which you started) or drag the mouse and the selection you are making back to your original starting point.
4. Hold the <Option> button (<Alt> in Windows) to access the Polygonal Lasso temporarily, discussed next.

To make a selection with the Polygonal Lasso Tool:

1. Open a new canvas. Any size will be fine (just make it big enough to have room to play).
2. Just click. A point will be created on your canvas.
3. Click anywhere else on your canvas. A straight line between the two points will be created. Continue this for as long as you want.
4. As with the Free Form Lasso Tool, the selection needs to close at the same point in which it was started. Either click on the original starting point to close your selection or just double-click at any point to create a straight line from that point to the starting point.
5. Hold the <Option> key (<Alt> in Windows) to access the Free Form Lasso temporarily, discussed previously.

Figure 3–2 gives an example of selections made with both of these tools.

Using the two Lasso Tools together can be tricky. In instances such as Figure 3–3, where both Lasso Tools would be needed, it can be somewhat frustrating to use the <Option> key (<Alt> in Windows) to toggle between the two. Don't get frustrated—a good rule to remember is to hold the mouse button down immediately before holding the <Option> (<Alt>) button and holding it down once again immediately before letting the <Option> (<Alt>) button go.

Sometimes, when using the Free Form Tool for a long while to make complex selections, your wrist will get tired or your fingers will ache from holding down the mouse key for so long. If that happens, you obviously can't let go without prematurely ending your selection. Just hold the <Option> (<Alt>) key and you can let go of the mouse and shake out the strain. Hold the mouse button down before you let go of the <Option> (<Alt>) button when you're ready to resume your work.

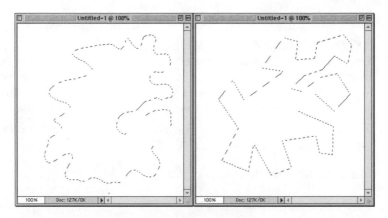

Figure 3–2: Sample selections made with various Lasso Tools.

Fig 3–3: Using the <Option> (<Alt>) key can help toggle between the Polygonal and Free Form Lasso Tools, helpful in making selections in images such as this.

Making Color-Based Selections: The Magic Wand and Magnetic Lasso

Color Figure 1 shows two other icons that appear in the Tools Palette for making selections. The first icon shown is the Magic Wand Tool, and the second is the Magnetic Lasso Tool. Neither tool does much good on a white canvas, because they both require color or varying shades to serve any useful purpose. We'll use the picture shown in Figure 3–4 and Color Figure 4 as the base picture for illustrating these tools.

The Magic Wand Tool

From a conceptual standpoint, the Magic Wand is a really cool tool. Let's suppose that I wanted to select the entire sky in my image. As you can see in the color figure, the sky in this desert image is blue. The varying shades of gray, however, illustrate that this sky is not made up of one solid shade of blue, but rather many shades of blue, with a few clouds also hovering around. I could use the Free Form Lasso Tool, as described earlier, but that might take a while, especially considering the uneven horizon and the clouds. The better choice for making the selection would be the Magic Wand.

The Magic Wand Tool makes its selections from colors and shades. You work with the Magic Wand Palette to increase the amount of colors that will be included in any given selection. To use this tool:

1. With the Magic Wand Tool activated, push the <Return> key (<Enter> in Windows) to access the Options Palette, shown in Figure 3–5. You can also activate it by double-clicking the tool icon in the Tools Palette or choosing Show Options from the Windows menu.

Figure 3–4: Base picture that I'll use for making color-based selections.

Figure 3–5: The Magic Wand Options Palette.

2. In the Options Palette, fill in the Tolerance level you desire. The Tolerance indicates the amount of shades of your chosen color that will be included in your selection. For example, if you fill in a Tolerance of 100 and click on a blue pixel in your image, that color plus all contiguous colors that fall within 100 shades of that blue will be selected. (go ahead—read that sentence over again. I'll wait...). You'll likely have a very large selection. If your Tolerance is set low, say, at a level of 5, then only your chosen color plus any contiguous pixels that fall within 5 shades will be selected. Figure 3–6 provides an example.

In short, simply remember that the higher the tolerance, the larger your selection will be.

3. Click anywhere in the sky portion of the image. The Marching Ants will appear to outline your selection, as illustrated in Figure 3–6.

4. You can add noncontiguous pixels within the color range of the selected pixel by choosing Select -> Similar. Other ways to add to your selection will be discussed later in this section.

5. In Photoshop 5.5 and previous versions, the Magic Wand Tool would take into consideration only the colors and pixels that existed in the active Layer. In 6.0, however, you can treat the image as a composite when using the Magic Wand Tool by activating the Use All Layers checkbox in the Options Palette. Anything that you do to your selection will still happen only on the active Layer, but the Wand Tool will make a selection of anything you click on, regardless of what Layer is active. Figure 3–7 illustrates this.

The Magnetic Lasso Tool

The Magnetic Lasso Tool also works with colors and/or shades to make selections. The Magnetic Lasso Tool, added to the toolbar in version 5.0 as a way to save time when making selections, will discriminate between colors and find the edge, creating a fairly accurate selection. I don't tend to use this tool very often, but it comes in handy once in awhile.

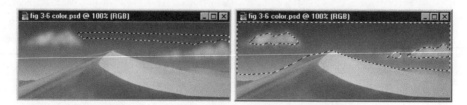

Figure 3–6: The image on the left shows the selection with a Magic Wand Tolerance of 100. The image on the right shows the selection with a Magic Wand Tolerance of 5.

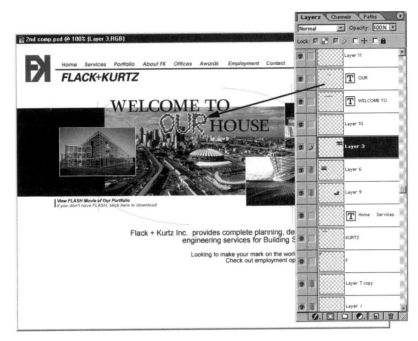

Figure 3–7: In this canvas with a lot of Layers, letters in the word "OUR" were selected by clicking on them with the Magic Wand Tool, even though a different layer is active.

Figure 3–8 shows a picture of my friend, Jackie. In this particular picture, I needed to do significant work to the skin tone, which seemed a bit too red. I tried to even it out. Because there is a good contrast between Jackie, her background, and her dress, the Magnetic Lasso Tool is helpful in making a selection of her.

You can make the Magnetic Lasso Tool more or less sensitive and accurate by manipulating the controls in the Options dialog box:

♦ Lasso Width will establish how sensitive the tool is to color differences in your image. The higher the number, the more sensitive and discriminatory the tool will be in its selection, so even shades of the same color will be separated.

♦ Frequency will set the number of points, or anchors, that will be placed as your cursor changes direction when you move it around your image. These can help you in the event of a mistake or an accidental wrong turn—simply retrace your steps to a previous point and click on it. You'll be able to resume making your selection in the proper direction.

♦ Edge Contrast will determine how drastically different surrounding and adjoining colors have to be for the Magnetic Lasso to include them. Use a high percentage if you have very stark color transitions.

This tool doesn't necessarily work by itself—some portions of an image may have more contrast than other portions, and setting your own points by clicking is often required. As you can see in Figure 3–8 and Color Figure 5 there are a few areas that have less contrast between Jackie and the background. These parts of an image need more detailed work and manually set points than the simple clicking and dragging that I had done to this point. Don't be surprised if your first few tries with a tool are a little frustrating.

Adding to, Subtracting from and Intersecting Selections

Well, if everything that you needed to select in Photoshop were as easy as making a rectangle or oval, we'd all be finished with our projects in a hour or so and have a lot more time to develop our social lives. Obviously, most projects are not that easy. More often, you'll need to manipulate your selections by adding to them, subtracting from them or creating an intersection between two selections. When you do these things, you don't necessarily need to be using the same tool each time; for example, if you make a selection with the Rectangular Marquee Tool, you can add a Free Form Lasso selection.

Doing any of these functions is rather easy—knowing when to use them and in what instances they can be helpful takes a bit of practice. Later on in this section, we'll examine a few instances in which selection tools can be used together.

In Photoshop 5.5 and previous versions, you needed to use keyboard commands to add, subtract or intersect selections. They're still the best way to go, but version 6.0 has also included a nonkeyboard way to do these functions. Figure 3–9 shows and describes the

Figure 3–8: The Magnetic Lasso Tool works well with images that have a good contrast from their background.

area of the Options Palette that deals with these commands (they're the same in all of the selection tools' Options Palettes). If you choose to use the Options Palette for adding, subtracting or intersecting, you won't need to hold any keys while doing so.

Adding to a Selection

To add to a selection:

1. With a selection made, choose a selection tool that you want to use to add to it.
2. Push and hold the <Shift> button down while you create your new selection, or push the "Add to selection" button in the Options Palette for that tool. Your cursor will have a little plus sign next to it (+). The new selection will be added to your original one. You can do this as often as you want or need. Figure 3–10 illustrates this.

Subtracting from a Selection

To subtract from a selection:

1. With a selection made, choose a selection tool that you want to use to subtract from it.

Figure 3–9: The portion of the Options Palette in version 6.0 that is used for adding, subtracting and intersecting (restricting).

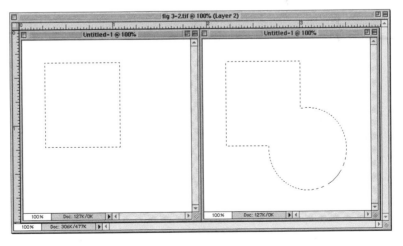

Figure 3–10: Adding one selection to another.

2. Push and hold the <Option> key (<Alt> in Windows) as you create your new selection or push the "Subtract from selection" button in the Options Palette for that tool. Your cursor will have a little minus sign (-) next to it. The area in which your new selection overlaps with the original selection will be subtracted from the original selection. Figure 3–11 illustrates this.

Intersecting Selections

To find the intersection of selections (probably the least useful of these functions):

1. With a selection made, choose a selection tool that you want to use to intersect with it.
2. Push and hold both the <Shift> and <Option> keys (<Shift> and <Alt> in Windows) as you create your new selection, or push the "Restrict selection" button in the Options Palette for that tool. Your cursor will have a little *x* next to it. The area where your new selection overlaps with the original selection will be the only area of each selection that is retained. Figure 3–12 illustrates this.

Combining Selection Tools and Functions

Using the various selection tools in conjunction with one another can be its own unique talent. The following examples show just a few of the creative ways in which you can use the different tools and functions together to achieve the selection that you want.

Example One

Figure 3–13 shows an image of a rudimentary fish. Notice that, for the most part, the fish is made of curved edges. The tail and mouth, though, are made up of straight edges and corners.

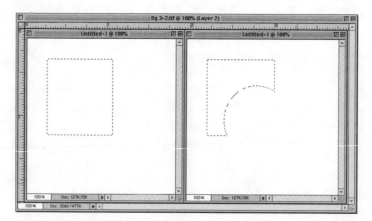

Figure 3–11: Holding the <Option> (<Alt>) key while making a selection will subtract from the existing selection.

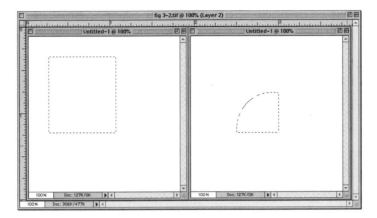

Figure 3–12: Holding both the <Shift> and <Option> (<Alt>) key while making a selection leaves just the intersection of the new and old selections.

Figure 3–13: This rudimentary fish will take a combination of the Free Form Lasso and Straight Edge Lasso to select.

To make this selection:

1. Choose the Free Form Lasso Tool to start making the selection.
2. Click on point A in the image and hold the mouse button down.
3. Begin dragging the mouse clockwise around the edge of the fish as best you can until point B.
4. Hold the <Option> key (<Alt> in Windows) to access the Polygonal Lasso Tool temporarily.
5. While still holding the <Option> (<Alt>) key, release the mouse button. You'll now begin to create a selection from points, rather than by dragging.
6. Click on point C. You'll see a straight line created between points B and C.
7. Click on point D. Another straight line will be created.

8. At this point, you'll need to access the Free Form Lasso Tool again to select the underside of the fish, just as you selected the top side of the fish. Release the <Option/Alt> key to access the Free Form Lasso.

9. When you reach point E, repeat the steps that you went through for the tail to select the mouth.

10. When you are back to point A, release the <Option> (<Alt>) key, then release the mouse button. The selection will be completed.

Example Two

Figure 3–14 shows an image of a multicolored pile of money on a white background. It is obvious that there are too many curves to use the Free Form Lasso Tool accurately with any sort of ease. At the same time, there are too many colors to use the Magic Wand Tool on it to capture the object directly. However, we can use the Magic Wand in conjunction with another selection tool to grab the object.

To make this selection:

1. Choose the Rectangular Marquee Tool to begin with.

2. Make a Rectangular Marquee selection around the pile of money.

3. Choose the Magic Wand Tool.

4. Rather than use the Magic Wand to try to select each individual color, we'll subtract the only solid color for the current rectangular marquee selection—the white background.

5. Hold down the <Option> key (<Alt> in Windows) and click on the white background. The selection that is left will be around the object.

Example Three

Figure 3–15 is a picture of a standard football. Although these are typically thought of as oval in shape, they're really not oval at all. They're oblong. But we'll use the Elliptical Marquee Tool to begin the selection process.

Figure 3–14: There are too many curves in this image to use the Lasso Tool.

Figure 3–15: The oblong shape of the football will make it challenging to select.

To make this selection:

1. Choose the Elliptical Marquee Tool to begin with.
2. Make an oval selection around as much of the football as you can. Your completed oval selection might look very similar to what I have done on Figure 3–16.
3. Choose the Magic Wand Tool.
4. Add to the selection by holding down the <Shift> key and clicking on the remaining brown area of the football that is not included in the original elliptical selection. If not enough of the remaining area was selected when you did this, push the <Return> (<Enter>) button to access the palette and manipulate the Tolerance.

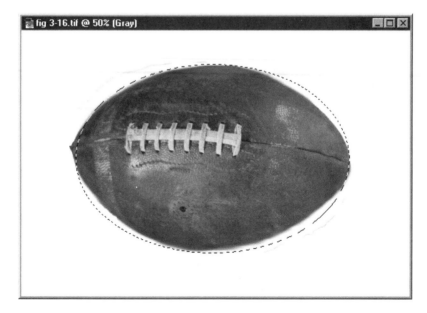

Figure 3–16: My oval selection around my football image includes some of the white in the background.

5. Continue to add to the selection until the entire football has been included.

6. As the figure shows, a few areas of the white background were also caught up in original selection. Remove the white areas by subtracting from the selection, similarly to how we did it in the previous example.

Moving Objects and Selections

Photoshop gives you the ability to move selections you have created, as well to as move the objects you have selected.

Moving a Completed Selection

1. Activate any of the selection tools, if one is not already active.

2. Put the cursor in the selection area.

3. Click and hold the mouse button as you drag the selection around the canvas. Release the mouse button when you've settled the selection where you want it.

Moving a Selection while Still Creating It (Elliptical and Rectangular Marquee Tools Only)

Sometimes, you'll start making a selection with one of the Marquee Tools, only to find that you've started making your selection in the wrong place, even if you're just a few pixels off. Instead of just starting all over again, you can move your selection while you are still in the process of making it.

1. Push and hold the space bar.

2. Drag the selection to the area you wish to place it.

3. Release the space bar and continue creating your selection as usual.

Moving a selected object or portion of an image

1. Select the Move Tool, if it is not already active.

2. Put the cursor in the selection area.

3. Click and hold the mouse button as you move the selected image. Release the button when you've settled the image in the place you desire.

If you want to move a selected image but have any other tool activated, you can temporarily access the Move Tool by pushing and holding the <Command> (<Ctrl> in Windows) key.

Instantly Copying a Selected Object or Portion of an Image

1. Select the Move Tool, if it's not already active, or push and hold the <Command> (<Ctrl> in Windows) key to access the Move Tool temporarily.

2. Push and hold the <Option> (<Alt> in Windows) button. You'll see that your cursor changes to two overlapping arrows, one dark and one light.

3. Continue holding these buttons as you drag the selected area with your mouse. As Figure 3–17 shows, the selected area will remain in place, but a duplicate of that area will be created for you to drag elsewhere.

Depending on the size of the selected area, the duplicate may appear on its own layer, as it does in the Layer Palette that is shown in Figure 3–18. See Chapter 5 for more about how layers work.

After you copy and move, the area that was originally selected won't be any longer. The selection will now be on the duplicate itself. The selection, however, will be hidden. Choose View -> Show Edges or press <Command + H> (<Ctrl + H> in Windows) to see the edges again.

You can constrain any of these commands, whether moving a selection or the contents of a selection, to straight lines or 45-degree angles by holding down the <Shift> key while dragging.

Figure 3–17: I can conveniently copy and drag a selected object using keyboard commands.

"Hey!" you're thinking, "Every time I try to move my selection to a straight line by holding the Shift key while dragging, Photoshop doesn't move the selection at all—it *adds* to the selection! What gives?" It's true—as we mentioned earlier, holding the <Shift> key down while a selection tool is active will add to the selection. Start moving the selection first, *then* hold down the <Shift> key. The selection will snap into place and you'll be able to move it in a straight line without adding to it.

Other Basics of Selections

As I said earlier, the ability to make selections in Photoshop is as diverse as the cast of "Real World," but not as contrived. And we're still on the basics! But before we move on to the harder stuff, there are a couple more loose ends that I want to cover; they just didn't seem to fall into any other category.

Select All

Pretty straightforward stuff here—Select All does exactly what the name implies. It puts a Rectangular Marquee around the entire canvas for one large selection of everything. (Everything on the active Layer, anyway. See Chapter 5 for more information on layers.)

To select the entire canvas, Choose Select -> All or push <Command + A> (<Ctrl + A> in Windows).

That was easy.

Deselect All

I'm not going to insult anybody's intelligence by telling you what this one does. To deselect your current selection: Choose Select -> Deselect, or push <Command + D> (<Ctrl + D> in Windows) or, with (almost) any selection tool active, click on a portion of the canvas that is not selected.

If you deselect using that last option, don't use the Magic Wand or the Polygonal Lasso Tools. Clicking on another portion of the canvas with either tool *will* deselect your existing selection, but it will also start a whole new selection.

Reselect

This one can be pretty handy. Let's say that you have a selection that you're working with. At some point, you deselect it and begin working on something else, when you realize that you need that selection back. Instead of making the selection over again from scratch, just Reselect it—the last selection that you had made will reappear.

To Reselect your last selection: Choose Select -> Reselect, or push <Command + Shift + D> (<Ctrl + Shift + D> in Windows).

> **There are other ways of reselecting selections, such as saving them as paths (discussed in Chapter 4) and saving them as Alpha Channels (later in this chapter).**

Inverse

You'll likely end up using this more often then you'd imagine. Inverse will turn your selection inside out, so that the area of your selection is no longer selected—the rest of the canvas is.

To inverse your selection: Create a selection with any of the tools we've discussed, and choose Select -> Inverse, or push <Command + Shift + I> (<Ctrl + Shift + I> in Windows).

Finally, there are two last selection tools that appear in the Tools Palette that I haven't mentioned yet. That's because these tools are about as important as the Professor and Maryanne in the early episodes of "Gilligan's Island."

Anyway, the Pixel Row and Pixel Column Tools are found hiding under the Rectangular and Elliptical Marquee Tools. Click once with either tool to select a full row or full column of pixels in your canvas. Pretty exciting stuff.

Ⓐ WALK-THROUGH EXAMPLE

Now that we have reviewed the basics, let's create a step-by-step project that utilizes some of these selection issues. We'll create the collage of items in and around the red wagon as shown in Figure 3–18 and Color Figure 6. We'll start with the individual images in Figure 3–19 to make our composite picture. We'll use different techniques to make the selections, even though it might seem easier to do it a different way than the way I am using. But that's the best way to practice.

1. We'll start by putting the beakers in the wagon first. I know, I know, why would there be a scientific beaker in a kid's wagon? Maybe the little monster stole it from chem class. Just pretend—we're practicing here. Anyway, we'll make the selection by using a combination of the Free Form and Polygonal Lassos. Start by activating the Free Form Lasso and, starting at the top of the beaker on the left at the point

Figure 3–18: The image that we will end up with.

Figure 3–19: The pictures that we'll use to create our final image.

marked A, make a selection clockwise to point at point B, hold the <Option/Alt> button down to access the Polygonal Lasso temporarily. Continue the selection down the side of the beaker and up to the top of the next one. At the top of the beaker on the right, release the <Option/Alt> key to return to the Free Form Lasso and make the curved selection of the top. Continue doing this for the remainder of the image, using the Free Form Lasso for curved areas and the Polygonal Lasso for straight areas.

2. With the selection made, activate the Move Tool and, placing the cursor over the selected image, drag it to the back corner of the wagon, as shown in Figure 3–20.

1. Choose Select -> Deselect to deselect your image.

2. Next we'll move and select the golf ball. Activate the Elliptical Marquee Tool. Holding the <Shift> key down for constraint (to make a perfect circle), start at the top left corner of the ball and drag downward to the right to select the ball. If you are off at all, move your selection by holding the space bar and dragging until you have the selection in the right place. Then release the space bar and continue dragging to finish the selection.

3. This time, instead of selecting the Move Tool from the toolbar, we'll move the golf ball by temporarily accessing the Move Tool. Hold the <Command/Ctrl> key down when you are done making your selection. You'll see that your cursor turns into the Move Tool icon. Continue to hold down the key and drag the golf ball until it is in the wagon, next to the beaker, as shown in Figure 3–21.

Figure 3–20: The selected beakers are moved to the back of the wagon.

Figure 3–21: The golf ball is moved to the wagon.

1. One golf ball, however, is not enough for this big wagon. So we need a second golf ball. With the golf ball you just moved still selected and while you are still holding the <Command/Ctrl> key, place your cursor (which is now a double arrowhead) over the selection, and drag. You'll see that an instant copy of the golf ball is created, as shown in Figure 3–22.

2. Release all buttons, and deselect everything, this time by using the keyboard command, <Command/Ctrl + D>.

3. With the knapsack, there are too many colors or shades of colors to use the Magic Wand Tool very efficiently and too many curves that would make using the Lassos kind of tiring. Instead, let's select it by first activating the Rectangular Marquee Tool and making a Rectangular selection around the knapsack, as shown in Figure 3–23.

Figure 3–22: Holding the <Option/Alt> key and dragging while temporarily accessing the Move Tool creates an instant copy of the selected image.

Figure 3–23: To select the knapsack, we first create a Rectangular selection around it.

1. With the Rectangular selection in place, activate the Magic Wand Tool. Although there are too many shades in the knapsack itself, there is only one shade of white in the selection around it. Holding the <Option/Alt> key down will force Photoshop to subtract from the selection. Click in the white area that surrounds the knapsack. The white will be deselected, leaving the selection around just the knapsack. Don't forget to do this same thing for the small areas of white in between the handles of the knapsack.

2. Once it's selected, use one of the methods described earlier to move it next to the wagon.

3. Once the knapsack is in place, deselect the selection.

4. Last is the crayon. Because it's a blue crayon, there are just a couple of shades—a darker shade for the crayon itself and a lighter shade for the paper around it. To select it, we'll use the Magic Wand Tool again, this time to make a selection instead of detract from one. Activate the Magic Wand Tool, and, with the Tolerance set to 25, click in the body of the crayon. Part of it will become selected.

5. To select the remaining parts, hold the <Shift> key down. This will add to your selection. Continue to click in parts of the crayon that are not selected. Do this until the entire crayon is selected.

6. Move the crayon into position and deselect it.

A Quick Guide to Selections

That was a lot of information in just a few short pages—especially with all those keyboard commands being barked at every corner. Table 3-1 provides a quick review of most everything that we just went over:

Function	Command (Windows in Parentheses)
To create an Elliptical or Rectangular Marquee from the center:	Option (Alt) while dragging
To create a perfect circle or perfect square (1:1 aspect ratio):	Hold Shift while dragging
To toggle between Elliptical and Rectangular Marquee Tools:	Shift + M
To move an Elliptical or Rectangular selection while making it:	Hold space bar while dragging
To create a Free Form Lasso selection:	Click and hold while dragging
To end a Free Form Lasso selection:	Release mouse button
To create a Polygonal Lasso selection:	Click once for each point

(continued)

(continued)

Function	Command (Windows in Parentheses)
To end a Polygonal Lasso selection:	Double-click, or click on start point
To access Polygonal Lasso temporarily while using Free Form:	Hold Option (Alt)
To access Free Form Lasso temporarily while using Polygonal:	Hold Option (Alt)
To toggle between all Lasso Tools:	Shift + L
To access the Options Palette for any selection tool:	Push Return (Enter)
To add to a selection:	Hold Shift
To subtract from a selection:	Hold Option (Alt)
To retain the intersection of two selections:	Hold Shift + Option (Alt)
To constrain movements to straight or 45-degree angle lines:	Hold Shift while dragging
To access the Move Tool temporarily:	Hold Command (Ctrl)
To copy and move at the same time:	Hold Option (Alt) while Move Tool is active
To select entire canvas:	Command (Ctrl) + A
To deselect current selection:	Command (Ctrl) + D
To reselect you previous selection:	Command (Ctrl) + Shift + D
To invert your selection:	Command (Ctrl) + Shift + I

WHEN STANDARD TOOLS WON'T DO THE JOB

So, with all those tools at your disposal, you're ready to select the world, right? Well, maybe. Depending on your eyes, your hands, your time and your patience, there's probably very little that you couldn't select using the previously described tools.

But what would you do with a picture like the one shown in Figure 3–24 and on the left in Color Figure 7? Let's say that you wanted to make a selection of just the polo player and his horse in the picture, to manipulate that without affecting the rest of the image. How would you do it? There are a lot of curves in the polo player and his horse, which would make the Marquee Tools and Polygonal Lasso useless. The Free Form Lasso has some possibilities, but unless you're on a strict no-caffeine diet, it would be tough to make all those twists and turns accurately without wasting a lot of time. In addition, the colors of the polo player and his horse are so close to the background colors in some areas that using the Magnetic Lasso or Magic Wand would also be extremely difficult.

Figure 3–24: Making a selection of the polo player and his horse in the image would be tough using the standard tools.

Your only real option, then, is to give up. Go to the beach. You're spending entirely too much time in front of the computer, anyway.

Still here? Well, I tried. If you're really going to be a stickler about this, there is something you can do to aid in making this selection (although I think my beach idea is *highly* underrated). You can use the brush tools in QuickMask Mode.

QuickMask Mode: Brushing Up Your Selections

QuickMask Mode allows you to use your brush tools, detailed in Chapter 2, as an additional arsenal of selection devices. It can be a semitough concept to grasp if you're not used to it, but it's really quite simple and very convenient. Let's take an image like the polo player and his horse seen in Figure 3–24. If we wanted to make a selection of him and the horse, we can easily see how it would be difficult to do this using any of the tools we've reviewed thus far. The number of colors would make the Magic Wand a poor option and it's obviously not a square or circle, so that leaves the Marquee Tools out, and there are too many curves to make the Lasso a great choice, either. Instead, we'll use QuickMask to make the selection.

To use QuickMask Mode for making this selection (or a selection like it):

1. Begin your selection by using any of the standard selection tools. For example, in this image, I have begun my selection by using the Magic Wand Tool in the center of my horse, with a Tolerance of 32, as shown in Figure 3–25. Continue to do this by adding to the selection until you get to a point that using the standard tools is no longer feasible.

2. Enter QuickMask Mode by pushing the QuickMask button on the toolbar, as indicated by Figure 3–26. You'll notice that there are a few changes that have been made to the canvas and the palettes:

   ◆ The portion of your canvas that is not selected now has a red film over it (50% red by default—we'll see how to change this later in this section), as shown on the right in Color Figure 7. The red works like an old-time rubylith, which artists would use to mask certain areas of their drawings.

   ◆ The *Marching Ants* that surrounded your selection while in Standard Edit Mode have disappeared.

   ◆ Any colors that you had in the Foreground or Background color have temporarily reverted back to black and white.

   ◆ A new Channel appears in the Channels Palette (detailed later in this chapter), named *QuickMask* in italics.

Figure 3–25: My initial selection using the Magic Wand Tool.

Figure 3–26: The QuickMask button on the Photoshop toolbar.

3. From here, on you'll create your selection using one of the brushes. Most likely, you'll use either the Airbrush or the Paintbrush Tool for this. Choose either one.

4. Choose Windows -> Show Brushes to open the Brushes Palette. The type of brush that you choose will depend on the complexity of the edges in the image that you are trying to capture. In most cases, you'll probably want to select a small brush with a hard edge. Soft-edged brushes don't grab edges very well, and large brush diameters make it harder to stay in the lines.

5. Begin to paint over the area that you want to select. Your paint tools will not work the same as they did when we detailed them in Chapter 2. The basic rules here are as follows:

   ◆ Painting with white adds to your selection (removes the red from the overlay).

   ◆ Painting with black subtracts from your selection (adds to the red of the overlay).

   ◆ These rules are reversed if you are painting with the Eraser Tool. (Don't paint with the Eraser Tool. It will only confuse you.)

   Paint with white until the entire area that you want to select is clear of the red overlay. If you have painted outside the lines, simply paint black in the areas you messed up. You might also need to change the brush size a few times to really get in there for detailed areas.

Don't be afraid to zoom in to an area you are trying to select while in QuickMask Mode. For some reason, I've watched nearly everyone in my agency try to select by painting with the image stuck at a small size. Not only does it make the image harder to capture, but you'll end up squinting and possibly hurting your eyes.

6. When you're done, simply click the Standard Edit Mode button on the Tools Palette to exit QuickMask Mode. The original Foreground and Background colors will be returned to normal, and the QuickMask Channel in the Channels Palette will disappear. More importantly, the red indicator color will be gone, and the Marching Ants will outline your entire selection.

7. If there is any part that you may have missed, return to QuickMask Mode or use a standard selection tool to finish the work. Do this as often as needed.

> **Depending on the type of image you are trying to select, I often find that I can save time by doing the edges in QuickMask Mode and using the Free Form Lasso Tool for the middle part. Since the edges of a curvy image are the hardest part to select, I use the brushes in QuickMask Mode to select them with as much ease as possible. I then return to Standard Edit Mode and hold the <Shift> key down to add to my selection, then use the Free Form Lasso Tool to outline the center part that I neglected in QuickMask Mode.**

Troubleshooting: Typical Frustrating QuickMask problems

Along with having a lot of options to complete any task, Photoshop also comes complete with an endless amount of things that can be wrong, too.

One of the problems that can be particularly frustrating when creating a selection in QuickMask Mode is that, as you paint, the red indicator color only partially appears or disappears.

If this happens—and believe me, it will—one of the following things is most likely the culprit:

If you're using the Airbrush Tool:

◆   The Pressure value is below 100%
◆   The Painting Mode is not on Normal

If you're using the Paintbrush Tool:

◆   The Opacity value is below 100%
◆   The Wet Edges option is checked on
◆   The Painting Mode is not on Normal

Somehow, the color you are painting with is not a solid black or white, but a shade of gray.

Another problem that you might encounter is that, even though you are in QuickMask Mode, you are somehow painting as you normally would—and the Foreground and Background colors are actually colors instead of black and white. If that happens, you've accidentally clicked one of the other Channels active. Fix this by clicking the Channel marked *QuickMask* to reactivate it.

You Can Use More than the Brushes

Although the brushes are the tools you'll use most often while in QuickMask Mode, they're not the only tools you can use. The Free Form and Polygonal Lassos, as well as the Marquee Tools, can also be helpful at times while in QuickMask Mode. The only difference is that you need to fill these selections with a color to make them work.

For example, make a Free Form Lasso selection on the mask (red) portion of your image while in QuickMask Mode. Fill it with white. The red mask disappears in this area, and it is added to your selection.

The Gradient Tool can also be used in QuickMask Mode. The results of creating a Black to White gradient can be especially interesting, as the grays that result in the transition between the two colors can have a cool effect. But I'm going to save this until our discussion of Channels later in this chapter, as I believe these effects are accomplished better in the Channels Palette than in QuickMask Mode.

Changing the Mask—Color and Area

As we saw earlier, by default, the QuickMask that was created was red and indicated the masked area outside the selection. There may be instances when you may need to change this. For example, an image that has a lot of red in it will undoubtedly make using a red mask difficult.

You can change this by double-clicking on the QuickMask icon to access the dialog box shown in Figure 3–27. The top portion allows you to decide whether you want the selection or the mask (the area outside the selection) to have the color overlay.

 You can change this more directly just by pressing <Option> (<Alt> in Windows) and clicking on the QuickMask button.

The lower portion of the QuickMask Options dialog box allows you to change the color and the color opacity of the QuickMask indicator. Click on the color swatch to access the Color Picker and choose a custom color. The Opacity area of the dialog box allows you to make that color more or less intense.

Figure 3–27: The QuickMask dialog box.

Making Selections with Color Range

QuickMask Mode is my personal favorite way to make selections. In any given situation, I would rather paint than try to carefully outline—which I do not have the patience for. But while the QuickMask option is great for solid objects, such as the polo player and his horse in the last example, that's not the only situation in which the standard tools won't be much help.

Consider the image in Figure 3–28 and Color Figure 8. What would you do if, for example, you needed to select all of the yellow in the players' uniforms? How would you do it? Well, let's go through the thought process as we did earlier. Obviously, it would take you quite a while to select them by hand using the Lasso Tools. QuickMask Mode isn't really an option, either, since it would take just as long to paint each of the stripes, especially since some portions are blurry. That would leave us with the Magic Wand Tool as the obvious choice. Choose one or more of the stripes, then choose Select -> Similar. The only problem is that because of the blurry areas, this too becomes difficult.

There is a way to do this more efficiently. The Color Range option is based on making the selection through color values, but it's far more powerful than the Magic Wand Tool.

To use the Color Range for making selections:

1. Make sure you have an image open

2. Choose Select -> Color Range to open the dialog box shown in Figure 3–29. You'll be using this dialog box to make selections based on color. The large black square in the center of the dialog box represents your image. The fact that it's black means that currently, nothing is selected. Once you begin selecting colors, the areas in which that color resides will turn white (or shades of gray, depending on how much of the selected color resides in any one area).

Figure 3–28: We'll need to make a selection of all the yellow in the uniforms.

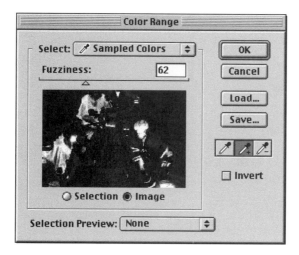

Figure 3–29: The Color Range dialog box.

3. You can see your image in full color instead of the black and white by using the radio buttons under the image preview window. By default, the Selection option is turned on. To see your full-color image, choose the Image radio button instead. You can also change it temporarily by pushing and holding the <Command> button (<Ctrl> in Windows).

Although it might help to see the full-color version in the preview window once in a while, it's not very practical to work this way. You're better off working in Selection Mode more often.

4. In the Select pull-down menu, make sure that Sampled Colors is chosen. The other options allow you a quick way to select specific predetermined colors (RGB and CMY), highlights, midtones and shadows. These can all be useful at times, depending on what you are trying to select and why. In this case, we're trying to select the yellow in the uniforms from our sample image.

If you are working in RGB mode, there will be one more option in the pull-down menu than if you are working in CMYK mode. In RGB mode, you'll also be able to make a selection of all Out-of-Gamut colors that exist in your image. As we reviewed in Chapter 1, colors that are out of gamut are colors that don't exist in the CMYK spectrum and therefore won't print.

5. By default, the Eyedropper Tool on the right of the dialog box will be selected. Use this to choose the color that you want to select. In this case, that would be the yellow. You can do this by any of the following methods:

- ◆ Clicking on the black preview window in a guess of where that color resides.
- ◆ Choosing Image rather than Selection to see the full-color image in the preview window.
- ◆ Moving your cursor outside the dialog box and actually clicking the color in the active canvas.

It's most helpful to do this last option. Ordinarily in Photoshop, you cannot do much of anything, really, until the dialog box that is currently open is closed. That is not the case here. Move the Eyedropper onto the canvas and click on the desired color.

6. Once you choose a color, you'll see the black preview window change. The portions of your image that contain that color are now white. Other portions that contain a percentage of that same color are gray. The white area constitutes your selection (the gray is a partial selection, which we'll get to in the section of this chapter that deals with Channels). Notice that it does not have to be contiguous pixels to be selected. You can allow more or fewer pixels in the selection by increasing or decreasing the tonal range of the selected color. You can do this by adjusting the Fuzziness slider. What, you say? "Fuzziness" is a pretty silly name for tonal range adjustments? Well, you said it, not me. Play with the Fuzziness slider and watch what happens to the white area in the preview window as you do so. Stop when the area you desire has been selected.

7. Let's suppose that, in this example, we would also like to select all of the maroon in the image, as well. We can add to our selection by changing our Eyedropper Tool. On the right of the dialog box, choose the Add Color Eyedropper (the one in the middle with the little plus sign next to it). Choose this new color the same way as you chose the maroon in step 5. The areas of the image in the preview window that contain that color are added to the selection and now also appear in white, as shown in Figure 3–29.

8. Finally, as you adjust the areas in the preview window to create just the right selection, you can also change the way you view your main canvas. By default, the Selection Preview drop-down menu is set to None, which means that your main image stays the same as you play in the Color Range dialog box. Try each of the other settings in the drop-down menu to see the effect they have. I personally prefer to work in the Black Matte option, as I find it to be the easiest on my eyes.

9. When you are done, click OK. The white areas in the preview window will now be selected and outlined with Marching Ants in your canvas.

Grabbing Selections from Layers

You should be proud of yourself—you're chapters ahead of your time. We're about to learn how to create selections with the help of the Layers Palette, even though we haven't reviewed Layers yet (rebels, ain't we?).

As Chapter 5 will describe in more detail, various objects and image portions will be kept in their own individual Layers. You can very easily make a selection around all items contained in any given Layer by holding the <Command> key (<Ctrl> in Windows) and clicking on the desired layer (more on this in Chapter 5).

Using this Technique for Making Polygonal Selections

As we saw in Chapter 2, Photoshop 6.0 has included Shape Tools, which allow you to make polygons that instantly fill with your Foreground color. But these are solid objects—there's still no tool that allows you to make a polygon selection. To do this:

1. Activate the Polygon Shape Tool.
2. Create a polygon on it's own Layer.
3. <Command> (<Ctrl>) + click on that Layer to grab the selection.
4. Save your selection as a Channel (read about how to do this later in this chapter), then erase the solid polygonal shape that you initially created.
5. Reload your polygonal selection.

BEING MORE SPECIFIC: ADJUSTING SELECTIONS

Once you have your selections made, there are things you can do to tweak and adjust them. Photoshop gives you ample opportunity to create the exact selection that you need.

The Modify Commands

There are four commands that are found under the Select -> Modify menu, each of which controls a different way to manipulate your selection:

- Border
- Smooth
- Expand
- Contract

Border

Choosing Border will create a selection area that borders the area of your original selection. The resulting dialog box which appears when you choose Border allows you to set a value between 1 and 64 pixels. The resulting border will distribute the pixels equally around the original selection and will be anti-aliased. This means that the selection edges will be soft—filling them with a color will not result in a hard edge.

Figure 3–30 illustrates the Border command on both a rectangular shape and a nonrectangular image.

Smooth

The Smooth command allows you to round the corners and hard edges of any active selection. Since the Elliptical Marquee Tool creates round-edged selections by virtue of itself, the Smooth command has no effect here. On all other selections, however, Smooth can be pretty useful. The dialog box allows you to set a value anywhere between 1 and 16 pixels. The more pixels you select, the smoother your selection will become. Figure 3–31 shows how the Smooth command can round the edges of a rectangular marquee selection.

Expand

Well, as though you needed me to tell you this, the Expand command will...well, expand your selection. Enter a value between 1 and 16 pixels to expand your selection by that amount. The expanded selection will be antialiased, so that the edges will be soft.

Figure 3–30: The Border command at work.

Figure 3–31: The Smooth command can round the edges of your selection.

Contract

The opposite of the Expand command, Contract, will…ahem, contract your selection. The rest of this reads just like the Expand command.

 Since each of the Modify commands has a maximum amount of pixels you can enter, they each have a more pronounced effect on low-res images. Obviously, an image that has only 72 pixels per inch will show a larger effect of a 10-pixel expansion than the same image which is 300 pixels per inch.

 If you need to set a value higher than the maximum allowed in any of the Modify commands, simply run the command at the max value, then run it again. Continue doing that until you reach the extreme that you need.

Other Fun Things in the Selection Menu

Well, I don't know if these are really classified as "fun," but they still have to be written about.

Feather

Feather is really a pretty neat function and one that you can have a lot of fun with. Feathering is a way to make the edges of a selection "soft." Choosing Feather from the Select menu gives you access to a simple box, which will allow you to set the radius value of the feather. A low value creates just a slight softness, while a higher value makes the edges very soft.

There are a number of things that feathering can be good for. Figures 3–32 and 3–33 provide a few samples of how you can use feathering for some cool effects. Figure 3–32 shows two instances of filling in a feathered selection with a color. In this case, I've filled it in with black, for a makeshift shadow. The selection on the left has a Feather radius of 2, while the selection on the right has a larger Feather radius of 16. (The image itself was 72 ppi—higher resolution images will require higher Feather radius values to see a visible effect.)

Figure 3–33 and Color Figure 9 shows how feathering can be used when pasting one image onto another. In both images, a biker has been cut out of one image and pasted onto another to create a picture. As you can see, the biker in the image on the left looks like it was literally pasted on—the edges are too sharp and distinct. The selection of the biker was not feathered at all—it was simply cut and pasted. The biker on the right, however, looks much more natural. After the original selection was made, the selection was feathered by 2 pixels, then cut and pasted. The softness of the selection keeps the biker from having an unnaturally harsh edge.

Figure 3–32: Feathering a selection and filling it with a color can have a cool effect. The image on the left shows a selection with only a slight feather, while the selection in the image on the right was more drastic.

Figure 3–33: Feathering a selection before copying or cutting will help make the image more natural-looking when it comes time to paste into another image.

Grow

The Grow command is kind of a combination of any selection tool with the Magic Wand Tool. From any given selection, the Grow command will expand the selection based on the surrounding contiguous colors. You can adjust how many shades of any contiguous color are added to your selection by changing the Tolerance value in the Magic Wand Options Palette. Figure 3–34 provides an example.

Transform Selection

Transform Selection gives you the ultimate control over manipulating any selection. This works basically the same as the more regularly used Transform function, which controls the shape of images. This is detailed further in Chapter 7.

Figure 3–34: My selection after the Select -> Grow command was used.

QUICK SAMPLE:
USING GUIDES FOR SELECTIONS

For lack of any place better to put this, I want to provide you a "quick" tip to grabbing simple selections. Let's say that you need to grab the soccer ball shown in Figure 3–35. It's a perfect circle. Using the Elliptical Marquee Tool, you can create a perfect circle somewhere in the vicinity of the edge (a pain).

Figure 3–35: We'll want to create a selection around the soccer ball.

To select this object:

1. Bring the rulers into view, if they aren't already, by choosing View -> Show Rulers, or pressing <Command + R> (<Ctrl + R> in Windows).

2. You can set a horizontal guide by placing your cursor in the top ruler and dragging downward. Place a horizontal guide so that it just touches the top of the ball.

3. Do the same with a vertical guide by placing your cursor in the left ruler and dragging to the right until it touches the left edge of the ball.

4. Activate the Elliptical Marquee Tool by clicking on it.

5. You'll be using the guides to help create your selection. Choose View -> Snap to Guides to make sure that the selection that you'll be creating will kiss up to the guides that you set.

6. Place your cursor at the point that the two guides intersect.

7. Hold the <Shift> key to constrain your selection to a perfect circle and drag downward to the right to create your selection, as shown in Figure 3–36.

Figure 3–36: Making a selection easily around a perfectly circular object.

WORKING WITH CHANNELS
PART ONE: SELECTIONS

In my years of teaching, the one aspect about Photoshop that had nearly all of the students at a loss was how to work with the Channels Palette. The problem, as I see it, is twofold: the Channels Palette is too often taught at the same time that the Layers palette is taught, which causes confusion between the two (the Layers Palette is conceptually easier to understand and arguably more fun to use in practice). The other problem is that the Channels Palette is often taught as one component when, in fact, it has two completely different functions—one for working with selections and one for working with colors.

If you skim over the table of contents in this book, you'll see that I have basically sectioned each important part of Photoshop into its own chapter. The Layers Palette has its own chapter; painting has its own, etc. The exception to this is the Channels Palette. Although this is one of the hearts of Photoshop, I've divided it into two parts. Part One, which deals with how the Channels Palette handles selections, is detailed in this section. Part Two, which concentrates on how the Channels Palette deals with color, can be found at the end of Chapter 6. Examples in that chapter will also provide instances when both functions of the Channels Palette will work together.

Saving Selections

You can see from all of this that making the appropriate selection can be tedious, time-consuming and complex. Imagine spending minutes or even hours creating the perfect selection, using it, deselecting it, then realizing a few days later that you need to work on that selection again. The thought of having to make that selection over again each time you need it would be enough to make you turn the computer off and take up water color painting as an alternative art form.

Fortunately, you don't have to keep recreating your selections over and over again. The Channels Palette, shown in Figure 3–37, will work like a vault for every selection that you make that you think you might use again (the color portion of the palette in Figure 3–37 is ignored until Chapter 6). Each Channel will retain the selections under a different name for easy retrieval at a later time.

Figure 3–37: The Channels Palette.

To save a selection as a Channel:

1. Create a selection in your image, like the selection that I've made around the snowboard guy in Figure 3–38.

2. You can save your selection directly by pushing the New Channel button at the bottom of the Channels Palette, or you can manually adjust some settings by choosing Select -> Save Selection to access the Save Selection dialog box shown in Figure 3–39.

3. Within the dialog box, you have three drop-down menus to work with. The first allows you to decide which document to save your selection in. If only one document is open, your only other option will be to save your selection in a new document.

    The second drop-down menu allows you to determine whether you wish to save your selection as a new Channel or to combine it with any existing Channels (except for the color ones, which we'll get to in Chapter 6). Choose New from the drop-down menu, and only one radio button (marked *New Channel*) in the lower Operation portion of the dialog box will be available. Choosing an existing Channel for your current selection activates all the Operation choices, allowing you either to replace the existing Channel, add to it, subtract from it, or intersect your selection with it.

    In the Name area, you may provide a name for your selection to help you remember what it was for. For example, in my image, I might name my selection *snowboarder*.

Figure 3–38: I've made a selection around the snowboard guy in my image.

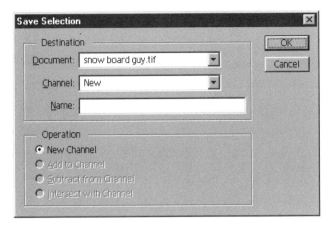

Figure 3–39: The Save Selection dialog box.

If you don't provide a name for your selection or if you bypass this dialog box by pushing the New Channel button at the bottom of the Palette, your Channel will automatically be named *Alpha 1*, *Alpha 2*, *Alpha 3* and so on.

4. Your new Channel will appear in the Channel Palette. The area of your selection will be white, and the area outside your selection will be black,

It's important to note that, as you create each new Channel, they will stack in the Channels Palette one under the other. I found that when teaching, this fact was a source for confusion among the students. Unlike the Layers Palette, detailed in Chapter 4, in which the stacking order matters, the stacking order does not matter in the Channels Palette. Hold on—let me power up the megaphone:

"ATTENTION ALL PHOTOSHOP USERS: DO NOT CONFUSE THE CHANNELS PALETTE WITH THE LAYERS PALETTE. THE STACKING ORDER OF THE CHANNELS DOES NOT MATTER. I REPEAT: THE STACKING ORDER DOES NOT MATTER."

Was that clear enough?

Retrieving Selections

The whole point in saving a selection is to keep it so that you can use it again later. (Well, there are a few other reasons why you'd want to save a selection, which we'll review in the upcoming section on cool Channel effects). Retrieving a selection is very simple:

1. To retrieve a selection directly, hold down the <Command> button (<Ctrl> in Windows) and click on the Channel that holds the selection that you need. You'll notice as you move your mouse over the Channel that the cursor changes to a hand with a Square Marquee selection in it.

2. To retrieve a selection with more options, access the dialog box shown in Figure 3–40 by choosing Select -> Load Selection. (Do I need to tell you that you must first have a selection saved before you can load one? I didn't think so.)

3. In the dialog box, first use the Document drop-down menu to indicate which open document you wish to load your selection from. The active canvas will appear as the first choice by default. From the Channel drop-down menu, select the name of the Channel from which you wish to retrieve your selection, if you have more than one.

   The Invert checkbox that appears below the drop-down menus will invert your selection if checked. When this is checked on, the selection that will appear will be around the black areas of your desired Channel and not the white part.

   If you don't have anything selected in your canvas at this point, the only radio button that will be available in the Operation area of the dialog box will be for New Selection.

   If you have an area of your image currently selected, all four radio buttons will be available. You'll have the choices of loading your Channel as a new selection (overriding the current selection), adding the Channel to your current selection, subtracting your Channel from your current selection, and intersecting your Channel with the current selection.

4. Hit OK when you've made your choices. The selection that you had saved earlier will reappear in your canvas.

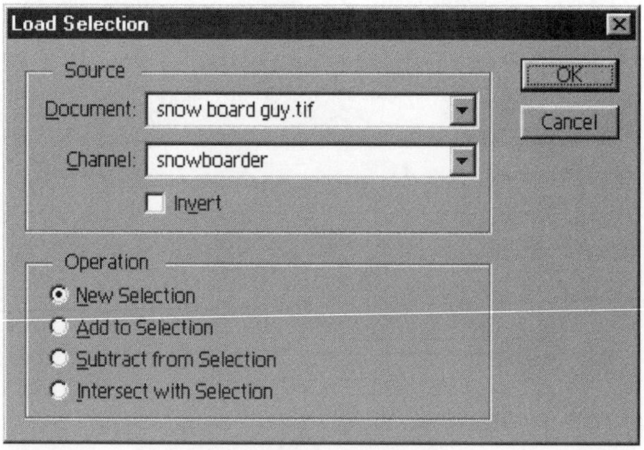

Figure 3–40: The Load Selection dialog box.

Odd Facts, But Important Notes on Channels

There are a few other things to note about using the Channels Palette for selections that we should review. Then we'll jump right into using these Channels for some cool special effects. None of the following info really deserves its own section, so I've just jumbled a bunch of odd facts into one group of bullets for you to read as needed:

♦ In the Channels Palette, you'll notice that the active Channels are the color Channels at the top. These Channels are what allow you to see your image in full color, also known as the *composite* image.

♦ When a Channel that holds your selection is made active (by clicking on one of them), your canvas will change, as shown in Figure 3–41. As you can see, the canvas now looks exactly like the icon of the active Channel, with the selection area in white and the area outside the selection in black.

♦ You can use this to help you complete your selections. For example, earlier in this chapter, when we were discussing how to make selections with QuickMask, we saw how a default red overlay washed over your image. You painted in white to add to your selection (removing the red area). Although this is a helpful way to make certain selections, it can be hard to see every speck of red that you need to paint. When you are done, you can save your selection, then make that Channel active. The small black specks, as shown in Figure 3–42, are the areas that were missed. Paint with white over these areas while your Channel is active to fill in the gaps.

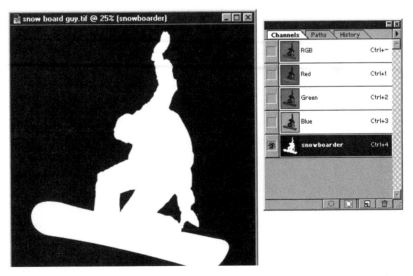

Figure 3–41: When a selection Channel is active, your canvas will change to be a black and white representation of your selection.

Figure 3–42: The small black specks are areas that I missed when making a selection with QuickMask. Small spots like these are easier to see in black and white than they are through a red rubylith.

I'd recommend that you save a version of your image *before* you go make adjustments. That way, if you mess up, you can revert back to the saved version.

◆ Painting in an active Channel is kind of the same as painting in QuickMask Mode. Your Foreground and Background colors will revert to black and white. Painting with white will add to your selection, while painting with black will take away from your selection. Painting with gray has an effect, as well, but we'll see what happens there in the upcoming section on special effects with Channels.

◆ If your color Channels (the ones at the top) are active, but one or more of the selection Channels is visible (by turning on the eye icon at the far left of the palette), the selection area will remain in full color, while the mask (outside the selection area) will be in the same red that you saw when working with QuickMasks. All of your tools and Foreground and Background colors will continue to work as usual.

◆ You can delete any Channel simply by dragging it to the trash can icon at the bottom of the palette.

◆ You can duplicate a Channel by dragging it to the New Channel icon at the bottom of the Channels Palette. Use this option as a precaution against screwing up and to double-check your work.

◆ Double-click on any Channel to open the Channel Options dialog box shown in Figure 3–43. This dialog box lets you do the following:

   ◆ Rename your Channel.

   ◆ In the Color Indicates section, the term *color* refers to both the black area that appears in the Channel, as well as the red that appears in the third bullet point of this section. The default is to have the color indicate the masked area. You can change this to have the color indicating the selected area instead (which gets confusing, and I would recommend against it) or any spot color area (which we will get to in Chapters 6 and 7).

   ◆ The Color portion of the dialog box allows you to change the red color and opacity, much as you could change it when we discussed QuickMask, earlier.

   ◆ You can change the order of the selection Channels by clicking on one and dragging it to a new location. Don't let this confuse you into thinking that the stacking order matters—it's just a matter of convenience. If you have a whole lot of Channels and there are some that you use more than others, you can move those toward the top, so you don't have to keep scrolling through the palette.

That about wraps up the discussion on Channels. Not too tough, right? Good. Now let's see how we can use this knowledge to create some really cool effects.

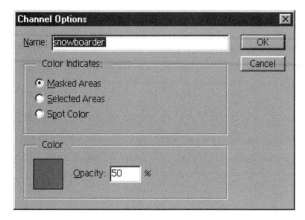

Figure 3–43: The Channel Options dialog box.

PUTTING IT ALL TOGETHER—COOL THINGS YOU CAN DO WITH SELECTIONS AND CHANNELS

Saving selections for later use isn't the only benefit you'll receive from the Channels Palette. There are many cool effects that you can accomplish once you get used to working with Channels and understand their properties.

Fade In, Fade Out

The trick to using Channels for cool effects primarily relies on knowing how the gray values work. As was pointed out earlier in this section, the white areas of a Channel are the areas that represent your selection. The black areas are the areas that fall outside your selection. I know that I'm saying that quite a bit lately, but believe me, repetition is the key to success.

When you load a selection, the Marching Ants form around the white areas. You can then go and manipulate these areas as you desire—paint them, cut them…you get the idea. Therefore, we can say that the white areas of a Channel are the areas that would ultimately be affected by any subsequent command, and the black areas are the areas that would not be affected.

For example, let's say that we wanted to use the Cloud on the snowboard guy that we've been working with. If I want to fill that selection with Clouds from the Clouds filter, I would take the following steps:

1. <Command> (<Ctrl> in Windows) + click on the Channel marked *snowboarder*. The Marching Ants appear around the snowboard guy to indicate that he is selected.

2. Choose Filter -> Render -> Clouds. The selected area fills with clouds. The area outside the selection remains unaffected. Figure 3–44 shows the result, accompanied by the Channels Palette again.

As you can see the, white area of the Channel was affected by the clouds, while the black portion wasn't. That would be fine if the world were just as simple as white and black, good and evil, Mary Matalin and James Carville. But sometimes there is a gray value to be considered, as well. The following example shows how the gray values work in Channels, and how we can use them to make a special effect or even a collage:

1. Open an image of your own like my snowboard picture. For the sake of this example, I'll start over again with this image from scratch. In this exercise, we'll make this image look like there are clouds in the sky.

2. Make a selection around the main object in your image. In this case, since my main object is in a field of blue, I simply used the Magic Wand to select the sky, then inversed my selection.

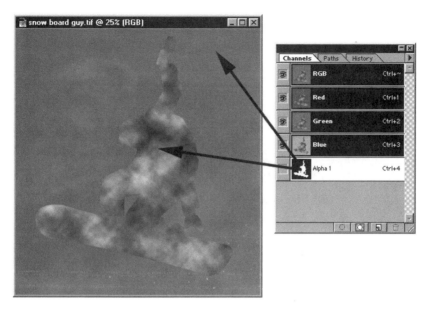

Figure 3–44: After reactivating my selection of the snowboard guy, I filled him with clouds. I've done this to demonstrate that the result occurred only in the portion of the Channel that appears in white.

3. Open the Channel Palette.

4. Save your selection as a Channel by pushing the Save Selection as Channel button at the bottom of the palette (see Figure 3–39).

5. If you used QuickMask to make your selection, make your new Channel active. Paint over any black specks that appear in the white portion with white. This will make sure that the entire image is, indeed, selected.

6. Double-click on the Channel to access the Channel Options dialog box discussed. Rename your Channel (currently called *Alpha 1* by default) *Main Object*. Click OK to exit the dialog box.

7. Click on the New Channel icon at the bottom of the palette. A new Channel, named *Alpha 1,* will appear. The entire Channel will be black.

8. Rename this Channel *gradient* the same way that you renamed the last Channel.

9. We're going to make a gradient from black to white, but before we do, we want to make sure that our main object (the snowboarder, in my case), is unaffected from anything that we will be doing.

   If your object is no longer selected, hold down the <Command> key (<Ctrl> in Windows) and click in the Main Object Channel. As you can see in Figure 3–45, the selection that was saved in the Main Object Channel is now loaded into the Gradient Channel.

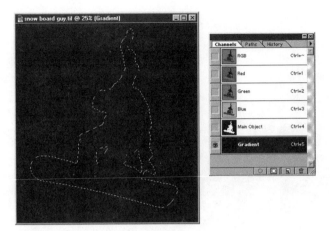

Figure 3–45: The selection saved in my Main Object Channel is now loaded in my Gradient Channel.

10. Invert the selection by choosing Select -> Inverse.

11. Make the Gradient Tool active and create a gradient from white to black, top to bottom, as illustrated in Figure 3–46. Hold the <Shift> key down while making your gradient to make sure that it happens in a straight line. Notice that now, for the first time, we are dealing with more than just black or white in a Channel—we are dealing with grays, as well. The gray areas are made up of mixtures of black and white. We'll soon see how this affects our work.

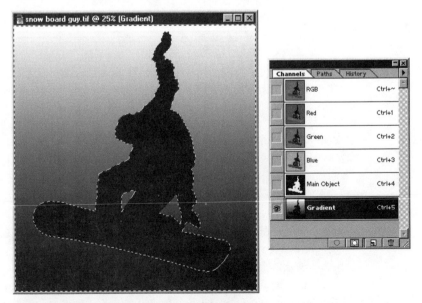

Figure 3–46: With the gradient applied from black to white, we now see grays appearing in the Channel.

12. So here's the tricky part to conceptualize. When you loaded your selection in Step 9, the white area of your Channel loaded. Now, load the Gradient Channel by <Command> (<Ctrl>) + clicking on it. You'll see that, as Figure 3–47 shows, your selected area is the top portion of your canvas. You'll also notice that it completely excludes the Main Object area.

The selected area is only loosely defined by the Marching Ants. As Figure 3–48 points out, there is still white in the gray areas below the center of the canvas. Conversely, there is a portion of black in the areas above the center of the canvas (within the Marching Ants). The Marching Ants selection starts at the top, where there is 100% white, and continues downward to point of neutral gray—the line at which there is 50% white and 50% black. Areas below this line will still be affected by anything you do with your selection, but to a lesser extreme.

13. Load the selection into your main image by clicking the RGB Channel at the top of the palette. (If your image is CMYK, click the CMYK Channel.) Figure 3–48 shows my composite image with the selection still intact.

14. Because I'm stuck inside, working on my computer while everyone is out having fun, I want to put clouds in the sky. With black and white as the Foreground and Background colors, choose Filter -> Render -> Clouds. Figure 3–49 and Color Figure 10 show the result. Notice how the clouds start off strong at the top (where there was 100% white), get fainter down to the bottom of the Marching Ants (where there was 50% white) and continue to get fainter until there are no clouds at all at the very bottom (where there is 100% black).

Figure 3–47: The selection now excludes my Main Object and appears to be limited to the top portion of the canvas. However, as the image indicates, because of the gray values in the gradient, a certain amount of white exists in the area not selected, and certain amount of black exists in the area that is selected.

Figure 3–48: My composite image with the selection loaded from the Channels Palette.

Note: **This will work with anything—not just the Clouds filter. Try any of the other Filters as well (Filters are reviewed in detail in Chapter 7). You can even try deleting your selection. If you are working on the Background layer, you'll see that it deletes to the Background color with the same varying intensity as we saw with the clouds.**

Tip: **You might want to Feather your selection before applying any filters to create a more realistic effect.**

Using this Effect for Collages

One of the best reasons to use this effect is to create collages. In the previous note, I mentioned that any number of effects beyond the Cloud Filter can be used to make cool things happen. One of the effects that I mentioned was to hit the <Delete> button (<Backspace> in Windows). As it said in the note, if you are working on the Background layer, the selected area will delete into the background color, as Figure 3–50 illustrates.

Figure 3–49: Notice how the clouds start off strong at the top (100% white in the Channels Palette) and fade out toward the bottom (0% white in the Channels Palette). Notice, too, that the snowboard guy, which remained 100% in the Gradient Channel, wasn't effected by the clouds at all.

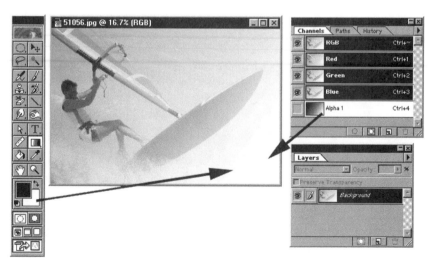

Figure 3–50: This time, I've created a diagonal gradient to a new Channel and loaded it into my composite, with the Background layer (the only layer, in this case) active. When I hit <Delete> (<Backspace>), my image fades slowly into white, which is my Background color (if my Background color had been red, my image would have faded to red).

Now, I know that we haven't reviewed Layers yet, but, regardless, I think we'll visit them briefly here to show how to use Channels to make a collage. Go through this now, then read the chapter on Layers and come back. It'll probably make more sense then.

1. Start with two images, such as the ones that I am using in Figure 3–51 and Color Figure 11. For the sake of this example, try to make them roughly the same size.

2. With the Move Tool active, drag one picture onto the other picture. In the Layers Palette, you'll see that the image you have moved is housed in its own layer. Use the Move Tool to center this image on the canvas, covering as much of it as possible (or hold the <Shift> key down when moving one image onto the other canvas to place it automatically in the center). New Layer 1 is created and made active.

3. Open the Channels Palette.

4. Complete steps 7-8 then 11-13 of the previous exercise (I'm skipping the part where we make a selection of the main object in our image).

 For this example, I've chosen to make my gradient diagonal, from top left to bottom right, instead of vertical. You can create your gradient in any way that you see fit.

5. Hit the <Delete> button (<Backspace> in Windows). The selected area disappears in varying intensities. However, instead of the deleted area being replaced by the Background color, the image on the underlying layer shows through, as shown in Figure 3–52 and Color Figure 12. This is the way many collages are done.

Making a Cool Frame

Framing images is a very popular thing to do with Photoshop. And some of the really cool ones can be made while in the Channels Palette. The following recipe will show you a really funky way to make a frame using a Channel and a number of Filters.

Figure 3–51: The two images that I'll use to create my collage.

Figure 3–52: My collage. Because I loaded the Gradient Channel onto a layer other than the Background layer (in this case, Layer 1), when I hit <Delete> (<Backspace>) the image fades to transparency, showing me the image that lies in a lower layer.

1. Open an image, like the one I am working with in Figure 3–53. If possible, try to use an image that has an object you would like to frame, and make sure that the image is in RGB mode (some Filters work only in RGB mode). Note that this exercise requires that you work in RGB mode.

Figure 3–53: I'll frame the biker in my picture.

2. With the Elliptical Marquee Tool, make a circular selection around the object that you want to frame.

3. Choose Select -> Feather and enter a value of 12 (I'm assuming you're using a low-res image, or around 72 ppi. If not, you may need to use a higher Feather value).

4. Open the Channels Palette.

5. Push the Save Selection as Channel button at the bottom of the palette.

6. Make Alpha 1 the active Channel.

7. Choose Select -> Deselect to release your selection.

8. Choose Filter -> Distort -> Wave to access the dialog box shown in Figure 3–54.

9. Use the following settings:

   ◆ Number of Generators: 5

   ◆ Minimum Wavelength: 1

   ◆ Maximum Wavelength: around 85

   ◆ Minimum Amplitude: 10

   ◆ Maximum Amplitude: around 35

   ◆ Horizontal and Vertical Scales: both 100%

   ◆ Repeat Edge Pixels should be on, and choose Sine for the Type.

Adjust any of these settings as necessary. Click OK when through. Figure 3–55 shows the canvas at this point.

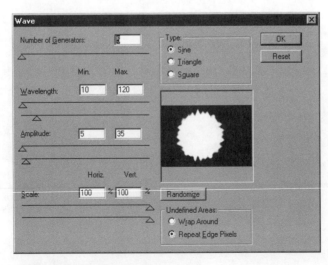

Figure 3–54: The Wave Filter.

Figure 3–55: My canvas after applying the Wave Filter.

 The Wave Filter is an odd one. Don't be surprised if your canvas looks different than the one in the figure. You might have to adjust the settings a bit, but if it doesn't look exact, that's okay.

10. Choose Filter -> Blur -> Radial Blur. Select Zoom for the Blur Method, and set the Amount value to around 75. Hit OK when done.

11. Choose Filter -> Pixelate -> Color Halftone. Hit OK on the dialog box (just leave the default settings). Your canvas will resemble the canvas shown in Figure 3–56.

12. Hold the <Command> key (<Ctrl> in Windows) and click on the Alpha 1 Channel to make a selection of all the white areas.

13. Choose Filter -> Distort -> Twirl. For the Angle, enter 999 degrees for the value. Click OK, and your image will look similar to Figure 3–57.

Figure 3–56: My canvas after applying the Color Halftone Filter.

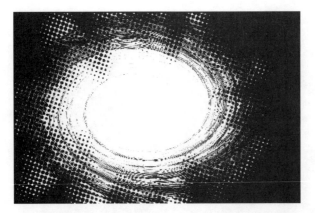

Figure 3–57: My canvas after applying the Twirl Filter.

14. Since the white area in your Channel has changed, reselect it by repeating Step 12.

15. Click the RGB Channel to see your full-color image again. The selection will still be there, with the center of it around the main object that you want to frame.

16. Choose Filter -> Render -> Lighting Effects to access the Lighting Effects dialog. This dialog box will be explained in detail in Chapter 11.

17. At the bottom of the dialog box, choose Alpha 1 in the Texture Channel pull-down menu. Make sure there is a checkmark in the White is High checkbox, and pull the Height slider to the far right (Mountainous). Click OK when through.

18. Push <Command + F> (<Ctrl + F> in Windows) to redo the Filter again for a more visible effect. Figure 3–58 shows the image to this point.

19. Choose Select -> Inverse to invert your selection.

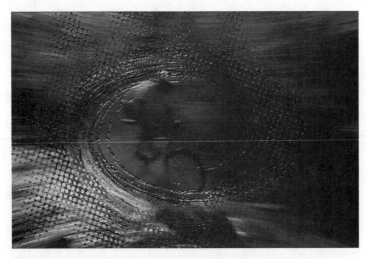

Figure 3–58: My image after the Filter has been applied twice.

20. Hit the <Delete> button (<Backspace> in Windows) to complete your frame, as shown in Figure 3–59. The whole process is shown in Color Figure 13.

THE CROP TOOL

The Crop Tool is the best and most convenient way to crop images. It's pretty easy to use— kind of a combination of the Rectangular Marquee Tool and the Free Transform feature.

Earlier versions had the Crop Tool hidden below the Marquee Tool in the toolbar. Version 6 has given the Crop Tool a place of its own.

To illustrate how the Crop Tool works, let's take the example that we have in Figure 3–60. The image in the figure was scanned into Photoshop on a desktop scanner and slid during scanning. The result, as you can see, is that the image appeared in Photoshop pretty crooked. In addition, there is too much extraneous background around the main subject of the image, which we'll want to do away with.

To fix this problem without rescanning, we would do the following:

1. Select the Crop Tool from the toolbar. It's hidden beneath the Marquee Tools, or you can quickly access it by pushing the <C> key.

2. Drag a selection around the portion of your image that you wish to keep. If you make a mistake, use the handles on the corners and sides of the bounding box to make changes. Holding the <Shift> key down while dragging will constrain the proportions.

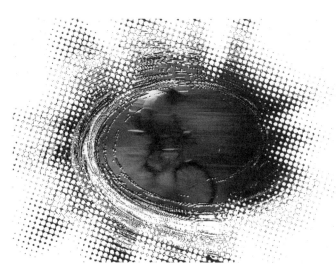

Figure 3–59: My final image, framed.

Figure 3–60: My scanned image is crooked, and there is too much background.

3. Outside the selection, your cursor will look like a curved line with arrowheads at either end. Drag your mouse in the direction of either arrow to crop at the appropriate angle. Figure 3–61 illustrates this.

To change the center of rotation, drag the point of origin (the center crosshair in the bounding box) to another area of the image.

Figure 3–61: Rotating the Crop Marquee for precision. The arrow shows the direction that I rotated my Crop Marquee.

4. Continue to manipulate the crop area by adjusting the handle bars until the area you want to keep is within the Marquee selection (the bright area), and the area you want to crop away is outside the Marquee selection (the dark area).

5. Hit the <Return/Enter> button to crop your selection, or use the <Esc> button to cancel your crop.

If there are specific dimensions that you need to crop to, you can do so by checking the Fixed Target Size box in the Crop Options Palette. You can set the desired Width, Height and Resolution in the appropriate value area. When you crop your image, it will crop to those settings.

Using the Marquee to Crop

You can use the Marquee selection to crop your image, as well:

1. Use the Rectangular Marquee to make a selection around the area you wish to keep.

2. From the menu options, choose Image -> Crop.

SUMMARY

There are many ways to go about nearly everything that you want to do in Photoshop. Making and working with selections is likely the best example of this. That's because, in a high percentage of all your Photoshop work, you will need to make a selection for one reason or another. This chapter has told you practically everything you need to know about making, saving, and working with selections. Just remember that there are many ways to select an image. Practice all of them, and see which selection path is best for you on a case-by-case basis.

As I'm often fond of saying (who talks like that?), one of the best things about Photoshop is that there is never just one way to do anything. There are usually millions of ways, it's just a matter of picking the right way for your specific purpose. That statement is probably never as true as it is when we're looking at making selections. Whether you are using the Lasso tools, the Magic Wand, or any one of the many other functions that you have to work with, the ability to create selections is one of the most important aspects to graphic design. This is what allows for real precision in your work, as well as interesting effects when used creatively.

chapter 4

WORKING WITH

PATHS AND USING

THE PEN TOOL

If you're the typical designer, especially a new typical designer, you're probably as excited to learn about using paths as I am to write about them. Paths, especially the Pen Tool, have an ugly reputation for being difficult to work with, and not worth the effort to learn. To be honest, as a designer I've always gotten by without heavy Pen Tool usage. But maybe it's just the kind of designs that I create. I'm sure that there are designers out there who find paths very useful.

The Pen Tool is, for the most part, another selection tool, while the paths they create are basically a selection-saving resource. Why, then, do paths and the Pen Tool get their own chapter, instead of being integrated into Chapter 3, which reviewed creating and saving selections? The answer is because the Pen Tool is more difficult and complex than the other selection tools, and the paths they create have different properties and purposes beyond simple selection saving.

Earlier in this book, we discussed that Photoshop is a raster-based program, dealing with pixels. Bezier Paths (the entire name), however, are vector-based and define selection areas through a series of lines and curves between any number of points. This means that you can create very smooth curves and odd-shaped edges that would be more time-consuming and difficult with other selection tools. Besides saving selections, paths are also used to isolate areas of an image and extract unwanted portions for use in page layout programs, and to gain maximum control over stoking and filling areas and selections. The paths that you create are stored in the Paths Palette, which is also the control center for what you will do with your paths once you create them.

CREATING PATHS

There are two ways to create paths—you can create them using the Pen Tool or from selections you have already made, using other selection tools.

Creating Paths with the Pen Tool

You see this tool all over the place, even outside of Photoshop. It's in Illustrator, QuarkXPress...it's even in some of those dinky paint programs that come bundled free with your new computer. From a psychological standpoint, it's interesting that such a universal tool can be so intimidating to so many people. The truth is, it's a tough tool to learn. But once you get the hang of it, it's really not that bad.

The following examples will give you hands-on experience with using the Pen Tool to create a number of different paths.

Creating a Straight Line Path

To create a simple path made up of straight lines:

1. Create a new canvas.

2. Choose the Pen Tool from the Tools Palette. When you move the Pen Tool over the canvas, there is a small *x* next to it to indicate that it is about to start a new path.

3. Click a spot on the canvas. You'll see a dot, or an Anchor Point, at the place you click. This Anchor Point is black because it's active. You'll also notice that the *x* next to the Pen icon has gone away, indicating that there is a path currently being built.

As soon as you create your first point, notice that a new Work Path is created in the Paths Palette.

4. Move the pen somewhere else on the canvas and click on that spot. Photoshop automatically draws a straight line segment from the starting point (point A) to the new point (point B). Notice that point A, which was black, is now white outlined. This is because it is no longer the active point in the path. Point B is black, to show that it is currently active—the line segment to the next point will come from point A.

5. Click somewhere new on the canvas. There is now a new straight-line segment from point B to the new point (point C). Point C is now the active point (it's black), and the next line segment will stem from it. Points A and B are both white outlined, since they are inactive. Point B, in fact, is *really* inactive—since there are already two line segments connected to it, there can't be any more.

6. Click somewhere new on the canvas. There is now a new straight-line segment from point C to the new point (point D). Point D is now—okay, this can go on for awhile. You get the idea, right? The whole thing is illustrated in Figure 4–1. New segments appear between the active point and the new point, and that new point then becomes the active point. This can go on forever—literally, until your fingers get tired of clicking the mouse or your computer just explodes. A path can have as many points as you want it to, until you end the path. Which leads us to….

Ending a Path

Before you can start a new path, you have to end your current one. You can end a path by doing any one of the following:

◆   Choose Edit -> Deselect.

◆   <Command> (<Ctrl> in Windows) + click on any area of your canvas away from your path.

◆   Click the Pen Tool in the toolbox.

Closing a Path

For the purposes of finishing the previous example, we'll go through the motions of closing the path:

1. Close the path. When you're done connecting the dots all over the canvas, end the path by clicking on the point of origin, or point A—the initial point. When you place the Pen Tool over the initial point, the cursor changes and includes a small *o* to indicate that it's about to close the path. Click on point A, and the final segment will be drawn between the active point and the starting point.

2. You can now begin a new path anywhere else. If you move the cursor to a new spot on the canvas, you'll see that the icon again has a small *x* in it, to show that there is no path currently being created.

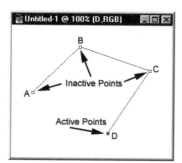

Figure 4–1: Making a straight line path is as simple as activating the Pen Tool and clicking.

Creating Curved Paths

Okay—straight lines were simple, right? Maybe all this talk about the Pen Tool being tough to learn is just an extreme overexaggeration. Well, keep telling yourself that...it'll make you feel better as you learn to draw curved paths.

1. Make sure your Pen Tool is active. If you want, start a new document to begin creating your curves without interference from the path in the previous example.

2. Click on any point in your canvas to place the first Anchor Point, much like you did in the previous example. This time, though, do not just click the mouse button and release. Instead, click and hold the button, and drag the mouse upward. You'll notice that, as you drag, you're creating a long solid line, with a small dark circle at the end, as displayed in Figure 4–2. This is called a *handle,* and we'll use it to set and adjust the direction and shape of the curve.

3. Click a new point (point B in Figure 4–2), approximately a quarter page to the right of your original point (point A). Again, don't just click and let go—click and drag your mouse downward, to create another handle. Your path should look like a semicircle, similar to that shown in Figure 4–3. There are a few other things you should note about the path that will help you understand how it works:

    ◆   The beginning of the curve is moving in an upward direction—the same direction that you originally dragged your mouse from point A and the same direction you brought your original handle bar.

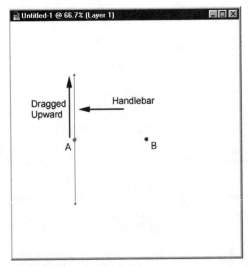

Figure 4–2: The length and direction of the handlebar will help to determine the arc of a curved path.

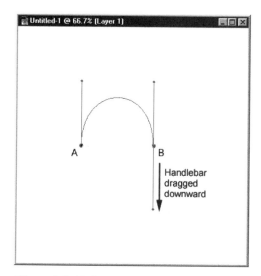

Figure 4–3: Making a semicircle.

♦ The path at this stage ended by moving downward to point B—the same direction in which you dragged the handlebar from point B.

♦ The extremity of the curve was directly related to the length of distance you pulled your handle bars.

You may want to recreate this path again, with these points in mind. In simple terms, curved paths will begin and end in the same direction that you drag the handles, and that the length of these handles will dictate the curvature of the path.

4. Create a new point on your canvas and drag your mouse in the direction of your choice. Without letting go, drag the handle bar to different areas on your canvas to see how it affects the curvature of your path.

Notice that only the path segment between point B and your new point is being affected—the path segment between points A and B remains still.

You can adjust the angle, curvature and severity of any curve, even after you have created it. Simply press <Command> (<Ctrl> in Windows) + click on a point associated with the curve. The handle bars that we worked with earlier will appear. Drag the handle bars to adjust and change the curve.

Changing the Direction of the Curve

The curve doesn't always have to move in the same direction as the last handle bar. To change the direction of a curve, such as in the dual-arched path shown in Figure 4–4, create the first arch from point A to point B, as described in the previous section. To create the second arch, from point B to point C, hold the <Option> key (<Alt> in Windows) and click and hold on the Anchor Point at point B. Drag your mouse to the upper right to create a new handle bar. When you're done, click point C and drag until you create the arch with the curvature you desire.

Working with Straight Lines and Curves

Most paths aren't made up of all straight lines or all curved lines. More often than not, you'll have to work with a combination of both to achieve the path you want to create.

Combining Straight and Curved Paths

Paths aren't an either/or situation: You can have both curved and straight lines in one path. Combining them is pretty easy: Figure 4–5 shows a path that goes from a straight line to a curved line and back to a straight line again. The straight line was made in the standard way between points A and B. To switch to creating a curved line, use <Option> (<Alt>) + click on point B and drag a handle bar in the desired direction. Click on point C to complete the curve. To go back to making a straight line, use <Option> (<Alt>) and click point C, but this time don't drag a handle bar. Simply click point D and a straight line will appear.

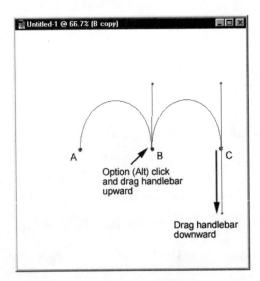

Figure 4–4: Use the <Option> key (<Alt> in Windows) to change the direction of a path.

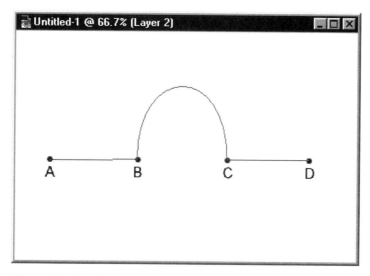

Figure 4–5: A path that combines straight lines and curves.

Changing an Anchor Point

Once a path is created or is in the process of being created, you can change the properties of any point within the path. Changing the properties will cause the lines from that point to change from curved to straight or vice versa. The path shown in Figure 4–6, for example, is made up of three Anchor Points and two straight line segments. To change the lines to be curved, instead, like the path in the right canvas of Figure 4–6, simply place your cursor over the middle point, hold the <Option> key (<Alt>) and drag. <Option> (<Alt>) + click the point again to turn the curved lines into straight segments. You can also do this by clicking on the point with the Convert Path Tool (the one that looks like the carrot).

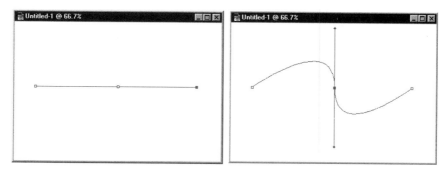

Figure 4–6: Making a straight path curved, and back again.

Creating Paths from Selections

This is a pretty quick and easy way to create a path when you might need to extract the exterior contents of an object for use in a page layout program, such as QuarkXPress. Take the image of the golfer in Figure 4–7. Let's say that I wanted to bring this into a page that I'm laying out in QuarkXPress, but I don't want to include all the extraneous stuff that's around it. The selection of the golfer is easy enough…I'd use a combination of the Magic Wand Tool, the Free Form Lasso and maybe even a QuickMask, if necessary.

Once my selection is made, turning it into a path is an even easier process:

1. Choose Window -> Show Paths to access the Paths Palette.

2. From the Palette pull-down menu, choose Make Work Path. This will open the dialog box shown in Figure 4–8.

3. The Tolerance that you need to set is how exacting Photoshop will be when turning your selection into a Path, which makes almost no sense in my opinion, because if you didn't want to be as exact as possible, you would have saved yourself the trouble of making a decent selection in the first place. Anyway, the lower the Tolerance value, the more precise your path will be.

More exacting paths will likely have more points, angles, lines and curves. This can put a greater strain on your computer, eating up more RAM, processing more slowly and creating larger file sizes. This is one of the reasons I prefer to extract unwanted images using Alpha Channels in TIFF files instead of paths in EPS files, as I describe in greater detail in Chapter 5.

Figure 4–7: I'll want to use a path around the golfer to extract him from the background later in QuarkXPress.

Figure 4–8: The Make Work Path dialog box.

You can also take the more direct approach to creating paths from existing selections. Push the Make Work Path button at the bottom of the Path Palette. This will create a path from your selection automatically, using the default or previous Tolerance setting.

4. As you can see in Figure 4–9, the new path that appears in the palette is *Work Path* by default. Double-click on it to access a dialog box that lets you rename it, if you'd like.

Filling and Stroking Your Path

Any path that you create can be a candidate for filling or stroking. Text, Marquee selections, and paths like the ones created in the previous examples all can be used. When you *fill* something, you are placing a body of color in its interior area, and when you *stroke* something, you create an outline for it. As Figure 4–10 shows, paths do not need to be closed in order to be filled or stroked.

Fill a path by doing the following:

1. Choose Fill Subpath from the Path Palette pull-down menu.

Figure 4–9: The new path that I created is named Work Path *by default.*

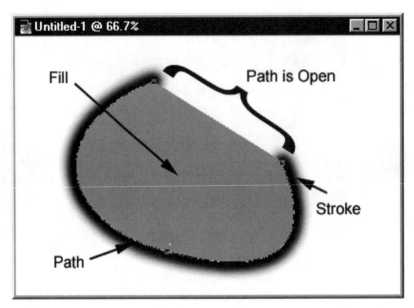

Figure 4–10: Filling and stroking a path. Paths do not need to be closed.

2. Arrange your desired settings from the dialog box that will appear, and hit OK to create your fill.

3. OR, click the Fill Path button at the bottom of the Path Palette.

Stroke a Path by doing the following:

1. Choose the color that you want to stroke with from any color source (such as the Color Picker), and make it your Foreground color (Photoshop will always stroke with the Foreground color).

2. Choose Stroke Subpath from the Path Palette pull-down menu.

3. From the subsequent dialog box, select the of tool of choice to use in making your path.

4. OR, click the Stroke Path button at the bottom of the Path Palette.

The brush size that will be used to create your path will be whatever the last brush was that you used for the tool that you chose. For instance, if the last time you used the Paintbrush you were painting with a soft brush with a diameter of 35 pixels, that is the brush that will be used to stroke your path if you choose Paintbrush as your stroke choice. Figure 4–11 shows a couple of paths stroked with different size brushes.

Figure 4–11: The stroke on the left was created by choosing the Paintbrush Tool that had a hard-edged brush of about 10 pixels. The one on the right used the same tool, this time with a soft-edged brush of 45 pixels.

A Quick Guide to Other Path Functions

There are many other functions that you can do with paths before we see how to utilize them outside Photoshop. Too many, in fact, to really describe in detail in this book (primers are written to be all the information that you need to know, without all the less necessary extras). But while this is not the format to detail these other functions, I didn't want to ignore them completely, either. So the following is a short list of some of other things you may need to know about working with paths:

◆ **To Add a Point:** Move your cursor over the line segment where you wish to add a point. Click to add an anchor, or click and drag a handle bar to curve the line segments.

◆ **To Subtract a Point:** Move your cursor over the point that you wish to subtract, and click it.

◆ **To Move a Point or a Line Segment:** <Command> (<Ctrl> in Windows) + click on a point or a line segment and drag.

◆ **To Move Multiple Point or Line Segments:** <Command> (<Ctrl>) + click on multiple points to move them or the line segments in between. Continue to hold the <Command> (<Ctrl>) key while you drag.

◆ **To Move an Entire Path:** Holding the <Command> (<Ctrl>) key, drag a Marquee selection around the entire path to select all Anchor Points. Continue to hold the <Command> (<Ctrl>) key as you drag.

◆ **To Hide a Path:** Click in the empty part of the Path Palette.

◆ **To End a Path without Closing it:** <Command> (<Ctrl>) + click in the canvas, away from the path you are creating.

◆ **To Save a Path:** Choose Save Path from the Path Palette pull-down menu and give your path a name in the dialog box. The Path will be saved and displayed in the Path Palette. Creating additional paths on your canvas will just add to the first one saved. To create a new path that won't interfere with other ones, first push the New Path button at the bottom of the Path Palette,

◆ **To Turn your Path into a Selection:** Click the Make Selection button at the bottom of the Path Palette or choose Make Selection from the palette pull-down menu.

◆ **To Create a New Path:** Choose New Path from the Path Palette pull-down menu, and provide a name for your new path. The stacking order of the paths within the palette won't matter (as it does in the Layers Palette).

Preparing a Path to Be Retained in EPS Format

Once you create a path, you'll be able to return to it as often as you'd like and easily make alterations to it. That's one of the inherent benefits of paths (besides the smoothness and simplicity of creating curves) that almost makes it worthwhile to bother learning. The other benefit is the ability to create a clipping path that I retained in the EPS format, which will exclude everything but the path interior when opening the image in a page layout program, such as QuarkXPress.

Although I am not a big fan of this method relative to using Alpha Channels in TIFFs (which are lighter in file size and more easily manageable), there are those (designers and service bureaus) who prefer to work with EPS images instead of TIFFs.

To manipulate a path for use in a page layout program, you would do the following:

1. Create your path.

2. Save your path by choosing Save Path from the Path Palette pull-down menu and naming your path (if you do not provide a name, *Path 1* will be the default).

3. Choose Clipping Path from the Palette pull-down menu (this will not be available until after the path has been saved) to access the dialog box shown in Figure 4–12.

4. Choose the Path that you wish to change to a Clipping Path from the Path pull-down menu. The enter a Flatness value (the lowest value that you can enter is .2)—this will keep your clipping path as close to the path that you have created as possible. Hit OK when you are done.

5. Save your image as an EPS. When you import the image into a page layout program, the portion of the image that falls outside of the path will not appear.

Figure 4–12: The Clipping Path dialog box.

SUMMARY

It's easy enough to blow off the Pen tool and skip Paths altogether. They can be frustrating to learn, and a huge pain to master. It's easy to blow off because many designers will just rationalize them out of existence: "I won't ever need to use them, and if I ever do, I'll just find some way to work with the other tools, instead." I know that designers say that, because for a long while I was one of those designers. But once you learn to use Paths, even just a little, you'll find that while not the absolute most important thing that you'll need, they are useful, and they will help to improve your work. The trick is just to not get frustrated.

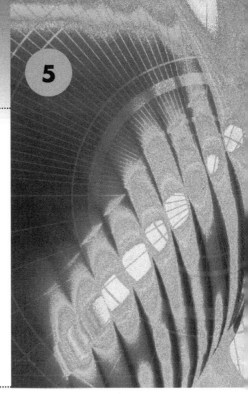

chapter 5

WORKING IN LAYERS: THE FUN STARTS HERE

With the introduction of the Layers Palette in version 3, Photoshop established itself far and away as the tool of choice for graphic designers. (There I go, sounding like an Adobe commercial again. Please accept my apology—I struggled for a clever opening but came up short). As newer versions were developed, Layers changed from a fantastic benefit to an absolute necessity; so much so that the program practically forces you to use them.

Layers allow you to work on one thing without having to worry about ruining something else. In the old days, when traditional artists ruled the design world, they did this by using acetate. A board would be used to start the project (the *background*), then significant additions would be made to the picture on numerous pieces of acetate, or transparent paper. As each transparency overlaid one another and the background, they would combine to produce one complete image. However, if any one portion of the image was not working or done incorrectly, it could easily be discarded without consequence to the rest of the image.

Layers in Photoshop work basically the same way, only better and more efficiently. Each file that you work on will begin with a Background Layer. As you add content to your image, such as text, other images, painted strokes, etc., you add them to their own individual Layers. In some instances, Photoshop creates the Layers for you (such as when your paste imagery onto you canvas or add text), and other times, you create the Layer yourself (such as when you paint or draw on your image). As you continue working, the Layers give you the flexibility to quickly delete, rearrange, change the opacity,

151

and otherwise manipulate specific content without damaging other elements in your image. Figure 5–1 gives a graphic representation of how Layers work, as well as a screen shot of the Photoshop Layers Palette, with descriptive tags. Don't worry if you don't understand everything in the palette right now—you'll be referring back to this screen shot throughout this chapter.

WORKING WITH LAYERS— A QUICK INTRO

Because the Primer series of books typically draws a more intermediate/advanced audience, I'll only spend a few pages discussing the more basic properties of Layers. Then we'll move quickly into using Layers in more challenging ways, including Layer Masks, grouping, etc. However, the information provided in this section should give any beginner users out there the ability to catch up rather quickly.

The Layers Palette

The Layers Palette may be tough to grasp at first on a conceptual level, but the palette is fairly straightforward. Shown and described in Figure 5–1, the Layers Palette shows

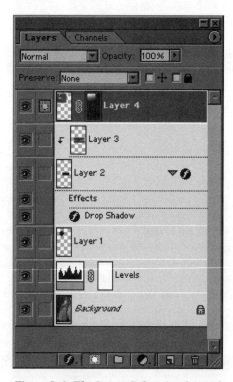

Figure 5–1: The Layers Palette is what makes images so easy to deal with in Photoshop.

how each Layer is set up in a stacking order. The images in the Layer at the top of the Palette are visible above all others, meaning that any images on underlying Layers may be obstructed from view.

Think of it almost as though you are viewing your canvas from different angles. The Layers Palette is as though you were viewing your picture from the side—you can see all the different elements stacked one on top of the other. Looking directly at the canvas, however, is like looking at your picture from an aerial view—you see all the elements from the top, working together (the *composite*) and as though it were one complete image, rather than a combination of many images stacked one on top of another.

Layer Properties

For the most part, there are two different types of Layers that you need to be concerned with at this point: the standard Layers and the background Layer. Other types of Layers, such as Text Layer and Adjustment Layers, will be discussed in more detail in places throughout this chapter and book.

Standard Layer Properties

A Standard Layer, which is, for the purposes of definition, any Layer besides the Background Layer can contain anything: text, photographs, illustrations, outlines, painting, etc. Each Layer can be manipulated primarily by three controls at the top of the Layers Palette:

◆ The Color Mode pull-down menu is set to Normal by default. You'll see this pull-down menu throughout Photoshop, as it also appears in the Options Palette for many of the individual tools. In the Layers Palette, the Color Mode options will affect how the colors of one Layer will affect and interact with the colors of another Layer. Each of the Color Mode choices will be fleshed out in the next chapter, when we take a close look at color correction techniques.

◆ The Opacity slider makes the active Layer more or less opaque (as it gets less opaque, it becomes more transparent). Opacity is measured in percentages, and you can enter your own value manually or click the small arrow to the right of the text area to use the slider. Sliding the marker to the left makes the Layer less opaque and more transparent. Sliding it to the right makes the Layer more opaque and less transparent. Making a Layer transparent allows you to see the Layer(s) underneath it right through your image, as Figure 5–2 illustrates.

Use the keyboard shortcut to enter a percentage. Each single number corresponds to a 10-measured unit, so that pushing 5 will set the opacity value to 50%, 7 = 70%, 1 = 10%, and so on. To set a value such as 12, simply type the number 12 quickly.

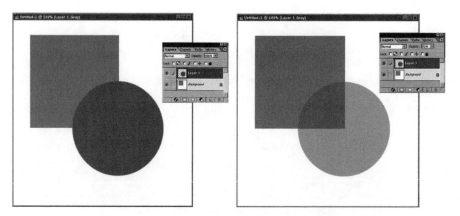

Figure 5–2: In the image on the left, the circle on Layer 1 is at 100% opacity and completely covers a portion of the underlying square. On the right, the opacity for Layer 1 has been reduced to 50%, making the circle partially transparent and allowing the square to show through.

◆ A small pull-down menu marked *Preserve* can be pretty helpful. Set to None by default, this pull-down menu also gives you the opportunity to preserve either the image itself or any transparency that may exist on a given Layer. Selecting either Image or Transparency, Photoshop will keep the respective portion of your Layer safe, so that any fills, painting, or other manipulations won't have any effect on those areas.

◆ Two features that are new to Photoshop 6.0 are the locking options. Clicking the Lock Move checkbox will still allow you to manipulate your Layer but will not allow you to move any item, locking them in place. Clicking the Lock Edits checkbox will completely lock your Layer from any manipulations or movements—this thing is the be all and end all of locks—all other Preserve and locking features will be grayed out. You won't be able to do anything at all—move items, paint, or manipulate images—a locked Layer. A small padlock icon will appear on any Layer that is locked.

Background Layer Properties (and How to Change Them)

The Background Layer is more solid than Standard Layers—think of it as the building block upon which all other Layers are created. The following holds true for the Background Layer:

◆ It is always at the bottom of the Layers Palette and can't be moved.

◆ The name *Background* is always written in italics.

◆   The option that we just reviewed for the Standard Layers is unavailable here. You cannot manipulate the Color Mode (because there is no underlying Layer for it to interact with), and you can't change the opacity, because the Background is solid. Because the Background is always solid, the Preserve drop-down menu and the lock options are grayed out, although you will notice that a padlock icon exists by default on the Background Layer, letting you know that the Layer is partially locked.

Considering these facts, as well as some of the useful features that we'll learn through this chapter, I would recommend that you don't do any work on the Background Layer if it can be helped. When you first start working on a new canvas, immediately create a new Layer (discussed in the next section) and begin work there. If you start painting or doing anything on the Background Layer, you'll have a hard time selecting it or manipulating it later in life.

You can give it all of the same functions that the Standard Layers have—opacity, transparency and Color Mode control, but, in order to act like a Standard Layer, the Background has to *be* a Standard Layer.

To change the Background Layer to a Standard Layer, simply change its name. Double click on it to access the dialog box shown in Figure 5–3. By default, the new name for the Background Layer will be Layer 0. Accept this or change it, but once you do, the Background Layer will act like any other,

Creating and Deleting Layers

As I mentioned earlier, there are certain times when Photoshop will literally force you into using Layers. This typically happens when:

◆   You move the contents of one canvas into the canvas you are working on.

◆   You paste anything at all into a canvas.

◆   You add text to your image.

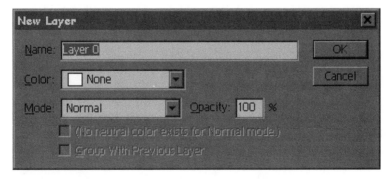

Figure 5–3: The New Layer dialog box. Changing the name of your Background Layer will alter its properties.

Beyond these instances, I would advise you to create and work in as many Layers as you possibly can. The more Layers you have, the more flexibility you will have when you need make changes.

The more Layers you have, the larger your image will be in terms of file size. Make sure you have the RAM capacity, as well as the available hard disk space necessary for large files.

To create a new Layer (without pasting or adding text):

1. Push the New Layer icon on the Layers Palette, as marked in Figure 5–1. This will create a new Layer immediately.

2. Choose New Layer from the Layers palette pull-down menu. Doing it this way will access the same dialog box shown in Figure 5–3. If you wish to enter a name for your Layer, you can do so here. Click OK when through, and your new Layer will appear in the Layers Palette.

Naming Layers will help you to remember where each element of your image is. For example, if you are going to put a red square on one Layer, you may want to name that Layer *red square*. Later on, when you have tons of Layers, you'll be thankful that you named them. More on this in the upcoming section, "The Layer Maze: Finding Image Parts."

Each time you create a new Layer, it will appear directly above the active Layer in the palette. The active Layer is the one highlighted in blue in the palette, as indicated in Figure 5–1. You can activate a Layer by clicking on it.

To delete a Layer, simply click and drag the Layer you want to delete down to the garbage can icon at the bottom of the Layers Palette. When you delete a Layer, however, you will also be deleting everything on that Layer, so make sure that you want those objects removed before you take this step.

Changing the Order of Layers

As you can see in the Layers Palette, each Layer is stacked on top of another. Because each acts as a transparency, the images on the topmost Layer can be seen in full, with underlying Layers possibly being (partially) hidden by Layers higher in the stacking order. Consider Figure 5–4: in the Image on the left, the circle is partially hidden by the triangle. The corresponding Layers Palette shows that the triangle Layer is higher in the stacking order. The image on the right, however, shows the opposite: Because the order of the Layers has changed, the triangle is now being partially hidden by the circle, which can now be seen in full.

Changing the order of your Layers is easy. Simply click and drag the Layer to its new position. As you are dragging the Layer (while holding the mouse button down), you'll notice that your icon, which is usually an open hand while in the Layers Palette, changes to a closed fist, as though it were gripping something (c'mon, people...use your imagination!). As you drag the Layer to its new position, a dark black line will appear between the Layers to indicate that this is where your Layer will reside. I know that that sounds confusing, but trust me, it really isn't. The process is illustrated in Figure 5–4.

> **If your active Layer is locked, you won't be able to relocate it at all within the Layers Palette. You won't even be able to throw the Layer out. I'm telling you, this new Lock feature is strong. Fort Knox should have a lock as strong as this....**

Making Layers Invisible

If only we could do this trick to ourselves! Wow—if I could make myself invisible, I'd have just set up camp in the women's locker room and called it a day. (Now, if any of you actually read that line, assume that my editor—who *hates* comments like that—just fell asleep on the job). **Nah—I'll let it slide... this time. –Ed.**

Making Layers invisible can be helpful when you need to see underlying portions of your image. More often, in my own work, I'll hide certain Layers after I create them, if I haven't decided whether or not I like their effect on the overall image yet. By making them invisible, they can be saved until you decide that you need them at some point in the future.

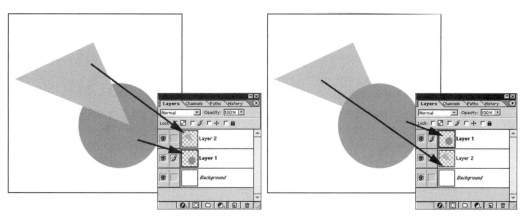

Figure 5–4: To change the order of these Layers, we simply click and hold on one of the Layers (in this case, Layer 1, with the circle), and drag to another position. Notice that, by putting the circle Layer on top, we change the way the composite image looks.

To make a Layer invisible, simple click the eye icon to the far left of the Layer that you want to hide. Click the box again to make the Layer visible again.

If a hidden Layer is also active, you won't be able to manipulate its contents at all. Make the Layer visible again to work in it.

You can make a lot of Layers visible or invisible at once just by clicking and holding the mouse button down, then dragging your cursor over all the Layers that you want to make visible or invisible. Further, if you <Option> (<Alt> in Windows) + click on the eye icon of any one Layer, all other Layers in the palette will become invisible, except for the Layer that you clicked. <Option> (<Alt>) + click on the Eye box again to make all of the Layers visible.

COPYING, CUTTING, AND PASTING ITEMS

If there is one set of commands that is universal between programs, it's the ability to copy (or cut) and paste items from one place to another. They're such universal commands that they're in most programs and not usually worth spending time or paper on. In Photoshop, however, the Layers feature provides a small reason to review the effects of cutting, copying and pasting, as well as quickly to describe a couple of alternate means of doing so.

Before you cut or copy something, you have to select it, using any of the selection methods described in Chapter 2 or a new method, described later in this chapter. When you paste it back, either onto the canvas you are working on or onto another canvas, it will be placed in a new Layer.

◆ If you select an object on a Layer and copy it without deselecting the selection, it will paste the object back onto a new Layer in the exact same position that it was originally.

◆ If you select an object on a Layer, copy it, then deselect the selection, it will paste the object back onto a new Layer in the center.

◆ If you select an object on a Layer and cut it from the Layer, the selection will be gone. It will paste the object back onto a new Layer in the center.

Sometimes, when you cut an object from a Layer, you'll still see a ring, or a thin "halo" of pixels where the object used to be, as displayed in Figure 5–5. To get rid of it, simply press <Command + A> (<Ctrl + A> in Windows) to select the entire canvas, and push <Delete> (<Backspace> in Windows).

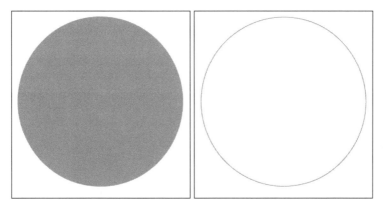

Figure 5–5: The thin halo of color that often exists after you select and cut something from a Layer can be annoying, but pretty easy to fix.

Layer Via...

To copy and paste onto a new Layer into the same position without having to actually select the commands from the Edit menu, simply activate the Layer that contains the object in question and choose Layer -> New -> Layer Via Copy.

If you want to cut instead of copy, you'll have to actually select the object, then choose Layer -> New -> Layer Via Cut.

Both of these options will create a new Layer, with the pasted object placed in the exact same position as the original object. Figure 5–6 illustrates. The original image is on the left, with the jumping boy selected. The image in the center shows the image and the corresponding Layers Palette after the Layer Via Copy command was used. Notice that, although he now appears on his own Layer, he also appears in the original Layer. This is unlike the image on the right, in which Layer Via Cut forced the selected boy to be removed from the original Layer (notice the white area in the Layer icon, where he used to be).

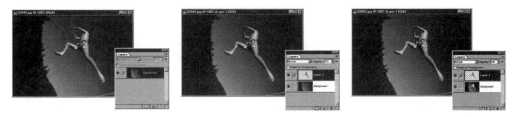

Figure 5–6: The results of using Layer Via commands for copying and cutting images from one Layer onto new one.

Paste Into

The Paste Into command can offer some neat results. Fairly uncomplicated, it lets you paste your image into a pre-made selection. For example, if the image on the far left of Figure 5–7 were selected and copied, then pasted into the selection (Edit -> Paste Into) in the center of Figure 5–7, the result would be the image on the far right of Figure 5–7. The image appears only within the selected areas.

The image will stay pasted into its own Layer. When you try this, you'll notice a distinct difference in your Layers Palette, as a new black and white thumbnail appears on the image Layer. This is called a *Mask*, and we'll review it in more detail during the Mask portion of this chapter.

MOVING ITEMS AND LINKING LAYERS

One of the nice things about using Layers is that you will have the ability to move items independently of each other. Photoshop makes the repositioning of items and objects simple by allowing you to move the contents of certain Layers individually or to link them and move them as a group.

Moving Items

Moving items on a Layer is a relatively simple task:

1. Click on the Layer that contains the item that you want to move to activate it.
2. Select the Move Tool (or, for the more efficient artists, hold the <Command> key (<Control> in Windows) to temporarily activate the Move Tool.
3. Drag your item to its new location.

Figure 5–7: When the image on the left is pasted into the selection of words in the center, the result is the cool effect shown on the right.

There are just a few things that you'll need to know while moving items on a Layer:

◆ Moving an item on a Layer with the Move Tool won't put it in front of or behind any item on another Layer. To do that, you would have to move the entire Layer either up or down in the Layers Palette (see "Changing the Order of Layers" earlier in this Chapter).

◆ If there is more that one item on your active Layer, dragging with the Move Tool will move all of the items on that Layer. If you want to only move one of the items on that Layer, you'll have to select it first, using one or more of the selection methods discussed in Chapter 2 (or, for even more selection options, check out the upcoming section, "Making Quick Selections and Finding Items in Layers" in this chapter).

◆ Hold the <Shift> key down while moving your item(s) to make sure that its movements is constrained to straight lines of 45-degree angles.

◆ If you move an item off the canvas (past the edges) so that it can't be seen any longer, it still exists. Its existence may not be visible, since it is no longer on the canvas, but it's still there. To bring it back onto the canvas, either increase the canvas size (Image -> Canvas Size) or drag with the Move Tool in the opposite direction until you see it again. For example, if you have moved your image off the left edge of the canvas, drag to the right until the image comes back into view.

Understanding the Move Tool

The Move Tool has had a face lift in the 6.0 version. The Options Palette, shown in Figure 5–8, now brings some previously understated features to greater prominence, as well as making the Transform function more accessible.

The tool itself is fairly easy to use. Simply activate it, click anywhere in the active Layer, and anything in that Layer will move along with your cursor. If you want only a portion of an active Layer to move, select the desired area first, then drag with the Move Tool. Holding the <Shift> key down will force your image to move in a straight line or a 45-degree angle. You can also move images by using the arrow keys on your keyboard.

 Each push of an arrow key will move your image by one pixel. Hold the <Shift> key while pushing the arrows to move your image 10 pixels at a time.

The first option available in the Move Tool's Options Palette is Auto Select Layer. This is a *really* annoying feature, and I would recommend that you keep it checked off. When it is checked on, the Layers Palette will automatically activate the Layer of any

Figure 5–8: The Options Palette for the Move Tool.

image that you click on. For example, let's say you have an image that has 10 Layers, with the Background Layer currently active. You want to manipulate a circle shape that resides in one of the other Layers, but you don't know which one. If Auto Select Layer is turned on, then all you have to do is click the circle shape in your canvas, and the Layer in which it resides will be activated.

It sounds pretty cool, but it really isn't. More often than not, you'll forget that you have that box checked, and go to move something on your active Layer but will accidentally click on something else, activating *that* Layer. This can build for a while in frustration, until you eventually uncheck the Auto Select Layer checkbox. Instead, I'd recommend using the keyboard command to auto-activate Layers by holding the <Command> (<Ctrl> in Windows) key and clicking on the desired image with the Move Tool.

The other checkbox that you'll find in the Move Tool's Options Palette is called *Show Bounding Box*. Clicking this checkbox on will create a bounding box around everything in the active Layer. The bounding box, with the handle bars that appear on the sides and corners, is nothing more than quicker access to the Free Transform features, which are covered in greater detail later in this chapter.

In the right-hand portion of the Move Tool's Option Palette are buttons for aligning and distributing images on "linked" Layers. While these options have appeared in earlier versions of Photoshop, they were pretty much lost at the bottom of the already cluttered Layers menu and, thus, kind of forgotten about. Placing them in the Options Palette for the Move Tool makes them far more visible and accessible—a real plus, considering how beneficial these features can be. All of the Align and Distribute buttons will be grayed out, however, until you have at least two Layers in your image that are linked together. Linking Layers and using the Align and Distribute features will be discussed later in this chapter.

Moving Items from One Canvas to Another

Moving items isn't limited to the canvas that you are currently working on. You can move items onto other images as well, simply by dragging the item off the active canvas and placing it onto another open image. There are some issues that you will want to be aware of when doing this (for the sake of explanation, let's say that you are moving an image of a car from Canvas 1 to Canvas 2):

♦   When you drag the car onto Canvas 2, the border of the entire canvas will highlight to let you know that there is an intercanvas move taking place. The move will end when you release the mouse button.

♦   The car will be placed on Canvas 2 in the location that you place it. You can have some control over the exact positioning, however, by holding the <Shift> key while you move the car:

   ♦   If Canvas 2 is the exact same size as Canvas 1, holding the <Shift> key while moving the car will cause it to be placed in the exact same position as it appears on Canvas 1.

- ◆ If Canvas 2 is a different size than Canvas 1, holding the <Shift> key while moving the car will cause it to be placed in the center of Canvas 2.

- ◆ As you are moving the car from Canvas 1, it will change positions (obviously, since you are dragging it). Once your cursor reaches Canvas 2, though, the original car in Canvas 1 will snap back into its original position.

- ◆ When you place the car in Canvas 2, it will automatically be placed in its own Layer. This Layer will be created immediately above whatever Layer is currently active in Canvas 2.

Linking Layers

As we can see, moving items while they are on a Layer is pretty simple stuff. But there can be more to it than that. Consider the canvas and its corresponding Layers Palette on the far left of Figure 5–9. You can see that the circle, square and triangle are on different Layers, yet they are working together nicely in the composite image. Assuming that you wanted to move them to another part of the canvas, moving the items of each Layer individually can take too much time. Even worse, if each object needs to be a certain distance from the other to work properly, moving each individually could permanently mess up your image.

To make this process easier, and more efficient, Photoshop lets you "link" Layers together. For example, in this image, you would do the following:

1. Make one of the three Layers that you wish to move active by clicking on it. As you can see, aside from the Layer in the palette being highlighted in blue, a small paintbrush icon appears in the box on the immediate left.

2. Click the second box in from the left of the two other Layers that you want to move. You'll see that a small chain icon appears. This means that your Layers are "linked", as shown in Figure 5–9.

3. With the Move Tool active, move the contents of the active Layer. You'll see that the contents of the linked Layers move, as well.

4. If you make one of the linked Layers active, the icons on the left trade places: The new active Layer now has a paintbrush icon, while the previously active Layer now has a chain link icon. They're all still linked; just the selection of which one is currently active has changed.

 If your active Layer is linked to a Layer that has either the Lock Edit or Lock Move checkbox on, you won't be able to make any moves on your active Layer, either.

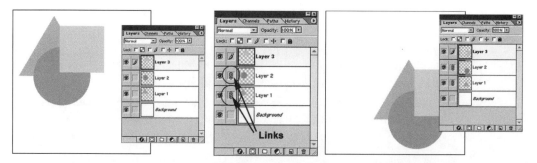

Figure 5–9: To move a number of images on different Layers at one time, link them together.

 Linking doesn't mean that *all* manipulations are universally made to the linked Layers. For example, if you painted on the active Layer, the other Layers remain unaffected—the paint does not happen to all Layers simultaneously. If you drag two or more linked Layers onto another canvas, as described previously in our discussion about Moving items, each Layer in the link will receive its own individual Layer in the new canvas.

Linking has a more dynamic range of uses beyond simply moving items around your canvas. Later in this chapter, you'll see linking play a role in transforming images, merging Layers, and pasting Layer Effects.

ALIGNING AND DISTRIBUTING IMAGES IN LAYERS

While the ruler and guides can be helpful tools in making sure that various aspects of your image are aligned and evenly distributed with one another, there is a decidedly more convenient method. With options found in the Layers menu and conveniently provided in the Move Tools Option Palette, you can automatically align and distribute images with one another, regardless of how many Layers they are on.

Aligning Images

Let's suppose that you have an image that looks like the one on the left in Figure 5–10. As you can see from the accompanying Layers Palette, the circle, square and the triangle are all on different Layers, and each in a different part of the canvas. What we want, though, is for our image to look more like it does on the right side of Figure 5–10, in which all of the objects are aligned with one another, both horizontally and vertically. To make this happen, we would do the following:

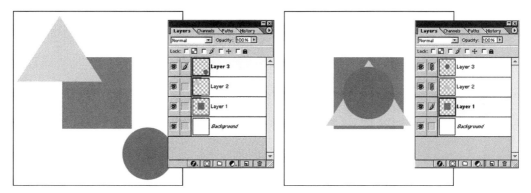

Figure 5–10: The Align Linked command makes it easy to line images on different Layers up with one another.

1. In the Layers Palette, make the Layer with the square active by clicking on it.

2. Link the circle Layer and the triangle Layer to the active Layer.

3. Choose Layer -> Align Linked -> Vertical Center (or activate the Move Tool and push the Align Vertical Centers button from the Options Palette). You'll see that, on your canvas, all of the images have moved vertically upward or downward to align with the center point of the active square Layer.

4. Choose Layer -> Align Linked -> Horizontal Center. All of the linked images now move left or right to align horizontally with the center of the active Layer.

Other choices in the Align Linked menu allow you to align linked Layers either at the top or bottom, or at the left or right sides. Although we used three Layers in this example, you are not limited to how many Layers you can use, as long as you have at least two linked together.

Distributing Layers

To distribute Layers, you'll need at least three Layers linked together. Unlike with aligning the Layers (which uses the contents of the active Layer to base the alignment of images), which of the linked Layers is active won't make a difference when distributing images. Instead, Photoshop will determine extreme edge or center positions and adjust the contents of whichever Layer falls in between.

For example, Figure 5–11 is a reprint of the left canvas of Figure 5–10. With the three shape Layers linked, let's say that we choose Layer -> Distribute Linked -> Horizontal Center (or push the button with the same name from the Move Tool's Option Palette). Regardless of which of the three linked Layers is active, Photoshop will determine that two middle points of the shapes are those of the triangle and the circle, and it will place the square so that the square's midpoint is in the dead center of those coordinates. The left canvas of Figure 5–12 illustrates this, with guides placed to show where the measurements are taken from. The right canvas of the same figure illustrates the effect of choosing to distribute based on the top edge, instead of the horizontal center.

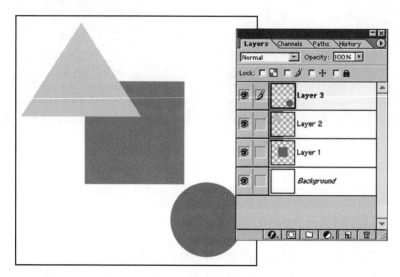

Figure 5–11: The original image—this time, the three shapes will be distributed instead of aligned.

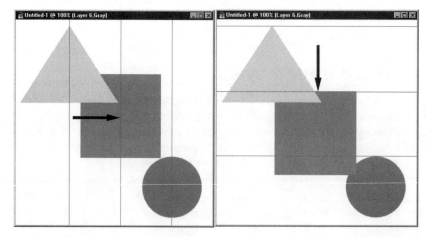

Figure 5–12: Distributing objects depends on the extreme measurements of the outer objects.

TRANSFORMING OBJECTS

Transforming objects can completely reshape an image—literally. Everything from Skew and Perspectives to simple resizing and stretching can be done through Transform functions.

In earlier versions of Photoshop, you needed to open the Edit menu to access either the Free Transform or the Transform submenu (or use the keyboard commands, of course). While you can still use these methods, version 6.0 has made accessing these features a little more convenient. In the Move Tool's Options Palette, click the box marked *Show Bounding Box*. The bounding box for the Move Tool provides instant access to the Free Transform features. In fact, once you begin making transformations, the Move Tool's Option Palette will be replaced by the Free Transform's Option Palette (to keep users of older versions sane: No, in older versions of Photoshop, the Transform features did not have their own Options Palettes).

If you want to manipulate the objects on a Layer with the Transform commands, make sure that your Layer is not locked. Locked Layers can't be transformed. In addition, make sure that any Layer that your active Layer is linked to isn't locked, either.

There are basically two separate Transform choices: a full transform menu, listing each feature individually, or the Free Transform option, which allows the nimble-fingered keyboard artist to use all of the Transform functions at once. We'll concentrate on the Free Transform at first, then later touch on the only two areas of the Transform menu that you'll ever really need: Numeric and Flip.

Free Transform

The first frame in Figure 5–13 shows a film reel, waving around in its own Layer. I have created it by using a Wave filter on it, which we'll discuss in detail in Chapter 7 and Chapter 11. In the background of Figure 5–13 is a fairly simple space scene, with a lone planet in the upper corner. I'm going to use the Free Transform features to make the wave seem to be coming from behind the planet and outward, toward the front of the canvas.

To accomplish this, we would do the following:

1. With the Film Layer active, activate the Move Tool and click the Show Bounding Box checkbox, or press <Command + T> (<Ctrl + T> in Windows). A bounding box outside of the filmstrip will appear, with handle bars on each corner and side (just like the one used for the Crop Tool). Notice that the bounding box will appear around whatever is selected, or, if nothing is selected, around everything on the active Layer.

2. The first thing we'll want to do is make the filmstrip a bit larger. Do this by dragging out any of the corner handle bars to increase the height and width at the same time. Hold the <Shift> key down to constrain the proportions. For this example, we'll just make it a little larger.

Making things larger through the Transform function can have the same effect as increasing the size through the Image Size dialog box. Take care to limit the amount that you increase anything, as you may run into blurring and pixelation problems.

3. Let's position the filmstrip so that it is coming from the direction of our planet. Move the cursor outside of the bounding box, and you'll see that it becomes a curved line with a double-headed arrow. Move your cursor in the direction that you want to rotate your image. In this case, I've rotated my filmstrip so that the left side is now positioned over or at least facing the planet.

The image rotates around its exact middle, as indicated by the center point of the bounding box. As we'll see later in this chapter, we can change the point of rotation by moving the center point.

4. If the filmstrip needs to be moved at all for better positioning, simply place the cursor within the confines of the bounding box and drag it to its desired location.

Now we need to give the image some depth. To make the filmstrip seem like it's coming from behind such a distant planet, we'll add perspective. With your cursor placed in the top or bottom left handle bar of the bounding box, hold down the <Option + Command + Shift> keys (<Alt + Ctrl + Shift> in Windows) and drag inward. You'll see that that portion of your image gets smaller while the opposite side retains its size. This causes the filmstrip to seem as though it's coming from a distance. To enhance this, continue holding the same keys and this time, place your cursor on the top or bottom right handle bar, and drag outward. Now the right side will get larger while the left side remains unchanged.

At any point during this process, you may need to make additional transformations. For example, in step 5, the perspective made my filmstrip seem smaller in length than I really wanted. I compensated for this by releasing all keys and dragging outward on one of the side handle bars to increase the length as needed. Or I might need to move the entire image again to reposition it properly. The point is that I am not confined to doing transformation in any particular order—I can do any or all of them at any time, as they are necessary.

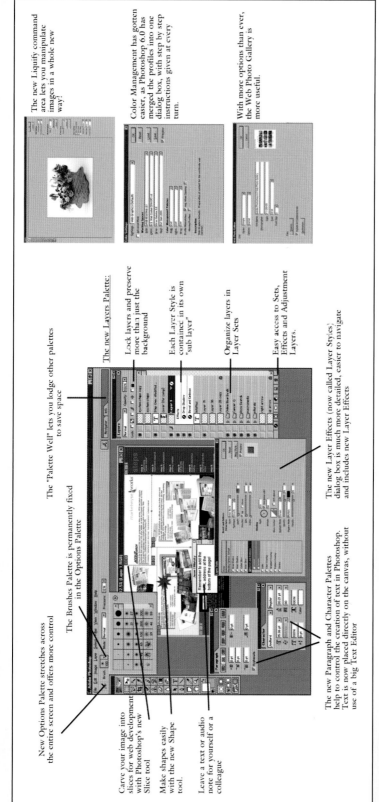

The new Liquify command area lets you manipulate images in a whole new way!

Color Management has gotten easier, as Photoshop 6.0 has merged the profiles into one dialog box, with step by step instructions given at every turn.

With more options than ever, the Web Photo Gallery is more useful.

The new Layers Palette:

Lock layers and preserve more than just the background

Each Layer Style is contained in its own "sub layer"

Organize layers in Layer Sets

Easy access to Sets, Effects and Adjustment Layers.

New Options Palette stretches across the entire screen and offers more control

The "Palette Well" lets you lodge other palettes to save space

The Brushes Palette is permanently fixed in the Options Palette

The new Layer Effects (now called Layer Styles) dialog box is much more detailed, easier to navigate and includes new Layer Effects

Carve your image into slices for web development with Photoshop's new Slice tool.

Make shapes easily with the new Shape tool.

Leave a text or audio note for yourself or a colleague

The new Paragraph and Character Palettes help to control the creation of text in Photoshop. Text is now placed directly on the canvas, without use of a big Text Editor

COLOR FIGURE I

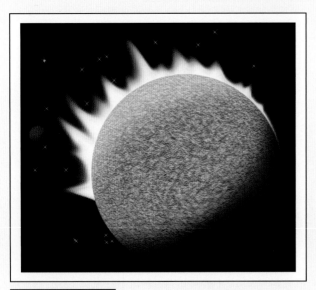

COLOR FIGURE 2
The flames of the fire were made with the Smudge tool.

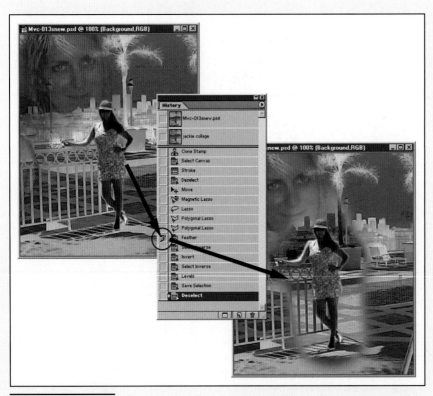

COLOR FIGURE 3
Effects created with the History palette.

COLOR FIGURE 4
Base picture that I'll use for making color-based selections.

COLOR FIGURE 5
The Magnetic Lasso tool works well with images that have a good contrast from their background.

COLOR FIGURE 6
The image that we will end up with.

COLOR FIGURE 7
Making a selection of the polo player and his horse in the image would be tough using the standard tools.

COLOR FIGURE 8
We'll need to make a selection of all the yellow in the uniforms.

COLOR FIGURE 9

Feathering a selection before copying or cutting will help make the image more natural looking when it comes to pasting into another image.

COLOR FIGURE 10

Notice how the clouds start off strong at the top (100% white in the Channels palette) and fade out toward the bottom (0% white in the Channels palette). Notice, too, that the snowboard guy, which remained 100% in the "Gradient" channel, wasn't effected by the clouds at all.

COLOR FIGURE 11

This time, I've created a diagonal gradient to a new channel and loaded it into my composite, with the Background layer (the only layer, in this case), active. When I hit Delete (Backspace), my image fades slowly into white, which is m[?] background color (if my background color had been red, my image would have faded to red).

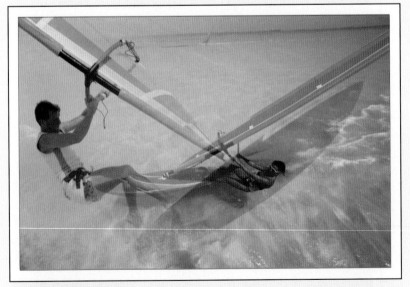

COLOR FIGURE 12

My collage. Because I loaded the "Gradient" channel onto a layer other than the Background layer (in this case Layer 1), when I hit Delete, the image fades to transparency, showing me the image that lies in a lower layer.

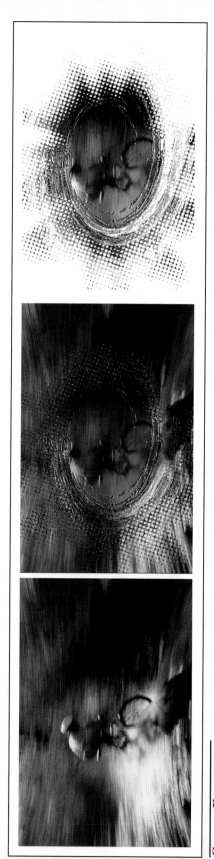

COLOR FIGURE 13
My final image, framed.

COLOR FIGURE 14

The lei would be too difficult to select with the Magic Wand tool (too many colors), or the Lasso tools (too many curves), but because it's in its own layer, we can easily select it by using Command (Ctrl) + clicking on its layer.

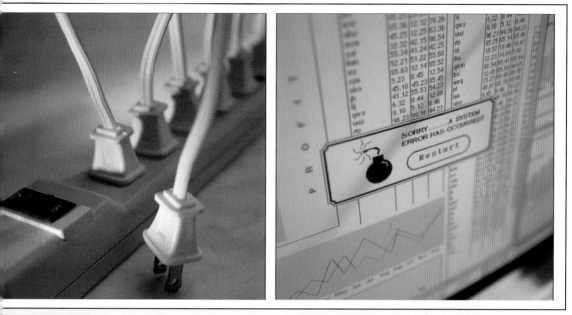

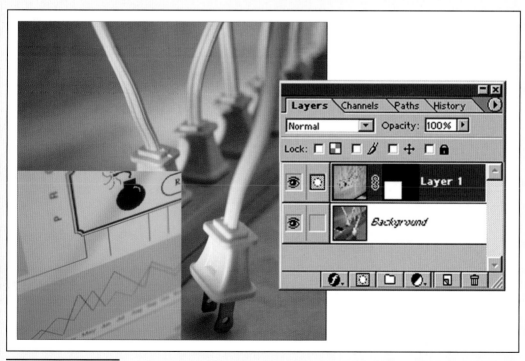

COLOR FIGURE 16

My background with the selection where I will add the mask.

COLOR FIGURE 17
On the left, the words "Layer Groups" will act as out mask for the center image. The right shows the result in both the Image and Layers palette when the CD layer is grouped with the text layer.

COLOR FIGURE 18
Problems with the fruit stand pic include that the fruit is too dark.

COLOR FIGURE 19

The colors in the flower basket are a bit faded, and we'll need to change some of the red roses to an alternative color.

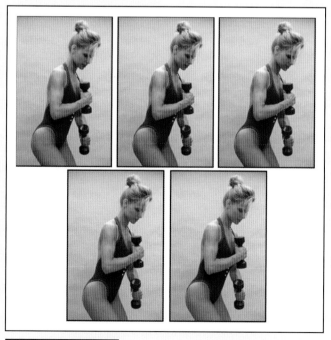

COLOR FIGURE 20

By the time we're done with this image, the girl will have a tan, a different color bathing suit, and some crazy color effects.

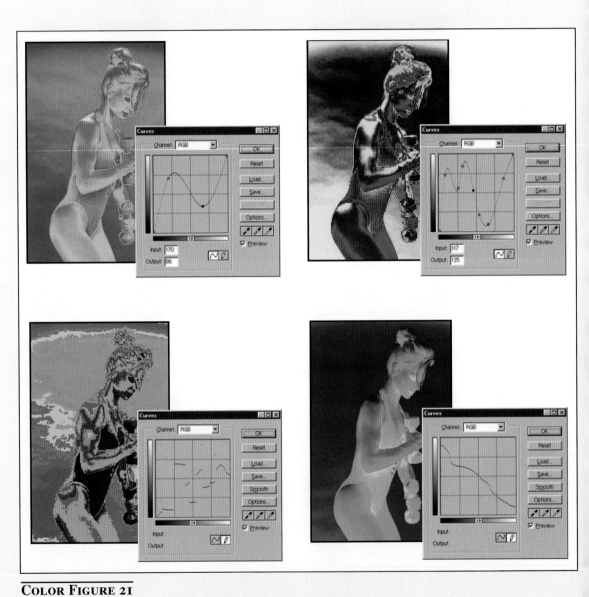

The Curves dialog box for a CMYK image. Notice the difference between this and the RGB version at the point of origin.

COLOR FIGURE 22
We'll make this picture look like it was taken around the turn of the century.

COLOR FIGURE 23
The Invert option can create a cool effect.

COLOR FIGURE 24
An example of the Posterize feature, with the tonal level set to 3.

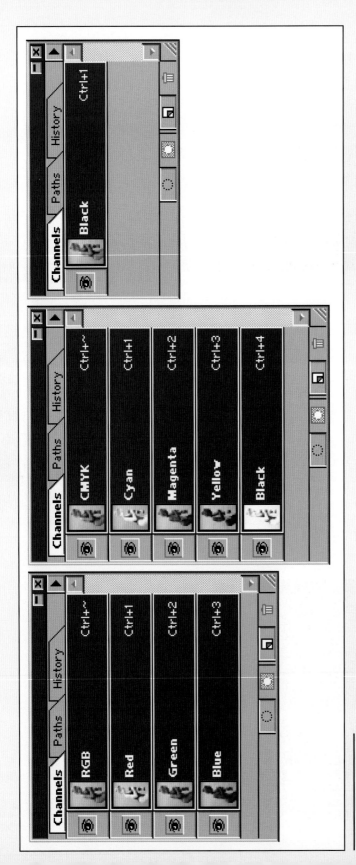

COLOR FIGURE 25

The Channels palettes as they appear for CMYK images (left), RGB images (middle), and Gray scale images (right).

COLOR FIGURE 26

Clockwise from upper left: composite, red, green, and blue channels. Individually, each channel appears in grayscale by default.

COLOR FIGURE 27

As you can see, by comparison to Color Figure 26, the channels are harder to work with in color.

COLOR FIGURE 28

This RGB image could use some sharpening and contrast adjustment.

COLOR FIGURE 29

The composite image after a few of the channels have been tweaked individual The red cast has been reduced in the image on the right.

COLOR FIGURE 30

The women in the forefront of the image pop off and become sharper when the channels are mixed (right image).

COLOR FIGURE 31

The images that I'll be using to describe the blend mode. I'll show the result with both the toast on top (in the Layers palette), and the computer on top.

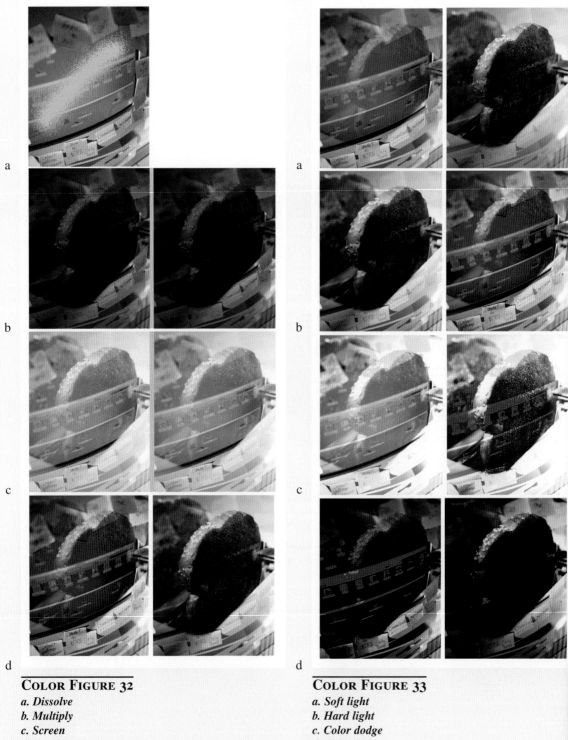

COLOR FIGURE 32
a. Dissolve
b. Multiply
c. Screen
d. Overlay

COLOR FIGURE 33
a. Soft light
b. Hard light
c. Color dodge
d. Color burn

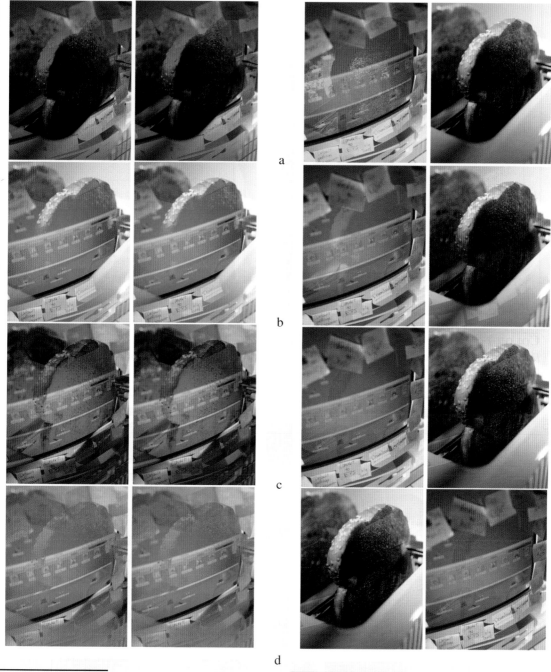

COLOR FIGURE 34
a. Darken
b. Lighten
c. Difference
d. Exclusion

COLOR FIGURE 35
a. Hue
b. Saturation
c. Luminosity
d. Color

COLOR FIGURE 40
The water droplets, when used with the proper blend mode,
make my glass and lime appear to be wet.

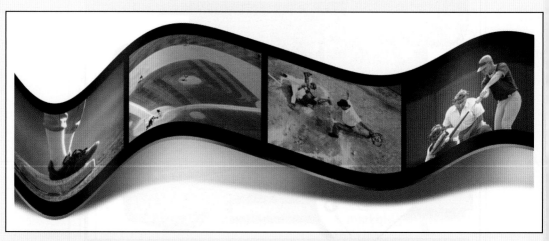

COLOR FIGURE 41
After adding the appropriate highlights and shadows, the wave finally looks realistic.

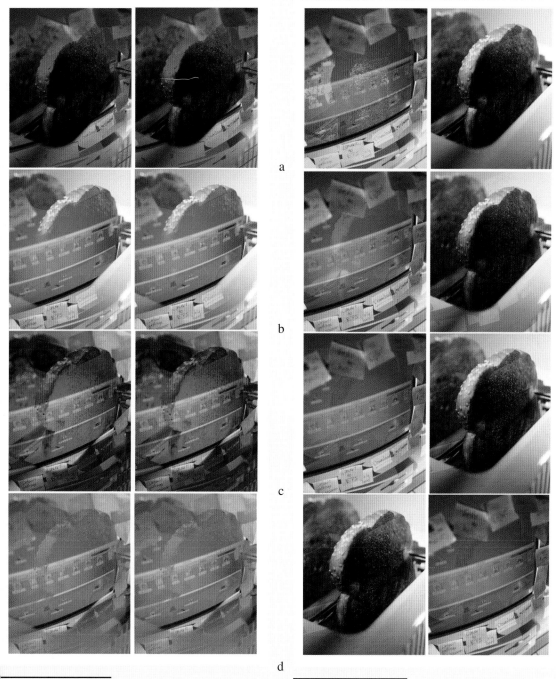

COLOR FIGURE 34
a. Darken
b. Lighten
c. Difference
d. Exclusion

COLOR FIGURE 35
a. Hue
b. Saturation
c. Luminosity
d. Color

Designing a flyer without bleeds (like the one on the left), can be a bit simpler. Full bleed images like the one on the right, need special treatment.

A typical tri-fold brochure. There are really three panels, not three folds.

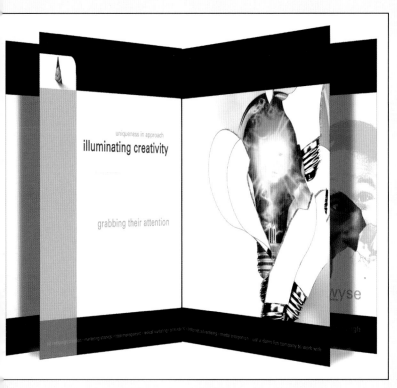

COLOR FIGURE 38
This eight-page brochure was made by folding two pieces of paper into one another.

COLOR FIGURE 39
A random collection of CD-ROM and DVD interfaces that were created in Photoshop.

COLOR FIGURE 40
The water droplets, when used with the proper blend mode,
make my glass and lime appear to be wet.

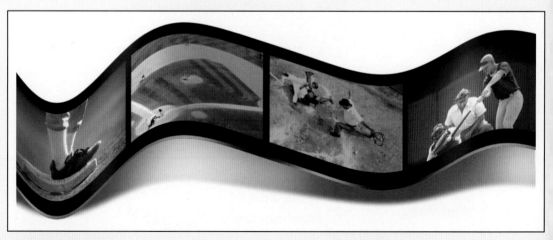

COLOR FIGURE 41
After adding the appropriate highlights and shadows, the wave finally looks realistic.

COLOR FIGURE 42
The result of the Lighting Effects filter on a feathered selection saved as a channel is a realistic bevel.

COLOR FIGURE 43
My canvas after filling it with Difference Clouds. Notice how the word "Neon" is effected.

COLOR FIGURE 44
The Motion Blur and Ripple filters really start to give the fire some shape.

COLOR FIGURE 45
Airbrush white over the blue icy letters.

COLOR FIGURE 46
The final collage, and its respective Layers palette.

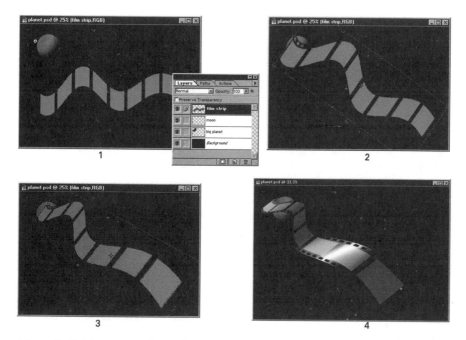

Figure 5–13: The steps used to make my wave seem realistically to be coming from behind a distant planet.

5. The perspective helped a lot, but now we just need to do a little extra tweaking to get the shape of the filmstrip just right. I'll employ a few different methods:

◆ Distort: By holding the <Command> key (<Ctrl> in Windows) and dragging one of the side handle bars of the bounding box, I can slant my image considerably. Dragging a corner handle bar will allow me to stretch my image one corner at a time.

◆ Skew: I can skew my image by holding both the Command + Option keys (Ctrl + Alt in Windows) and dragging any of the handlebars.

6. When all of the tweaking is completed, we can accept the transformation by pushing <Return> (<Enter> in Windows). If you don't like the transformation that you've made, you can get out of it and start all over by pushing the <Esc> key.

 You will have only one undo while you are transforming. Make a mistake, and you can choose Edit -> Undo, but only once. The History Palette is not retaining the changes that you make while in Transform Mode.

Once your transformation is completed, you can continue to work on your image. In the case of my filmstrip, my continued work included painting a slight back that wrapped around the planet and adding shadows and shimmer in their proper places to lend depth to the filmstrip, The process is illustrated in Figure 5–13.

For anyone interested, the shadow and shimmer were made by grabbing a selection of the film strip and painting either white or black in
the appropriate places on a new Layer, using a soft-edged brush and
the Airbrush Tool. I then lowered the opacity of the new Layer to
make the shadows and highlights more realistic.

For your convenience, all of the Free Transform functions and their associated keys
are listed in Table 5–1. When I refer to a "corner handle," I'm usually referring to any
corner. When I refer to a "side handle," I'm usually referring to the handles on the side
as well as the top and bottom of the bounding box. Try each one.

Table 5–1: Transformation Functions

Function	Command
Scale	Just drag any handle bar. To constrain the proportions, hold the <Shift> key while dragging a corner handle. Similar to making a marquee selection, you can Scale from the center by holding <Option + Shift> (<Alt + <Shift> in Windows) while dragging a corner handle.
Move	Place your cursor within the confines of the bounding box, and move the selection to its desired location. As usual, hold the <Shift> key down to ensure that you're dragging in a straight line or at a 45-degree angle.
Rotate	Place your cursor outside the bounding box. You'll see that it becomes a two-headed, curved arrow. Move your mouse to the left to rotate left, or to the right to rotate right. Hold the <Shift> key while rotating to constrain the rotation limits to 15 degrees at a time.
	Notice that your image rotates around the center point of the bounding box. To change the circumference of your rotation, drag the center point to some-where else within your canvas (it can be outside the confines of the bound-ing box). Your image will now rotate around the center point wherever you have placed it.
Flip	Flipping isn't really a function, it's more just overdoing the Scale com-mand. To flip an image horizontally, for example, drag the handle bar on the left or right side of the bounding box past the opposite handle. It's easy to do, but chances are you'll never get it to flip with the same exact mea-surements as it was originally. A more effective way of flipping is to choose Edit -> Transform -> Flip Horizontally (or Flip Vertically). You can do this even with the Free Transform bounding box active.
Skew	Drag one of the side handles while holding the <Command> key (<Ctrl> in Windows).

(continued)

Table 5–1: (continued)

Function	Command
Perspective	Hold the <Command + Shift> keys (<Ctrl + Shift> in Windows) while dragging a corner handle bar for a one-point perspective. For a two-point perspective, hold the (get your carpal tunnel syndrome insurance card ready) <Command + Shift + Option> keys (<Ctrl + Shift + Alt> in Windows) while dragging on a corner handle bar.
Distort	This is probably my favorite Free Transform function, since you can really do some funky stuff to your image. Hold the <Command> key (<Ctrl> in Windows) ...do I really need to keep saying this?) and drag a corner handle bar. All other handle bars will remain in place as you stretch your chosen corner like a digital piece of Silly Putty.
	Hold the <Command + Option> keys (<Ctrl + Alt>) while dragging a corner to stretch the opposite corner symmetrically.
Undo	Pushing <Command + Z> (<Ctrl +Z>) or choosing Edit -> Undo while using Free Transform will undo the last transformation that you did. Pushing <Command + Z> (<Ctrl + Z>) or choosing Edit -> Undo after you have accepted your changes will undo the entire transformation.
Accept Transform	If you're happy with your work and want the transformation to apply, either double click within the bounding box or push the <Return> key (<Enter> in Windows).
Cancel Transform	If you are unhappy with the changes you've made and want your image to go back to the way it was before you started the Free Transform function, simply push <Esc>. This will get rid of the bounding box and return your image to its original state before you started Free Transforming.

 You can choose to perform each of the above commands individually through the Edit -> Transform menu. Personally, I can't see the use in simply choosing the Skew command all by itself when Free Transform allows you to do each function at once with just a little practice with the keyboard commands. But to each his own....

Using transformations, especially the Free Transform function, will probably be especially helpful as you work but can also be especially frustrating. My ultimate advice would be not really to concern yourself with which keys perform which function in terms of memorizing them, but rather to simply try using Free Transform with various combinations of the <Option>, <Command> and <Shift> keys (<Alt>, <Ctrl> and <Shift> in Windows).

Other Transform Features

Everything that we just did in the previous example could also be done individually by choosing the proper command from the Edit -> Transform menu. There are two options in this menu that do come in handy, however, and that you can't accomplish as efficiently through the Free Transform option.

The Transform Options Palette

The Numeric dialog box, shown in Figure 5–14, allows you to move, scale, skew and rotate by entering a numeric value. This is helpful when exact positioning is needed in the transformation of an object.

Click on any of the small white boxes in the Reference Point Location icon on the far left of the Options Palette and fill in the X and Y values in the corresponding areas accordingly. The portion of icon that you clicked will move to the X and Y coordinates on your canvas. For example, if you clicked on the small white square in the bottom left corner (it will turn black to indicate that it has been clicked), the bottom left of the image you are transforming will move to whatever point on the canvas that corresponds to the X and Y axis values that you set.

The next area in the Options Palette allows you to scale the image numerically by percentage. Click the chain link between the width and height to maintain the aspect ratio and keep them relative to each other.

Other areas of the dialog box allow you to alter the angle and skew of your image. A checkmark on the far right allows you to accept the changes you have made, while a large X will reject the changes and take you out of Free Transform mode.

Flipping

By choosing either Flip Horizontal or Flip Vertical, you turn your image to become a mirrored reflection of itself. You can do this by playing with the Free Transform function as well, but chances are you would never get it exactly right when doing it by hand.

Be careful when you flip things. Some objects are fine when flipped. Other objects will give it away immediately (assuming that you don't want your audience to know that you've flipped something). While images containing words might be obvious when flipped horizontally, watch out for less apparent problems, like flipping a man with a coat on (the buttons on a man's suit are always on the right), or flipping a woman with an engagement/wedding ring (traditionally worn on the left hand).

Figure 5–14: The Transform Options Palette.

Some Final Thoughts on Transformations

As with most anything else in Photoshop, there are always a few extra points to keep in mind when transforming an object:

◆ When transforming text, you will be limited to which functions you can use. Check out the next section for details on how to remedy this.

◆ If your Layer is linked to other Layers, and you choose to transform the images on your Layer without selecting them first, all of the images on every linked Layer will be transformed as well.

◆ Choosing Edit -> Undo while in the middle of making a transformation will undo the last transformation that you made. Choosing Edit -> Undo after you have accepted the transformation will undo the entire transformation.

◆ After you complete a transformation, if you want to do the exact same thing again, choose Edit -> Transform -> Again.

WORKING WITH TEXT
AND TEXT LAYERS

The New Type Tool: A Brief Editorial

If you read this whole book cover to cover and have any sense of insight, you probably get the feeling that 6.0 is not my favorite upgrade. You can't please everybody, right? It's not that this is a bad upgrade, and, like the Layer Sets that we read about in Chapter 1, it has a few good points. But for the most part, the changes made just seem kind of extraneous. I was happy enough with the Options Palette the way it was before, and I really kind of liked being able to access the Brushes Palette, even if I wasn't using a painting tool. The Shape Tool was a nice addition, but I run out of breath trying to create my own custom shape and really don't understand the need for Shape Layers and Photoshop's sudden fetish for paths. And the new Liquify feature...well, that's really nothing more than Kai's Power Goo repackaged and less interesting.

But those things are just the kind of stuff that makes you shake your head and wonder if each upgrade is about improvement or just an excuse to get users to spend more money. Where I have a problem is with the areas in which they have dismantled something that was fine to begin with, and rebuilt it to be worse than it was before.

As I wrote in the intro to this chapter, Type has never been particularly easy to place in Photoshop. But while the traditional Text Editor may have been a bit bulky, by the time they released Photoshop 5.5, they had it working really well—all of the options were there in front of you, you had far more control over the size and style of the text you were placing, the Move Tool worked in conjunction with the Editor, changing type you had placed was as easy as double-clicking the Layer it was on and (for me, at least) the fact that the Editor was open forced you to finish what you were typing before you moved on to perform other functions.

Photoshop 6.0, however, has abandoned the Text Editor completely. Now when you want to place text, you just activate the Type Tool, click the area of your canvas where you want to place your text, and begin typing. It seems like a great idea, but start working with it a bit and you'll likely get frustrated. The options available, such as color, font style, size, etc., are spread out over three separate palettes, one of them being the Paragraph Palette. Who writes entire paragraphs in Photoshop? Buy that guy Microsoft Word, for crying out loud!

Simple things have been changed, also. The often-used "force" attributes, such as underline, bold and italics, which went from nonexistence (5.0—"boo!") to prominence (5.5—"yay!") to obscurity (6.0—"huh?"), hidden in a submenu of one of the three palettes. Why, were these a little too simple to find before? Nothing like some adventure when designing under a deadline.

Re-editing your type has changed, as well. In earlier version, double-clicking on a Type Layer, regardless of what tool was active, opened the Text Editor and allowed you to change the copy you'd placed. In 6.0, you first have to activate the Type Tool again, then click within the Type that you placed to do any revisions. Maybe that's simple enough, but if you want to place new type on your canvas, don't inadvertently click on the canvas within 10 pixels of any other body of type, or you'll find yourself editing copy that you didn't mean to change.

But the worst part of all is the fact that the new Type Tool works counter to the way most long-time designers have trained themselves to work. Photoshop is primarily a keyboard-command program. Even though you need a mouse of some sort to paint, draw, etc, the program is really much faster and richer with liberal use of keyboard commands and shortcuts. Use any tool in Photoshop, and you can immediately activate any other tool by pressing a single button. Say you're using the Airbrush, for example, and suddenly need the Lasso tool. Just release the mouse button and push the <L> key. Simple enough and universally true for every tool in Photoshop. But the Type tool is not like every other tool. In the past, you wouldn't think to access the Lasso Tool while the Text Editor was open. But the lack of an Editor box in 6.0 creates the impression that the Type Tool is like any other, and, more often than not, you'll find yourself trying to access the Lasso Tool, only to type a long series of LLLLLLL's on your canvas. It's annoying.

Lastly, and along the same lines, designers like myself who are used to keyboard shortcuts are prone to working without any palettes open and in Full View Mode, without the menu bar. Try to place type on your canvas under these conditions. Then try to change the Font Style. It's an extremely frustrating process.

It's unfortunate that a program like Photoshop, which has been largely responsible for the advanced state of modern graphic design, doesn't know when to stop. Maybe it's because a lack of any real competition has made it too comfortable for its own good. But, hopefully, this lackluster upgrade and a retreat from the last best attempt to provide a decent Type Tool is more of an unfortunate glitch, rather than an indication of what's to come.

Because this book is supposed to be more tutorial than editorial, I'll provide the rest of this chapter with as few negative quips and opinions as possible.

Placing Text

In previous versions, text was placed through the use of a Text Editor dialog box, which, although large, kept everything united in one nice, neat, compact area. In version 6.0, text is placed directly onto the canvas. Activate the Type Tool, click on your canvas in the area that you wish to place your text, and start typing. Text will appear on its own Layer, marked by a large T, as shown in Figure 5–15, and be created automatically on your canvas, without the Text Editor used in the past. Every new piece of text that you write (each time you click in a unique location with the Type Tool) will be placed on its own Layer.

To accept the text that you write and move on to other things, either choose another tool, make another Layer active, or click the checkmark on the upper right corner of the Options Palette, shown in Figure 5–16. The Options Palette gives you the ability to change the font style, size, color, justification, etc. It also includes a button marked _Palettes_ to access the Character and Paragraph Palettes that we'll review in just a bit (yes, everything that _used_ to be located within the Text Editor is now broken up and spread across three individual palettes. Brilliant). One saving grace, however, is a button that looks like a frowning T—even though I've made it pretty clear that I am not a fan of the changes to the Type Tool, I have to admit that this particular feature is pretty cool.

To go back and edit any text that you have placed, activate the Type Tool and click any place within your desired copy. The Layer for that text will be activated, and you can begin typing, deleting or otherwise editing any area of what you had written.

 The new way of selecting text to edit, though, causes a problem. Be careful when placing new text on a canvas—if you click to place new text within about 10 pixels of existing text, you'll end up editing the old text, instead of starting new copy as you had planned.

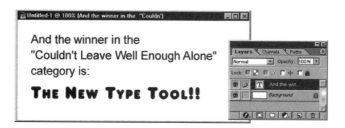

Figure 5–15: Placing text on your canvas is more direct than in previous versions of Photoshop.

Figure 5–16: The Type Tool's Options Palette.

To move your copy to another area of your canvas while you're placing or editing text, move your cursor to another part of your canvas, away from the text, to access the Move Tool temporarily. Drag to the new location and move your cursor back to the text to continue typing.

There is a major drawback to this new-fangled way of placing text—a big drawback. Once you start placing text on your canvas, your keyboard shortcuts pretty much become useless. For example, if you are finished typing and want to use the Rubber Stamp Tool, pressing the <S> key to access it will only type another S in the copy you have placed. You'll either need to accept the change by pushing the checkmark in the Options Palette or manually choose another tool.

The Character Palette

Any "tweaking" or cosmetic settings that you'll make to your text will be done through the Character Palette, as shown and described in Figure 5–17. Fairly straightforward, this palette allows you to establish the font(s) you'll use for your copy, as well as any attributes (such as bold, underline or italics).

Anyone who was happy to see the return of the forced bold, italic or underline features in version 5.5 doesn't have to panic—they're still here, just not as prominent. These options, plus an option for strikethrough, subscript and superscript are available in the Character Palette's options menu.

Other areas of the Character Palette provide new features for text, none of which really take a rocket scientist to figure out. The center command area of the palette lets

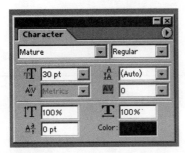

Figure 5–17: The Character Palette.

you set the values for the characters themselves and how they will relate to one another. These include setting the point size of the text, as well the pixel distance between lines and the letters themselves. Each option gives you the chance either to insert the value manually, or to use the drop-down slider.

The lower command area is for the more aesthetic adjustments to your copy, including color adjustment and somewhat pointless horizontal and vertical text stretch areas (pointless because you can achieve better results quicker by using the Free Transform commands).

You don't need to settle for one set of values for any one area of text that you create. Instead, you can set lines of text at a time, with varying font styles and sizes, kerning, tracking, stretching, color, etc.

To change any of the settings or attributes on text that you have already placed, simply use the Type Tool to highlight the copy that you wish to change, then make your changes in the Character Palette.

The Paragraph Palette

The Paragraph Palette, shown and described in Figure 5–18, is a great new feature to version 6.0 that is almost a little beyond itself, depending on the application. In earlier versions of Photoshop, your only real options in terms of placing multiple lines of copy were to justify left, right or center. What was always missing was the ability to justify both left and right at the same time, with the ability to force the justification for the last line (either left, right or centered). Those choices have now been added and appear in the Paragraph Palette.

What has also been added are features that you'd be more likely to find in a standard text editor or page layout program, such as MS Word or Quark XPress. These include paragraph indents on the left or right, indention of the first line of copy, or adding a set value of space before or after a paragraph. The Paragraph Palette's pulldown menu even provides the opportunity to make a drop cap, where the first character in a paragraph is larger.

The problem here, as I see it, is that there really shouldn't even *be* paragraphs in Photoshop. Photoshop is a bitmap program and should primarily be used for graphic

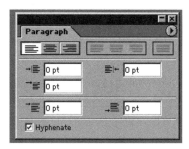

Figure 5–18: The Paragraph Palette.

design—not for writing book reports or brochures. Typical text that is placed in Photoshop should be for effect only and used sparingly. These new features are good to have around and to understand on a *just-in-case* basis, but my advice to you is not to allow yourself to get lazy and begin placing too much copy within Photoshop itself. For printed pieces, text will come out a lot sharper if it's set in a page layout program such as QuarkXPress (and it will be easier to adjust in the long run), and, for Web sites, setting as much text as you can in standard HTML will help to keep your file size down.

Is This Photoshop or Illustrator?

Although Adobe's other monster product, Illustrator, is a key graphics tool in its own right, one of the main reasons a lot of designers would use it is for special text effects. Curving text, waving it, bloating it—none of that was ever very easy or successfully accomplished in Photoshop until 6.0 hit the shelves. The new Shape button in the Type Tool's Option Palettes reveals the dialog box and menu shown in Figure 5–19. These options allow you the freedom to manipulate your text more creatively without having to Render the Layer (as you would need to do if you wished to use a filter on your text, which we'll review in the next section).

To use one of the options on your text, simply place your text in your canvas, and, with the Type Tool still selected, push the Shape button and choose the shape you wish to apply to your copy. Sliders and other standard dialog boxes will appear with any shape that you select to help you adjust the shape accurately. Figure 5–20 shows a few sample shapes.

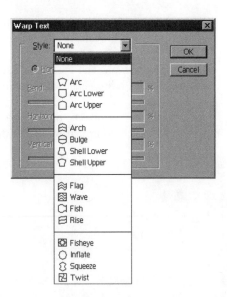

Figure 5–19: The Warp Text menu gives you more control over your text.

Figure 5–20: Look! Cool Text effects!

Making a Text Layer into a Regular Layer

Did you ever see one of those television commercials for a new drug that prevents some ailment nobody has ever heard of? After 25 seconds of how great this new drug is, the final five seconds contains a voiceover speaking very quickly and alerting you to such a long list of awful side effects that most people would be better off sticking with the original ailment.

The ability to edit text is kind of like that. You gain the ability to make changes to text that you've placed, but you end up paying a substantial price for it in a lack of manipulation ability. In the end though, it's a worthwhile trade-off:

◆ You can't use any effects from the Filters menu. Go ahead, try it. None of them work.

◆ If you try to Transform the text (see "Transforming Objects," earlier in this chapter), you will be limited to what you can do—skews and perspectives, for example, are not going to happen.

◆ If you want fill with a color, by either using the Paint Bucket Tool or pushing <Option + Delete> (<Alt + Backspace> in Windows), you don't need to click the Preserve Transparency button on the Layers Palette—the transparency is automatically preserved.

◆ You can't paint, rubber stamp, place a gradient or otherwise manipulate this Layer.

◆ You can try to select a portion of the existing text and copy it, cut it or move it, but it won't work.

◆ You can't merge this Layer with other linked Layers (we'll get into merging Layers in the next section and the silly way around this problem).

You can regain any of these functions if you need them by giving up your right to edit the text. To do this, simply choose Layer -> Rasterize -> Type. The text Layer retains its name but loses the giant T on the far right. From this point on, you can no longer change the text (but you can filter the hell out of it).

MAKING QUICK SELECTIONS AND FINDING ITEMS IN LAYERS

Whoa! You mean, there are more selection options than the 20 billion described in Chapter 3?. Yep, the list goes on, and using the Layers Palette may make some of your selecting chores at least a little easier. A similar method also helps you to find which Layer an item is located on, in case you have too many.

Making Selections from Layers

This is actually a pretty neat feature. Let's say that you want to select the lei in the picture in Figure 5–21. There are a lot of colors in it, and you really don't want to waste time with the Magic Wand Tool or the Lassos. Figure 5–21 and the left image in Color Figure 14 show that the lei is in its own Layer, it's very easy to select. Simply hit <Command> (<Ctrl> in Windows) + Click on the Layer that contains the lei. When you move the cursor over the Layer with the <Command> (<Ctrl>) key pressed, the cursor becomes a hand with a square marquee next to it. Clicking the Layer will cause the items in this Layer to be selected.

If you have more than one item in your Layer, <Command> (<Ctrl>) clicking will cause them all to be selected. Use one of the other selection tools that we discussed in Chapter 2 while holding the <Option> (<Alt> in Windows) button to deselect the unwanted images.

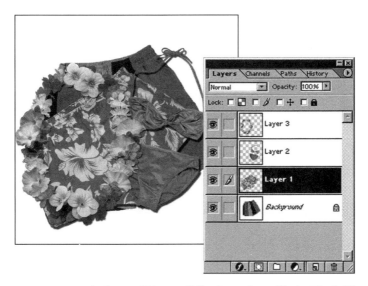

Figure 5–21: The lei would be too difficult to select with the Magic Wand Tool (too many colors) or the Lasso Tools (too many curves), but because it's in its own Layer, we can easily select it by <Command> (<Ctrl>) + clicking on its Layer.

Any of the addition, subtraction or intersection features that we discussed in Chapter 2 hold here, as well. For example, if you want to add the selection of an object on another Layer to the selection that you just created, simply hold the <Command> (<Ctrl>) + <Shift> keys when you click on a Layer. To subtract from your current selection, hold the <Command> (<Ctrl>) + <Option> (<Alt> in Windows) keys when you click on a Layer. Hold all three buttons to intersect selections.

Using this Feature To Create a Shadow

You don't need to have the Layer be active to "grab" the selection from it. For example, let's say that you wanted to create a shadow below the lei in Figure 5–21. As you can see in the accompanying Layers Palette, the lei is located in the Layer called *lei*, directly above *bikini*, which contains the bikini. Ordinarily, one would probably use Layer Effects to create a shadow for the lei (we'll be getting to Layer Effects in just a bit), but for the sake of this example, let's pretend we want to create a shadow from scratch.

1. With Layer 2 active, create a new Layer by clicking on the New Layer button at the bottom of the Layers Palette. This new Layer, which will be named *Layer 4*, will be active upon creation. This is the Layer upon which we will create our shadow.

2. <Command> (<Ctrl>) + click Layer 3. This will create a selection around the lei, even though the Layer containing the lei is not active.

3. Activate any of the selection tools, preferably one of the Marquee Tools or the Free Form Lasso Tool.

4. Use the arrow keys to move the selection down and to the right by a few pixels.

5. Choose Select -> Feather, and fill in between 4 and 16 for the pixel radius.

 The amount that you choose will be determined not only by how soft you want your shadow, but also by the resolution of your image. Higher-res images will need a higher radius to see any significant effect.

6. Fill your selection with black.

7. To make the shadow more realistic, reduce the opacity setting on Layer 2. Figure 5–22 and the image on the right in Color Figure 14 provide an example of the result.

Finding Items Quickly in Layers

If you're like me, and may God help you if you are, most of your images will have a ton of Layers, and not one of them will be named. Consider the Layers Palette for the print ad in progress, shown in Figure 5–23. As you can see, it's very long—so long, in fact, that even when the palette is stretched to its longest on my 21-inch monitor, with my screen resolution set to 1072, I still have to scroll up and down to see all of the Layers.

Figure 5–22: The result of using my selection to add a drop shadow.

Figure 5–23: Too many Layers, like the one in this example, can make an image difficult to work with.

Let's say that I want to work on the object that appears in the lower left corner of my image. I know it's on it's own Layer—I remember putting it there. But like most everything else in my life (my keys, my wallet . . .), I seem to have lost it.

I could scroll forever up and down the Layers Palette, squinting into the small icons trying to find it, (or rather, have my secretary do it for me), or I can take the shortcut: <Command> (<Ctrl> in Windows) + click on the object in the canvas. The Layer that the object resides in will become the active Layer.

As I mentioned earlier in the section about using the Move Tool, you can also click the checkbox marked *Auto Select Layer* in the Move Tool's Option Palette, but this becomes more of an annoyance and should generally be left unused in place of the keyboard shortcut.

CREATING LAYER SETS: THE MECCA OF "CLUB ORGANIZATION"

Talk to anybody who knows me, and they'll all agree that I am not an organized person. Creative people, I explain, are not supposed to be organized. At least, that's my story and I'm stickin' to it. But those geniuses over at Adobe are making it very difficult for me to maintain a separation between organization and creativity. Layer Sets are a new feature that give you the ability to be both at the same time, and, well, I hate to admit it, but it's a real headache saver.

But no matter how organized I may get in Photoshop, I still refuse to clean out the back of my car.

For better or for worse, most of my designs tend to use an inordinate number of Layers. Let's say that I am using Photoshop to lay out the ad that we looked at in Figure 5–23. The globe has a number of different elements to it, with each explosion needing specific attention and graphic requirements. By the time I'm done, the design of this ad alone could be 50 or so Layers.

Now, let's say that I take some time off from this project, then come back to work on it a few days later. As you can see by the Layers Palette in the figure, I have a bad habit of not labeling my Layers, and with so many of them, it's hard and time-consuming to find all the ones that relate to the specific areas of the design.

Believe it or not, this is not an unusual scenario, as many designers tend to forget to label Layers and use a multitude of Layers to accomplish any given design. That's where Layer Sets come in. Creating a set, which I can do by clicking the Layer Set icon at the bottom of my Layers Palette, is like creating a folder, or directory, in my Layers Palette. As you can see in Figure 5–24, this folder can be opened or closed by clicking on a small arrow to the left of the folder icon.

Within each folder that I create, I can organize the Layers for any given area of design. For example, in the set I've illustrated in Figure 5–24, I've placed all of my Layers that are associated with the various areas in sets under specific names, such as *Earth and Space*, *CD Explosion* and *Keyboard Explosion*, which is currently open to show the Layers in the set. This is helpful in two ways:

◆   By placing all of these graphics into one folder, they're very easy to find again.

◆   When I'm not working on this portion of the overall design, I can keep the folder closed, making the Layers Palette more manageable to work with.

To place existing Layers into a folder, simply click and drag the Layer as you would if you were moving it to a new location. Place it right on top of the Set Layer until the Set Layer is highlighted. Release the mouse button, and your Layer will be placed within the set.

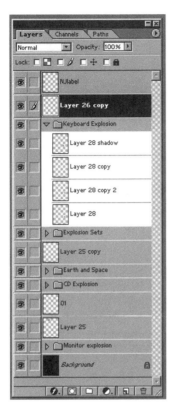

Figure 5–24: Organizing Layers in sets helps to organize complex images.

In the figure, other Layers are kept outside the sets, either because of needing to be in a specific place or just because they don't need to be in a set.

To create a name for your set, simply double-click the Set Layer to access the dialog box shown in Figure 5–25.

Type a name for your set to really be at the forefront of organizational efficiency.

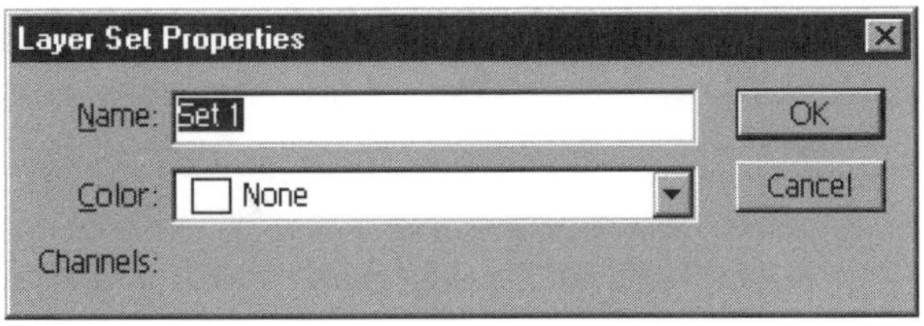

Figure 5–25: The Set Properties dialog box allows you to change the name of your set and the color of its bounding boxes.

When you throw out a set, you are throwing out every Layer within that set, too. So make sure that you really want to discard all of those Layers before trashing an entire set.

MERGING AND FLATTENING LAYERS

There are times when you may have too many Layers, and you need to condense things down a bit. Two of the ways you could do this (aside from throwing some Layers out or using Layer Sets) are as follows:

◆   Merge Layers: Merging Layers is the process of taking the contents of two or more Layers and condensing them into a single Layer. This is helpful if you have too many Layers and not enough memory (remember, the more Layers, the heavier your file and the more RAM and disk space it uses). You may also merge Layers if you have certain items that are so locked into their position that you no longer need to keep them separated.

When you merge or flatten Layers, any image or part of an image that was previously unseen because it was off of the canvas will be destroyed, and you'll no longer be able to get it back.

◆   Flatten Layers: Flattening Layers means taking the contents of all Layers and merging into one (the Background) Layer. Once you do this, you will no longer be able to manipulate objects independent from each other (unless you undo or go back with the History palette). You would typically do this when you are ready to publish something, either to the Web, to Print, or to some similar destination. Although programs such as Illustrator an InDesign (Adobe's answer to Quark Xpress for page layout) can now read Photoshop's Layers, this is not universally true. However, it probably won't be long before even non-Adobe programs, such as Xpress, can read them, as well. Flattened images can be saved in any number of formats, including EPS or TIFF (for print) or JPEG or GIF (Web).

Although it's not well known, Photoshop 6 can save TIF images with Layers still intact. However, Xpress doesn't recognize them, and the file sizes are increadibly huge.

Flattening Layers

Both Flattening and Merging are pretty easy. Because flattening Layers is by far one of the most brainless tasks you can undertake in Photoshop, we'll start with this one.

To flatten an image:

1. Start with an image that has multiple Layers.
2. From the Layers Palette pull-down menu, choose Flatten Image.
3. If you have hidden Layers (hidden Layers are Layers that are invisible), a warning box will appear to ask whether you want to discard the hidden Layers. Because hidden Layers can't be part of the flattened composite, you really have only one option. So as long as you are sure that you want to flatten your image, hit OK.
4. Done. Now you can save your image in practically any format you would like.

If you want to retain your Layers but save as a format other than Photoshop at any given time, choose File -> Save Copy.

When you flatten your image, all flexibility in editing type Layers or changing the values of Layer Effect (coming up later in this chapter) will be lost.

Merging Layers

Merging Layers is just as easy as flattening them, except that you have more ways to do it. Just as we did in the previous example, you'll merge your Layers with the choices found in the Layers Palette pull-down menu:

◆ Merge Visible: This choice will merge all the visible Layers. If every Layer is visible, your image will be flattened.

◆ Merge Linked: If you have two or more Layers linked together, this command will link them together. If all Layers, including the Background Layer, are linked together, your image will be flattened.

◆ Merge Down: This option will merge your active Layer with the one immediately below it. Merge Down is available only if your active Layer is not the Background or linked to any other Layer and if the Layer immediately below it is visible.

If you merge any Layer that has a Layer Effect on it (we'll discuss Layer Effects later in this chapter), you'll lose your ability to go back and manipulate their values.

Merging Text Layers

Text Layers have different properties when it comes to merging. When a text Layer is active, the only merging option that will be available is Merge Visible. You won't be able to Merge Down or to merge it with any linked Layer, until you turn it into a "normal" Layer, by choosing Layer -> Rasterize -> Type, as discussed previously in this chapter.

 If you really want to merge a text Layer with a linked Layer without taking the extra step of rasterizing it, simply make the nontext Layer that it is linked to active. Then you can choose Merge Linked from the Layer Palette pull-down menu. It seems kind of silly that you can't merge a text Layer with a nontext Layer that it linked to when that text Layer was active if you can do it simply by changing the active Layer, but who am I to judge? Oh, by the way—when you merge Layers this way, you will still lose the ability to edit the text later.

LAYER EFFECTS: THE LAZY MAN'S GUIDE TO DESIGN

Layer Effects were introduced in Photoshop 5.0 and instantly made the creation of popular effects quick, efficient and easy enough to turn even the worst artist into the next Claude Monet. Okay, maybe Monet would be pushing it, but it helps make a hell of a drop shadow.

The Layer Effects are accessed either by choosing Layer -> Layer Effect -> (your desired effect) or simply clicking on the Layer Effects shortcut button at the bottom of the Layers Palette, as indicated in Figure 5–24, or just double-clicking on any non-Background Layer. This last option is new to Photoshop 6.0, and kind of convenient. There are 10 total effects that you can choose from, five of which are brand new to Photoshop 6.0.

One of the nice things about using Layer Effects is that, like text, nothing you do is set in stone. This has been made even more easy in this latest Photoshop release, with each individual Layers Effect being contained in it's own "sub" Layer below the Layer you are applying the effect to. As Figure 5–26 also shows, the sublayers are indicated with a small, italicized "f" in a circle, and each can be made invisible by clicking off the eye icon on the far left. Double-clicking on the Layer Effect icon in any of the sublayers will let you adjust or edit the settings for any effect you have applied.

Each of the Layer Effects has its own dialog box with specific value options and settings specific to that effect. Each of these dialog boxes, though, makes it easy to go from one effect to the other, so that you can combine effects for really awesome results.

There are too many Layer Effects to give a full description of each one within this chapter, and they are not such a main function of Photoshop that they would deserve their own chapter either. Instead, please review Appendix A for a more thorough review of Layer Effects, how they work, and what they can do.

Figure 5–26: Layer 1 has had a Layer Effect added to it. The small circle with the "f" in the center indicates that an effect has been added.

DESIGNING WITH LAYER MASKS

Well, that's a lot of information on Layers to this point. If you've been reading this straight through, I'd recommend you take a rest here. Put the book down, turn the computer off, maybe even go outside for a bit. This next section starts to get a little tougher to grasp from a conceptual standpoint, so make sure your brain is fresh before diving in.

Working with a Mask within a Layer

Masks tend to be a confusing aspect of Photoshop. Think of the Lone Ranger or Batman. Traditionally we think of their masks as covering their eyes. But in reality, their masks are actually covering the part of their faces *around* their eyes—the eyeholes aren't technically part of their masks. The same goes for when we discuss masks, such as the Layer Masks, in Photoshop. The dark areas that hide a portion of your image are the masks, while the nonblack areas are equivalent to the eyeholes.

Creating a Layer Mask

To understand how masks work, try the following example:

1. Open two images, that are roughly the same size. The two images that I am using are displayed in Figures 5–27 and 5-28. Both are shown in Color Figure 15.

2. Drag Picture 2 onto Picture 1. Hold the <Shift> key while doing so to ensure that it is placed in the center of the canvas. You'll see that Picture 2 resides on a new Layer, and (if your pictures are the same size), it completely hides Picture 1.

Figure 5–27: My background image.

Figure 5–28: The image I'll use for the mask. Good idea!

3. With the Rectangular Marquee Tool, create a square marquee selection in the lower left corner of your canvas. Make it cover about a quarter of the canvas.

4. Click the Layer Mask button at the bottom of the Layer palette. When you do this, you'll notice the following changes, all of which are illustrated in Figure 5–29 and Color Figure 16.

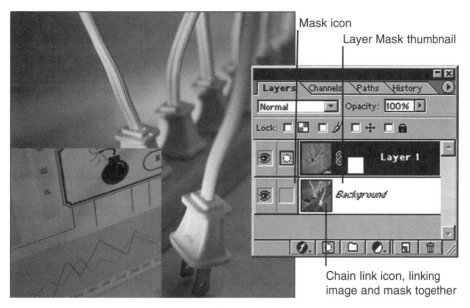

Mask icon

Layer Mask thumbnail

Chain link icon, linking
image and mask together

Figure 5–29: How a Layer Mask changes your image and your Layers Palette.

◆ The three-quarters of your image that was outside of the selection that you made
has disappeared, and you can now see Picture 1 in its place. Only the area that you
had selected remains.

◆ In the Layers Palette, you'll see that Layer 1 looks different—a new black-and-
white thumbnail appears on the right. This is the Layer Mask thumbnail. The black
portion of this thumbnail represents the mask.

◆ A small chain link icon sits between the image thumbnail and mask thumbnail.

◆ The small paintbrush icon to the left of the Layer that used to indicate that that
Layer was active has changed to a Layer Mask icon (the same as the one you
clicked at the bottom of the Layers Palette).

◆ Your Foreground and Background colors have reverted to black and white, respectively.

You might ask why we'd even bother to create a mask in the first place. After all,
wouldn't we have achieved the same result if we had inverted our selection and then
hit the <Delete> (<Backspace> in Windows) button? Visually, the answer is yes—we
would have achieved the same effect. But if you did that, you would essentially be
eliminating that portion of your image. When you create a mask, you are simply hiding that portion of your image and not discarding it forever.

Figure 5–30: Holding the <Shift> key while clicking on the Layer Mask thumbnail temporarily hides the mask, indicated by a large red X.

Temporarily Hiding the Layer Mask

As you're designing, you may, at some point, want to see what your image looks like again without the Layer Mask. To do this, hold the <Shift> key down and click on the mask thumbnail (indicated in Figure 5–26). As Figure 5–30 shows, a big red X appears over the mask thumbnail, and you can once again see the entire image on that Layer.

The reason you would do this and not just click the eye icon is that clicking the eye icon hides the whole Layer. <Shift> + clicking the Mask thumbnail just hides the mask.

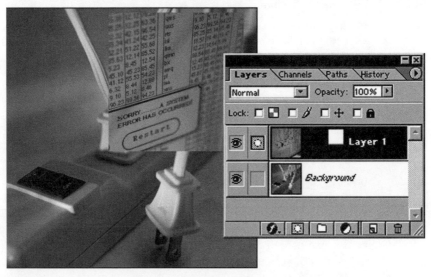

Figure 5–31: Notice that, with the chain link icon gone, when the mask is moved to the upper right corner, a different portion of the underlying image is revealed.

Press <Shift> + click on the mask thumbnail again to remove the big red X and once again view your image with the Mask activated.

Editing a Layer that Has a Mask

As long as the mask is activated and the mask icon appears to the left of the Layer in the Layers Palette, you won't be able to color correct or paint your image as you ordinarily would. At this point, all you can do is manipulate the mask, which we'll get to later in this section.

If you want to color correct or otherwise manipulate your image without eliminating the mask, simply click on the image thumbnail. You'll see that the mask icon to the left of the Layer is once again replaced by the paintbrush icon.

The Chain Link Icon

The chain link icon that exists by default between the image thumbnail and the mask thumbnail indicates that if you were to move either the image or the mask, they would move together. When the chain link icon is not there, the image and mask could be moved independently from each other.

Try it, using the last example as a testing ground:

1. Click on the mask thumbnail to make sure that you are in Mask Mode. Make sure that the chain link icon is still there between the two thumbnails.

2. Activate the Move Tool by clicking on it.

3. Put your cursor anywhere in the canvas, and move the mask. You'll see that both the mask and the image move together. (The same would have happened if you were in edit mode, instead of mask mode. If you want to try it, click the image thumbnail and move your image—you'll see that the mask moves right along with it.)

4. Choose Edit -> Undo to put the image and the mask back to their original positions.

5. Click on the chain link icon to make it go away. Now, anything that you move will move by itself.

6. Move the mask with the Move Tool. You'll see that different parts of your image, which were hidden by the mask are made visible as you move the mask around your canvas. Figure 5–31 illustrates this.

7. Choose Edit -> Undo to put the image and the mask back to their original positions.

8. Click on the image thumbnail, and move the image. You'll see that the mask remains in one place, and your image moves within it.

Adding to and Subtracting from a Layer Mask

You don't have to live with the original mask that you create, nor are you limited to creating masks in square shapes, as we did in the previous example. If you've read

Chapter 3, or if you're familiar with making selections using QuickMask, you'll have no problem manipulating a Layer Mask—for the most part, they work the same way, just with different results.

Look at the mask thumbnail in Layer 1 (working off the previous example). You can see that the parts that are black are the portions of your image that are hidden, and the white square represents the portion that you can see. Use this as a cheat sheet for manipulation:

◆ Paint (using any of the paint tools) with black to expand the mask and hide more of the image.

◆ Paint with white to reduce the mask and reveal more of the image.

◆ If you use the Eraser Tool, the above two points are reversed (use black to reduce the mask and white to expand it).

◆ Use a selection tool to make a selection, and fill it with either black or white to expand or reduce the mask with specific edges.

Deleting and Applying a Mask

◆ Move your cursor to the mask thumbnail and drag it to the trash can icon at the bottom of the Layers Palette. The message box will appear on your screen, giving you the option to Apply the mask, Delete the Mask or Cancel the whole thing. Choosing Apply will cause the mask that you've made to stay permanent—the area that is covered in black (the mask), will be the part of your Layer that is deleted.

◆ Choosing Discard will delete the mask that you created, and the entire image on that Layer will be visible again.

Using One Layer as a Mask for Another—Grouping Layers

Creating masks from selections on any given Layer is often a necessity, as we'll see later in this chapter when we create a collage. But for other effects, we can also use one Layer to act as a mask for another Layer. This allows you to easily control the confines of your mask for specific shapes, designs, or, as we'll see in the upcoming example, words.

1. Create a new canvas, 5" x 3.5", 72 ppi, RGB color.

2. With black as your Foreground color, activate the Type tool and place the words *Layer Groups* in the center of your canvas. Use a large font that is somewhat bold in nature, as illustrated in the left of Figure 5–29.

3. Open any image that you have that will cover the entire canvas, such as the image that I am using, in the center of Figure 5–29.

4. Use the Move Tool to move your newly opened image onto the original canvas. Hold the <Shift> key down to make sure that it is placed in the center of the canvas. It will appear on its own Layer above the text that you've placed.

5. Regardless of what tool you have activated, hold the <Option> key (<Alt> in Windows) and place it in the Layers Palette in between the two Layers that you want to group, in this case, the text Layer and the Layer containing your image. When I say in between, I mean in between. You have to get the cursor right on the thin line that separates the two Layers. It can be frustrating, but when you finally get it, your cursor will change to the two intersecting circles with a tiny arrow pointing to the left. Click your mouse when you finally get it. The resulting image is shown on the right of Figure 5–32.

If you don't like this method because it's too hard to hit the line right in between the two Layers, you can go about this from another direction. Make the image Layer (the top most Layer that you want to group) active, and choose Layer -> Group with Previous. If you have a number of Layers that you want to put in a group, link them together (we reviewed linking Layers earlier in this chapter), and choose Layer -> Group Linked.

When you group your Layers together, the images in the *base* Layer—in this case, the text Layer—become the mask for the Layers in its group. You'll notice a few distinct differences in the Layers Palette, as illustrated and described in Figure 5–29:

◆ The line separating the Layers in the group has changed to a dotted line.

◆ The name of the base Layer is now underlined.

◆ The image thumbnails and names on the Layer(s) that have been grouped with the base Layer is indented.

On the canvas, you'll see that your image has changed, as well. The picture that you moved onto your canvas now fits within the confines of the text on the underlying

Figure 5–32: On the left, the words **Layer Groups** *will act as a mask for the center image. The right shows the results in both the image and Layers Palette when the CD Layer is grouped with the text Layer.*

Layer. You can use the base Layer as the mask for as many Layers as you wish to group with it. As you'll see in the next chapter, you can even group Layers to control the effect of certain color-correction techniques.

All Layers in a group must be contiguous. You can't group Layers that are not one right on top of the other.

To ungroup Layers, simply hold <Option> (<Alt>) + click in between the Layers that you want to remove from the group. If you have a large number of Layers in a group and want to deconstruct the entire group, remove <Option> (<Alt>) + click in between the base Layer and the first Layer in the group. All the other Layers will fall out of the group, as well (as we saw in the last note, this happens because grouped Layers must be contiguous).

If you don't want to bother trying to find the exact spot that you need to click in between the Layers, activate any of the Layers that you wish to remove from the group and select Layer -> Ungroup. That Layer, plus all of the Layers above it, will be removed from the group.

SUMMARY

Layers are what separate Photoshop from the crowd. At their most basic, they will allow you to add to a composite image without doing any damage to the existing work. At its most complex, Layers will allow you to completely manage your workflow, enhance design and special effects, and go completely nuts with experimentation. Mastering Layers is an important part of not only taking control of Photoshop itself, but also expanding your creative work and doing so with the timely efficiency that most designers to need to maintain.

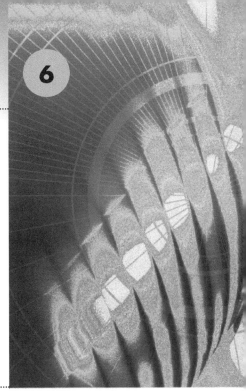

chapter 6

COLOR CORRECTION AND IMAGE ENHANCEMENT

Color is a funny thing. Used properly, it can spread happiness and tranquility throughout an entire population of people. Used improperly, it'll start a religious war that can span centuries.

Okay, maybe that's a bit overdramatic. But the truth is, religions, cultures, corporations and individuals take color very seriously. No matter what people see, whether it is a flag, a bible, a photograph, menu or brochure, the way that color is used will influence what they think and feel.

Perhaps that reason, above all else, is why many designers start off their Photoshop careers by learning color correction. Some never get beyond that—they never have to. Entire careers can be built on the talent that it takes to take an image with dull, tired color and give it new life and vibrance. Photoshop's arsenal of color correction tools allow designers to enhance, subdue, alter, fold, spindle and mutilate colors as they see fit, with fantastic results.

So...have I overplayed color correction enough to fulfill my "generalized and pointless" chapter intro requirements? Good. Then let's move on.

REASONS WHY...

The first and most obvious question is, Why in the world would I ever need to alter the colors on my image? There are many, including just individual or client tastes, which might mandate a need for a color change. But tastes aside, there is a bevy of problems that might cause you to need to alter your colors.

One of the primary reasons is an inadequacy of technology. Somehow, the great tech minds of our time, which have conquered the trials of placing a man on the moon over 30 years ago, can't seem to come up with a desktop scanner that won't put a color cast over a photograph. Scan beds are also the culprits behind dust particles that appear on a photograph.

Scratches, tears or other mishandled photographs account for some other problems, as does problematic photography: blurry images or shots taken without the proper lighting. And don't forget the dreaded "red eye" in lower quality photos.

Of course, one other major issue that accounts for the need of image enhancement or retouching is image usage. Images typically scan into a computer in RGB color. If you are using your image for print, you'll be forced to convert it to CMYK, which, as we learned in Chapter 1, has a small color gamut. CMYK color tends to be less vibrant that RGB color. If you are building a Web site, RGB is just your thing…but you still have a platform issue to contend with. Macs will read colors one way, while their Windows counterparts will read those same colors just a few shades darker. And if your audience will be coming from Web TV or some other television-based Internet viewer, you'll of course want to stay away from reds and yellows.

As you can see, there is a plethora of reasons one might need to color enhance or otherwise manipulate an image. Fortunately, Photoshop provides the tools for practically every situation.

DOWNLOADING THE IMAGES

Don't skip this section!

The easiest way to learn about color correction is to see it in action and play with the features. This chapter is unique from the others in this book, as we'll be learning about color correction by enhancing some specific pictures. Other chapters in this book teach lessons either by creating content from scratch or by using any image that you might currently have on your computer.

For this chapter, however, it'll be easier if we're all using the same imagery. Please download the necessary pictures, as listed throughout this chapter, for this book's Web site, www.pfsmarketwyse.com, or from my agency's site, www.pfsmarketwyse.com/primer.

REAL LIFE EXAMPLES

Although there is no end to the color problems you might encounter, the following examples provide a few situations which you may encounter when you work with Photoshop. At the beginning of each, I'll list which color correction tools you'll be working with.

It's important to remember in this chapter more than any other that the directions I give for making any color corrections are just one way of many that you can choose from. Photoshop provides you with numerous options to achieve any color effect, and the only "right" way to do it is whichever way you are most comfortable with.

The Fruit Stand

This image came into the computer with a few problems that need correcting, as we'll see in a moment. The tools that we're going to use to make any changes in this example will be:

◆ Levels

◆ Dodge Tool

◆ Sponge Tool

◆ Rubber Stamp

◆ Replace Color

So, let's go through the steps, examine some of the problems, and see how we correct them.

1. The first problem with the image, as you can see in Figure 6–1 and Color Figure 18, is that it is simply too dark. None of the fruits at this point really seem very appetizing (personally, I'm more of a cupcake and ice cream fan, so there really aren't many fruits that seem very appetizing to me). To make them more palatable, let's give them a little more color and life.

Figure 6–1: Problems with the fruit stand pic include that the fruit is too dark.

We'll do this by adjusting the Levels. Choose Image -> Adjust -> Levels or push <Command + L> (<Ctrl + L> in Windows) to access the dialog box shown and described in Figure 6–2.

The most prominent part of the Levels dialog box is the center with the row of black vertical bars, in the Input Levels portion. This is called a *histogram*. In creating this histogram, Photoshop is essentially turning your color image into a grayscale image, and assigning each pixel a brightness value, from 0 (pure black) to 255 (pure white). The left side of the histogram represents the shadows, or darker pixels, while the right side represents the highlights, or lighter pixels. The center shows the midtones, or neutral grays. Each vertical bar in the histogram shows how many pixels are present at any given brightness level.

As we can see by the histogram in our dialog box, there is an abundance of darker pixels (although, since the histogram does not extend all the way to the left, there is no pure black in the image). There is a severe lack of light pixels, as the histogram slopes downward to the right and ends far short of the extreme right.

2. To make the image more vibrant, we need to adjust the levels and balance out the histogram. Typically, a vibrant picture has a relatively even histogram that extends all the way to the right and all the way to the left.

Make sure that the box on the right marked *Preview* is on, so that you can see changes as they happen. Drag the shadows marker (the left most arrow) to the right, or insert the numeric value of 100 in the shadows value area. As you can see, the image gets very dark. Basically, what's happening is that all the pixels with a value of 100 or less are now pure black. Obviously, this is too much. Reduce the shadows level to where it should be, which is 17.

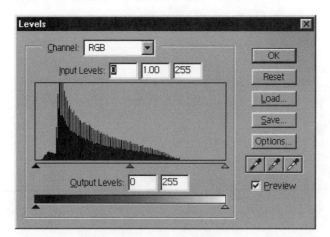

Figure 6–2: The Levels dialog box. This histogram in the center maps the brightness of your images' pixels.

Drag the highlights marker (the rightmost arrow) to the left to increase the highlights, or insert the numeric value of 70 in the highlights value area. As you can see, the image gets very light. Similar to what we saw when we overdid the shadows, every pixel with a value of 70 or higher is now pure white. Again, this is too much. Reduce the highlights value to the proper level of 166.

How do we know that 17 and 166 are the proper values? Well, there's no law that says they *are* the right values—I made them up. But as a rule, I chose values that were around the areas where the histogram starts on either side, as shown in Figure 6–2. In this case, to make the shadows and highlights a bit more pronounced, I went a bit further than the end points on either side.

Add just a bit more lightness to the overall image by dragging the midtones slider (the center arrow) to the left, until the value area reads 1.25. Push OK when through.

In case you're wondering about the bottom portion of the Levels dialog box—the Output Levels—I rarely ever use them. Honestly, they've got a fairly obvious effect, but I've never had an instance in which manipulating them would be useful. Basically, the Output Levels deal with the shadows (left slider) and highlights (right slider) of all pixels simultaneously. So as you pull the shadows slider to the right, you reduce the shadows and make the entire picture lighter. If you pull the highlight slider to the left, you extract the brightness from all pixels and make your image darker. The result is usually a flatter-looking picture, which is fine for achieving some sort of special effect, but rarely needed for enhancing an image.

3. To see the effect that the levels had, choose Edit -> Undo, or push <Command + Z> (<Ctrl + Z>). You'll see that the change is fairly dramatic. Push <Command> (<Ctrl>) again to redo your levels. To see how this change has affected your histogram, either open the Levels dialog box again, or choose Image -> Histogram. You'll see that it is far more even than it was before. Figure 6–3 shows the new Histogram.

4. At the bottom of the fruit stand are some long green things. I'll have to ask my mom for sure, but I'm fairly sure they are zucchinis or cucumbers. Either way, they're long, green, and you wouldn't catch me alive putting one of them in my mouth. Especially not the way they look. Even though adjusting the levels made my image more colorful, the green things still seem too dark to be edible.

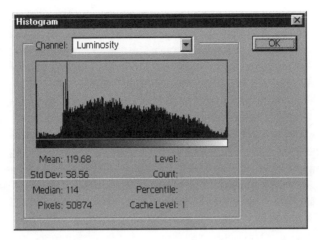

Figure 6–3: The histogram is spread out a bit more evenly than before.

To change the brightness of one particular item, such as the green things, we'll use a more controlled tool. Activate the Dodge Tool for the toolbar. If your Brushes Palette isn't open, choose Windows -> Show Brushes to access it. Choose a brush that has a soft edge, with a 45- or 65-pixel diameter. Hold the mouse button down and run the cursor around the green stuff. You'll see as you do this that the darkness gives way to a lighter color. Continue running your cursor over the fruit until you are satisfied with the result, as shown in Figure 6–4.

Figure 6–4: The brightness of the green things has improved.

5. One last thing we want to do to really make the green stuff work is, well…make them more green. We'll use the Sponge Tool for this job. The Sponge Tool is hidden beneath the currently active Dodge Tool, so push <Shift + O> to scroll through the options until the Sponge Tool is active (or just click and drag out the Dodge Tool on the toolbar to the Sponge Tool underneath it). Push <Return> (<Enter> in Windows) to access the Options Palette for this tool. In the pull down menu on the Options Palette, choose Saturate. Make sure the Opacity is set to 100% (you can set it to less, but you'll have more work to do).

6. With the same brush as you used for the Dodge Tool, hold the mouse button down and run the cursor over the green stuff again. Instead of getting darker or lighter, you'll see that they're getting more green. Continue doing this until you're satisfied with the result, as shown in Figure 6–5.

7. Okay, I can almost eat the green things now. But the one food in this image that I simply can't even look at are those big, ugly black things right in the center. I think they're eggplants. In any case, we need to get rid of them. I don't mind tomatoes, which are located right next door, so let's just fill the eggplant bin with more tomatoes.

We'll do this by using the Rubber Stamp Tool, which runs neck and neck with the Magic Wand for the title of "coolest Photoshop tool." The Rubber Stamp Tool is used for cloning images or portions of an image from one place to another—kind of a "copy and paste" in real time.

Select the Rubber Stamp Tool from the toolbar. From the Brushes Palette, select a hard-edged brush with a diameter between 10 and 15 pixels.

Figure 6–5: Saturating the green things made them more green.

8. Move your cursor over the tomatoes and hold down the <Option> key (<Alt> in Windows). Your cursor will change to look like the icon shown in Figure 6–6. Click in the area from which you wish to start cloning (around my agency, I usually refer to this as "sucking up" the image, but no one ever knows what I'm talking about when I say that, so I'll refrain…), which would be the tomatoes. After you've clicked in a portion of the tomatoes, release the mouse button. Your normal brush icon will return.

 If your cursor looks like the Rubber Stamp Tool as you work, you should change some of your settings—it tends to be very difficult to work in Photoshop if all of your icons appear as actual tools. Check out "Changing Tool Icons" of Chapter 1 to learn how to make the icons easier to use.

9. Begin cloning the tomatoes by holding the mouse button and dragging your brush over the eggplant. Now there will be two different cursors on the canvas, as shown in Figure 6–7. Your brush cursor continues to indicate where you are cloning to, while the crosshair shows you where you are cloning from. As you move your brush, the crosshair will move, as well.

 Cloning can be very obvious and detract from the image quality if not done properly. Make sure that you don't clone too close to the source, or an obvious pattern will appear.

If you let go of the mouse button, your cloning will end. Hold down the mouse button again to resume cloning. However, where you begin cloning from may not be optimal. Push <Return> (<Enter> in Windows) to access the Rubber Stamp Options Palette. If the checkbox marked *Aligned* is clicked on, Photoshop will remember your positioning and restart the cloning as though you had never stopped in the first place. If the checkbox is clicked off, then each time you release the mouse button and begin again, your cloning source will always start from the original point, no matter where you want to clone.

Figure 6–6: Your Tool icon will change when you are deciding where to clone from and hold down the <Option>/<Alt> key.

Figure 6–7: One cursor shows where you are cloning from, while the other shows where you are cloning to. Even on screen and in color, these can be hard to see. The black arrows point out where each cursor is—the one on the left, where I'm cloning to, is the circular brush I am using. The plus sign on the right is where I am cloning from.

For this example, continue cloning until all of the eggplant is covered. It's okay if some of the tomatoes overflow into the onions, but make sure that you don't leave any tomatoes unfinished, or it could look weird. Also, don't ignore the bottom of the eggplants' wood box—you may have to clone a few times from a few different sources to get it right. Figure 6–8 gives an example of what my image looks like.

Figure 6–8: With the Rubber Stamp Tool, I was able to replace the eggplant with more tomatoes.

And there you have it. Much more editable fruit and good stuff for you like that. Color Figure 18 provides a full example at each major stage. For purposes of example, this was pretty good, but for purposes of appetite, I'll still take a dessert cart over a fruit stand any day.

The Flower Basket

Fruits, flowers…this chapter isn't doing much for my masculinity, is it? Well, after this one, I'm going to do my best to get a sports- or travel-oriented image in here for an example. I don't like getting this close to my inner woman.

The flower basket in Figure 6–9 really isn't too bad—the colors are a bit faded, and I've come to hate red roses, so we'll want to solve both problems. To do this, we'll use the following:

♦ Levels (with a little more control than we had in the fruit stand example)

♦ Replace Color

As with the last example, we'll start this one by enhancing the colors to be more vivid.

1. Just like we did in the fruit stand example, we're going to use the Levels to enhance the colors. But this time, instead of just jumping in and using them, we're going to make sure that we protect our image by using what are called *Adjustment Layers*. Adjustment Layers let you make your changes to the image on a completely separate Layer. That way, you won't be doing any permanent harm to your image if you later decide that you don't like the Levels adjustments you had made.

Figure 6–9: The colors in the flower basket are a bit faded, and we'll need to change some of the red roses to an alternative color.

In the Layers Palette, choose New Adjustment Layer from the Palette menu to access the dialog box shown in Figure 6–10. In the Type pull-down menu, make sure that Levels is selected, and push OK.

Your Layers Palette, which previously had only the Background Layer, now has a new Layer, which is active, marked *Levels*. In addition, the Levels dialog box that we saw in the fruit stand example also appears.

2. This time, instead of simply moving the shadows and highlights sliders, we're going to have a little more control over the enhancement of our image. Drag the Levels dialog box to an area of your monitor so that you can also see the flower basket image.

   Double-click on the Shadow Eye Dropper Tool, as shown in Color Figure 1. The Color Picker appears, allowing you to set a color. If it's not already chosen, select a deep black, and hit OK.

3. Click in an area of the flower basket that looks like it should contain a deep shadow. I've marked the point that I've chosen in Figure 6–11. The color that you had selected from the Color Picker will be inserted in that point, and the brightness values of the remaining pixels will be redistributed accordingly, as shown in Figure 6–12. Notice that the histogram in the Levels dialog box has adjusted.

4. Double-click on the Highlight Eye Dropper Tool. This time, choose a bright white from the Color Picker and hit OK.

5. Figure 6–11 shows that the point I've chosen to insert my highlight is the background. Once again, as Figure 6–13 shows, the bright white that I selected from the Color Picker is inserted, and the brightness value of the remaining pixels is redistributed.

Just for fun, access the Color Picker with any of the Eye Dropper Tools again, and this time, select a medium color, such as blue or green. Click on any spot within the image and see what happens.

Click OK on the Levels dialog box when you're finished. You'll see that your new Layer, marked *Levels*, is still active. So what's the point? We've still added a lot of vibrance and color to the image, just as we did in the fruit stand example…and we didn't need an extra Layer there. So why did we bother with an Adjustment Layer here, instead of applying the Levels directly to the Background?

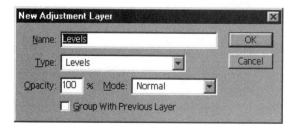

Figure 6–10: The New Adjustment Layer dialog box.

Figure 6–11: I've marked off the points in the image where the shadows should be darkest and the highlights should be brightest.

Figure 6–12: When I add the shadows, the dark pixels are redistributed.

Figure 6–13: When the lighter pixels are redistributed, too, the results are obvious.

The answer is simple. In the fruit stand example, once the Levels were set, that's all she wrote, unless you used either the Undo or the History Palette (read Chapter 2 for more info on the History Palette). But with the Adjustment Layer, you can always, no matter how long you work on your image, get rid of or change the Levels settings.

To go back and see what your image looks like without the Levels settings, simply hide the Levels Layer by clicking the eye icon to the left in the Layers Palette. Click the icon a second time to make it visible again. To change the settings completely, double-click the Levels Layer. The Levels dialog box will appear again, with the last settings that you made. You can make any necessary adjustments. You can't do those things without using Adjustment Layers.

6. Okay, so now that we have color back, let's get rid of some of these red roses. We don't have to get rid of all of them—we can leave a few for the romantic readers in the crowd. Make the Background Layer active by clicking on it and select the Rectangular Marquee Tool from the toolbar.

7. Make a selection around the left side of the flowers. Since we want to isolate the colors as much as possible without too much work, I created a rectangular marquee selection, then subtracted out a few smaller rectangles to reduce my overall selection, as shown in Figure 6–14. We'll change the red roses within the selection to green, leaving the roses on the right in their original red.

Figure 6–14: I've made a selection around some of the roses on the left, making sure I'm selecting as few of the other flowers as possible, without causing tons of selection work.

8. Choose Image -> Adjust -> Replace Color to access the dialog box shown as described in Figure 6–15.

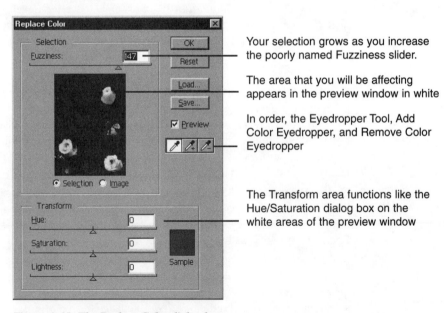

Your selection grows as you increase the poorly named Fuzziness slider.

The area that you will be affecting appears in the preview window in white

In order, the Eyedropper Tool, Add Color Eyedropper, and Remove Color Eyedropper

The Transform area functions like the Hue/Saturation dialog box on the white areas of the preview window

Figure 6–15: The Replace Color dialog box.

For those of you wondering why we are about to apply a change directly to the Background Layer about 10 seconds after preaching the benefits of using Adjustment Layers, it's because Replace Color is not one of the things you can do on an Adjustment Layer.

The black and white box in the center represents your selection. To change this, click the radio button for Image, right below. The black and white representation will be replaced by a full-color image of your selection. It's almost impossible to work like this, so change it back by clicking the radio button marked *Selection*.

9. With the Eyedropper Tool, selected by default, click on one of the roses on your canvas. Although you can try to guess where it is in the large black box, it's easier just to move the cursor onto the actual image and click on one of the red roses within your selection. The black and white representation within the Replace Color dialog box will change, and all of the pixels within your selection that share that color of your selected pixel will appear in white.

10. Drag the stupidly named Fuzziness slider either to the right or the left to increase or decrease the number of pixels that will be affected. As you drag the slider to the right, you increase the number of shades of your selected color that will be included, and the white areas in the preview window will expand. As you drag the slider to the left, the white areas contract, because you reduce the number of shades that will be included.

   Continue to drag the slider until you have as much of the red roses represented in white as you can, while keeping a minimum of other areas from being included. Figure 6–15 shows my preview window after the first try.

11. If your white areas look similar to mine, it's obvious we have more work to do. Not every area of the roses has been selected, and portions of the basket and other flowers have been inadvertently included. Use the Add Color Eyedropper and the Subtract Color Eyedropper Tools to tweak your selection as best you can. With either tool, you don't have to just click once—you can click and drag to add or reduce a number of colors.

   Continue this until you've done the best that you can. If you really can't select the roses without including a significant portion of the basket, you may have to hit Cancel and redo your marquee selection. I've tweaked my image enough to get the selection shown in Figure 6–16, which seems to be the best that I can do. All of the roses are completely selected, and the other areas that have also been included won't make a huge difference.

12. We'll change the color of the areas that are in white by adjusting the sliders below the preview window. The Hue slider arranges the entire 360-degree color wheel into a linear blend, so as you move the slider in either direction, the color of your selection will change. Drag the slider to, or manually enter the value 121. That'll give you a nice green.

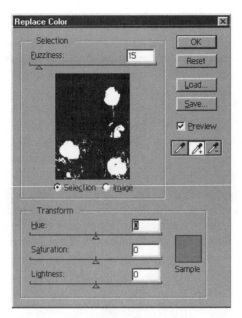

Figure 6–16: The roses have been selected in full by using a combination of the Eyedropper, the Add Color Eyedropper, and the Fuzziness Slider.

As your roses change color, if you notice some red areas still peeking out, you can continue to use the Add Color Eyedropper and select the areas that you need.

The Saturation controls the intensity of the color. Sliding it to the left will reduce the intensity until, eventually, all of the color is eliminated and you're left with a shade of gray. Set the slider to 17 to make the green a bit more intense.

Although there is no such thing as a naturally green rose, the ones we have created so far look especially unrealistic. Make the green deeper by reducing the lightness to –7.

Push OK when through. Figure 6–17 and Color Figure 19 show the result, as well as the major highlights throughout the process.

There you have it. Your flowers are now brighter, cheerier, and...greener.

The Body...Builder

Once again, my editor hates these quasi-sexist remarks or titles that I put in my book, so if you actually read this the way I wrote it, I'll be impressed. But you really can't deny that the girl in Figure 6–18 has a great body—after all, she is working out. But while the girl might be perfect, the image isn't. In this example, we'll make three changes: we'll begin by giving her a tan, then we'll change the color of her bathing suit and, finally, we'll create some funky effects with the colors, just for the fun of it.

Figure 6–17: The green roses are the result of changing the hue in the Replace Color dialog box.

Figure 6–18: By the time we're done with this image, the girl will have a tan, a different color of bathing suit and some crazy color effects.

We'll do these things by using the following tools:

◆ Color Balance (then we'll do it again using the Variations dialog box)
◆ Curves

Let's start by giving her a tan.

1. Using one or more of the methods described in Chapter 3, make a selection around the girl's skin. Don't include her bathing suit, hair or the weight she's lifting. Figure 6–19 shows my selection.

Although there are dozens of ways you can make your selection, I made mine by first selecting the Background with the Magic Wand Tool. I then inverted the selection and used the Magic Wand again to subtract the bathing suit and weights from my selection. Finally, I used QuickMask to deselect her hair.

2. Hide the marching ants by pushing <Command + H> (<Ctrl + H> in Windows). This isn't totally necessary, I just find it hard to view changes with all those marching ants around my selection.

Figure 6–19: The selection that I made around the girl.

3. Choose Image -> Adjust -> Color Balance to access the dialog box shown in Figure 6–20. The dialog box lists the CMYK values on the left side (minus the "K") and their RGB counterparts on the right. Just as the world of color and print should work, as you add to one color component, you take away from another. For example, in the Color Balance dialog box, if you move the topmost slider to the right, you'll add red, while simultaneously subtracting cyan.

4. The three radio buttons at the bottom in the Tone Balance area allow you to make color changes to either Shadows, Midtones or Highlights. The Highlights will be active by default. To give our girl a tan, we're going to want to add red, a bit of magenta and yellow. Try the following values:

Midtones: +22, -18, -19

Highlights: +10, -6, -10

Shadows: +23, 0, -14

Push OK when through.

5. Undo your changes to see the difference. If you feel like you may have gone a bit overboard (sometimes too much color can reduce detail in your image), choose Filter -> Fade Color Balance to access the dialog box shown in Figure 6–21. Move the slider to the left as much as necessary to achieve the effect of the Color Balance. The second and third images in Color Figure 20 show my image before and after I did this.

6. Undo your image again (so that all the tan has been removed. Either choose File -> Revert to start from the beginning, meaning that you'll have to make your selection again or check out how to use the History Palette in Chapter 2). Even if it's perfect just the way you have it, we can use this opportunity to explore another way to achieve our goal of tanning the girl. The Variations dialog box, shown in Figure 6–22 and accessed by choosing Image -> Adjust -> Variations, is a simpler and more basic means of adjusting color. As you can see, the Variations dialog box basically holds your hand as you adjust the colors.

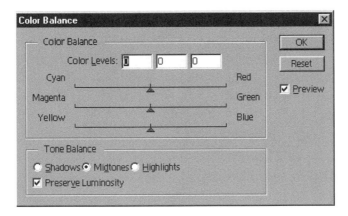

Figure 6–20: The Color Balance dialog box.

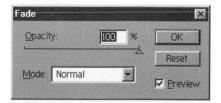

Figure 6–21: The Fade dialog box.

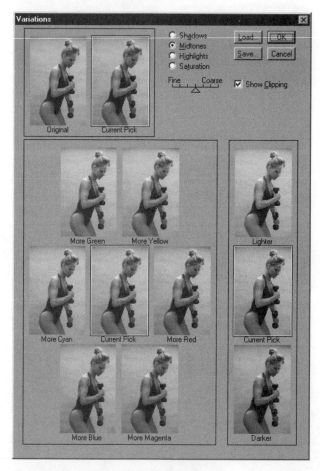

Figure 6–22: The Variations dialog box.

Once again, radio buttons allow you to choose among making changes to the shadows, midtones or highlights. The two image windows at the top of the dialog box show the Original image as it is before any corrections have been made, while the Current Pick shows the image as it changes with each color added. This is the same image window that appears in the center of the main box (bottom left). Each surrounding image window in the main box is marked with a CMYK or RGB color. Unlike with the Color Balance, adding one color doesn't necessarily subtract from another.

You add colors to your image by clicking on one of the color-labeled image windows. Click once to add one "drop" or multiple times to add more "drops." Each color-labeled image window shows what your image would look like if you added that particular color. For example, the image marked *Blue* provides you a preview of what your image will look like if you add one drop of blue.

On the right side of the Variations dialog box is the opportunity to make your image either lighter or darker—a trick that could come in handy if you want to change her tan from "New Jersey Salon" to "Genuine Tahitian."

Continue to add red, magenta and yellow in varying amounts until you give her your desired tan. Click OK when through. The fourth image in Color Figure 20 provides an example of my results.

When using the Color Balance, you should first create an Adjustment Layer. Unfortunately, you can't use an Adjustment Layer when manipulating through Variations—with this tool, you'll just have to work on the image Layer itself.

7. Now that we've given her a more healthy skin tone, let's change the color of her bathing suit. Once again, use one of the methods we learned in Chapter 3 to select her bathing suit (I used the Magic Wand Tool). Choose Image -> Adjust -> Hue/Saturation to access the dialog box, shown in Figure 6–23.

If you've worked through the last example with the flower basket, this might look vaguely familiar. We've already seen this, or a semblance of this, in the Replace Color dialog box. Well, the Hue/Saturation dialog box works in exactly the same way, except that you can't make your selections while it's open.

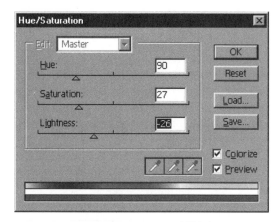

Figure 6–23: The Hue/Saturation dialog box.

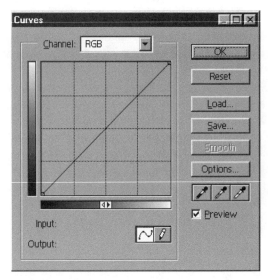

Figure 6–24: The Curves dialog box.

I won't bother detailing it here, since we've already reviewed it in our last example. Make sure that the Colorize box is checked, and move the sliders around until you come up with a color for her suit that you like. I chose a Hue of +99, a Saturation of 27 and a Lightness of –26 to give her the dark green suit you see in the final image in Figure 6–20.

8. Deselect your selection.

9. My image is pretty much finished at this point. But now I might want to do something kind of…funky to it, just to play. Although the Curves dialog box is usually used for creating tonal adjustments, as a stronger alternative to working with Levels, we're going to use Curves in this case to create a cool special effect.

Open the Curves dialog box by choosing Image -> Adjust -> Curves to access the dialog box shown in Figure 6–24.

That big graph in the middle of the dialog box is where you will be doing the bulk of your adjusting work. The gradient bar on the left (the vertical axis) measures the output levels, and the gradient bar at the bottom (the horizontal axis) measures the input levels. The curve, which starts out as a diagonal line from bottom left to top right, describes how each output level value measures against each input level value. Exactly how your image will change when you alter the curve will depend on what Color Mode you're in:

♦ If your image is in RGB mode (such as the one we're currently working with), the values will be measured as brightness values, and the point of origin (the bottom left, where both input and output values are equal at 0) will be black (no brightness). Both the input and output gradient bars will gradate from black to white outward and upward, so that the further along the curve you go, the brighter your image is.

◆ In CMYK (and Grayscale) mode, the curve will measure the ink coverage in an image. Both gradient bars are opposite their RGB counterparts, as the point of origin now measures the level of ink applied to an image (0% at point of origin) and increases to full ink coverage as you move outward along the curve. Figure 6–25 shows the CMYK Curves. Compare this to the RGB dialog box shown in Figure 6–24.

◆ There are two tools that you can use to change the shape of the curve. The default is the Point Tool, which allows you to place points on the curve by clicking on it. Place a point and drag it upward (increase the value), and your image will become darker. Drag it downward (decrease the value), and your image will become lighter. You can set as many points as you'd like to manipulate your image at different levels. Color Figure 21 shows a number of manipulations to my image, and their respective curves. You can also use the Pencil Tool to draw a customized curve. Click on the Pencil Tool in the dialog box to activate it. To use it, simply draw a curve freehand through the graph, which may or may not be one continuous line. You can get some pretty crazy results from it, though, as Color Figure 21 demonstrates.

◆ Play with the Curves to get various effects. Depending on how you use the curves, you can either get some very realistic looking enhancements in the shadows and highlights areas (usually with more depth than by using the Levels dialog box) or you can get some cool special effects. Click OK when through.

A Few Last, Typical Uses

There's still a ton to discuss when it comes to color, so we'll quickly cover just two more examples, with issues that you'll undoubtedly have to deal with at some point before finally moving on.

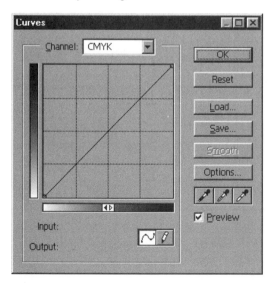

Figure 6–25: The Curves dialog box for a CMYK image. Notice the difference between this and the RGB version at the point of origin.

Making a New Image Old

The secret's in the sepia tone. Taking a new image and making it look like it was taken around the turn of the century can be a fun, neat-looking effect. You can do this with any picture, really (well, except a picture of the space shuttle or something—I'd doubt that'd pass for turn of the century…).

1. Open any picture, such as the one I have open in Figure 6–26.

2. Remove all the color from it by choosing Image -> Adjust -> Desaturate. This will remove all of the color from your image in one step, instead of having to open the Hue/Saturation and reduce the Saturation to 0, or without having to change the color mode to Grayscale and then back again to RGB.

3. Open the Color Balance dialog box. Add a conservative amount of red and yellow to each of the three tones to achieve a sepia, or light brownish color.

4. Choose Filter -> Add Noise to give it a little texture (The Add Noise filter is explored in Chapter 8). Because mine was a particularly dark image to start with, I enhanced its age by reducing the shadows in the Output Levels, as well. My end result, as compared to the original, is shown in Figure 6–5.

Some Color Correction Odds and Ends

Before we move on to Color Modes and Channels, let's review a few of the remaining color correction/enhancement items found in the Image menu. While all of these have their place and importance, it's just as easy to explain them without going through an entire example.

Figure 6–26: We'll make this picture look like it was taken around the turn of the century.

Image -> Calculations

Calculation, shown in Figure 6–27, is quite a bit like Apply Image, with one important difference: there is no set target image. While Apply Image places a source image on top of a target to create a composite, Calculations mixes two distinct *Channels* together. The result is placed in a target Channel. There is a lot more leeway with Calculations: The target can be completely separate from the sources. Although both sources will still need to be the same size as in Apply Image, the target doesn't need to be an existing image at all—it can be used to create a brand new document.

But more importantly than that, is that while Apply Image works with the entire image (all Channels that make up a composite), Calculations works by combining individual Channels only. As a result, only one Channel in the target will be affected by anything you do in Calculations. To use the dialog box, select your sources from the Source 1 and Source 2 pull-down menus. Each source will have to be open, and each will have to be the same size. Choose which Layer from each, then which Channel. Select how you want each to blend from the Blending pull-down menu (Blend Modes are discussed in detail in Chapter 5) and, finally, select your target in the Result dialog box.

Image -> Adjust -> Auto Levels (and Auto Contrast)

These are pretty much cop-outs for allowing Photoshop to do what you should do yourself using, either Levels or Curves. Doing it yourself will almost always give you better results than trusting Photoshop to do it for you.

Image -> Adjust -> Brightness/Contrast

The Brightness/Contrast dialog box, as shown in Figure 6–28, will, as you might guess, allows you to adjust the brightness and the contrast. From what I can tell there's nothing you can accomplish with this tool that you can't do more effectively with the Levels or Curves Tools.

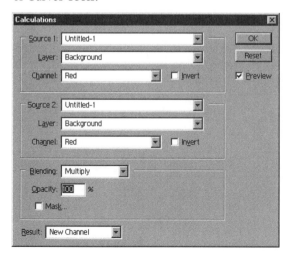

Figure 6–27: The Calculations dialog box.

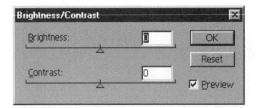

Figure 6–28: The Brightness/Contrast dialog box.

Image -> Adjust -> Selective Color

The Selective Color dialog box, shown in Figure 6–29, gives you control over the amount of any particular color in an image. To tell the truth, I rarely use it, and don't think it a very important function. It's somewhat tough to really know how much of any one color to add or subtract, and both the Color Balance and the Variations will do a better job.

Image -> Adjust -> Invert

This can be a pretty cool effect all by itself. When you choose Invert from the Adjust submenu, you turn your positive image into a negative, or vice-versa. Figure 6–30 and Color Figure 23 provide an example.

Image -> Adjust -> Equalize

Equalize acts almost like having Photoshop adjust your levels for you. When you choose Equalize, Photoshop will take the darkest pixel in your image and make it black, and take the brightest pixel and make it white. Then it distributes the remaining pixels evenly in between. Figure 6–31 shows an example.

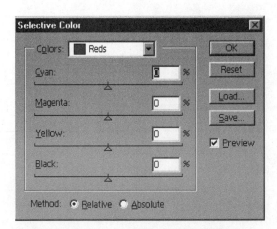

Figure 6–29: The Selective Color dialog box.

Figure 6–30: The Invert option can create a cool effect.

Figure 6–31: An example of the Equalize function.

Image -> Adjust -> Threshold

The Threshold command will turn your image into pure black and white. The Threshold dialog box, shown in Figure 6–32, provides the Histogram of your image, similar to what you might find in the Levels dialog box. All of the pixels whose brightness fall to the left of the slider will be represented in black, while pixels to the right of the slider are represented in white. Figure 6–33 gives an example.

Image -> Adjust -> Posterize

By choosing Posterize, you're in essence reducing the number of tones per Channel (we'll be examining Channels later this chapter). The result is usually a cool effect that provides large areas of flat colors. The fewer tonal levels you set, the more dramatic the result. Figure 6–34 and Color Figure 24 gives an example with a tonal level set to 3.

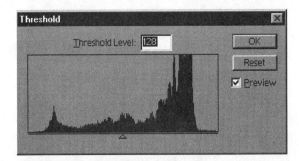

Figure 6–32: The Threshold dialog box.

Figure 6–33: The Threshold function at work.

Figure 6–34: An example of the Posterize feature, with the tonal level set to 3.

Image -> Adjust -> Gradient Map

This is a new feature for version 6.0. It's kind of neat, but I'm not sure that it has much value except for special effects purposes. Basically, when you choose Gradient Map, Photoshop will pretend that your color image is Grayscale and give each pixel a brightness value to determine where the shadows, highlights and midtones are.

When you apply the Gradient Map, you'll be able to choose the type of gradient you want from a dialog box. The colors on one end of the gradient will map themselves to the shadows, while the colors on the other end will map themselves to the highlights. The colors in between both ends will obviously map themselves to the midtone areas. Play around with it—you can get some pretty wild effects!

The two checkboxes in the Gradient Map dialog box give you a little control over how the colors apply themselves. Choose Dither to add some random noise to your gradient. This will help alleviate any banding that could happen (especially when you're printing oversized pieces—see Chapter 7 for more info). The other choice is to reverse the gradient so, that the opposite ends map to the shadows and the highlights. To change the gradient that you are applying, use the pull-down menu and select from the dialog box. A few gradients are provided for you. Other gradient libraries are available in the submenu, or you can simply click on the gradient itself to access the Gradient Editor. Instructions on how to use the Gradient Editor are in Chapter 2.

CHANNELS PART 2: COLOR

We've already seen in Chapter 3 how the Channels Palette helps you work with selections. But just as important, if not more importantly, the Channels Palette is where the information for color is stored.

You can use the color information stored in each Channel to gain even more control over color correction and enhancements. We'll also see how you can use the Channels Palette to set up for spot color printing.

The Channels Palette looks different depending on which color mode you're in. Figure 6–35 shows the differences in the Channels Palette for CMYK, RGB and Grayscale color modes. As you can see, the Palette for the Grayscale image require just one Channel—a black Channel to hold the information for the blacks and gray tints.

In both the CMYK and RGB images, however, there are a number of color Channels. The topmost Channel in each is the composite—a representation of all the colors in your image mixed together. Each of the underlying Channels holds the information for a specific color. In an RGB image, then, there is one Channel for Red, Green and Blue, while a CMYK image has one Channel each for cyan, magenta, yellow and black.

Changing the Views

Open an RGB image and open the Channels Palette by choosing Windows -> Show Channels. The four color Channels, red, green, blue and RGB (the composite Channel), are all highlighted, meaning that they are active, and your image will appear on your monitor in full color.

Unlike working with Layers, which only lets you activate one Layer at a time, you can activate multiple Channels at once. In fact, all of the color Channels need to be currently activated in order for you to view the composite.

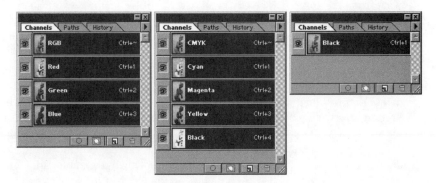

Figure 6–35: The Channels Palette as it appears for CMYK images (left), RGB images (middle) and Grayscale images (right).

Click on the Red Channel. No, don't worry—Photoshop isn't broken. Your image is supposed to be in black and white, even though you probably expected it to appear in all red. Click on the green or blue Channel. You'll see that they are in black and white, as well, although with different highlights and shadows in each. Color Figure 26 shows how each color looks.

Ordinarily, if you were going to change your image to Grayscale, you would simply have your CMYK or RGB image open and choose Image -> Mode -> Grayscale. But not all Grayscale is alike. You can choose from any of the Grayscales that generate from the individual color Channels and make one of those your Grayscale image. Simply activate the Channel that has the best Grayscale appearance (in the current example, that would be the blue Channel), then select Image -> Mode -> Grayscale.

The reason why the color Channels appear in black and white is because it makes them easier to work with. If you want to see them in color, though, you can by choosing File -> Preferences -> Display and Cursors. At the top of the dialog box, check the box marked *Color Channels* in Color. Push OK.

Color Figure 27 shows how the Channels appear when viewed in their respective colors. Looks pretty awful, doesn't it? While you can see the colors this way, it would be practically impossible to work like this, so you should open the Display and Cursors dialog box again and change it back.

Adjusting Colors in Channels

Now that we see how the Channels Palette is designed, we can see that when we used certain color adjustment tools, such as Levels, we were applying them to the composite Channel and having an effect on all of the color Channels at once. However, we can be more precise than this by applying certain correction techniques to one or more color Channels individually.

Let's take the image in Color Figure 28 as an example. The image could obviously use a little sharpening and some adjustment to the overall contrast. Instead of just whipping open the Levels dialog box, though, let's look at each of the individual color Channels first.

Figure 6–36 shows the three color plates: red, green and blue that make up the color in my image. From these, I can see that the green Channel seems to have the best overall contrast and definition, especially for the girls in the forefront of the picture, while the blue seems to do the best job with the guys in the back (who appear blurry in the composite). The red Channel probably the worst, being slightly oversaturated and lacking real definition.

Figure 6–36: The individual color Channels for my image. Red is on the left, green in the center and blue on the right.

By adjusting the tonal difference either through the Levels or the Curves to the blue and red Channels, I didn't risk disrupting the other Channels, which were already in good shape. Color Figure 29 show my image after I finished applying the color adjustments to the red Channel.

> You don't always have to have just the individual Channel active to apply a color correction to it. Some color correction tools, such as Level and Curves, provide you with a pull-down menu that lets you decide which Channel you which to edit.

Mixing Channels

Wouldn't it be great, though, if you could take the better parts of one Channel and mix it with the better parts of another Channel? Well, you can.

In my opinion, mixing Channels is one of the most effective ways of enhancing a picture. It takes a discerning eye, and it may take some time to really see subtle detail between Channels, but once you get the hang of it, you'll find it's worth the effort.

For this example, let's concentrate on making the girls in the foreground pop out a bit more from the photograph and make them just a bit sharper.

With the Channel Mixer, you can use the strengths of one Channel to compensate for problems in another Channel. To use the Channel Mixer for a situation as I have illustrated:

1. Make a selection around the girls or in the problem area in the image you are working with. For this particular case, I used the Magnetic Lasso Tool—even though I'm not a huge fan of the tool in general, it does come in handy once in awhile.

2. Choose Image -> Adjust -> Channel Mixer to access the dialog box shown in Figure 6–37.

3. For Output Channel, choose Green from the pull-down menu, since that had the best contrast for the area we've selected. In the Source Channels below, the Green slider jumps to 100%.

4. Keep the Monochrome box unchecked. Even though we saw earlier that it was easier to work with Channels when we view them as Grayscale images, clicking Monochrome will turn the selection to Grayscale permanently.

5. I've added just 10% more red to the selection and 22% more blue. Unless your Channels are really out of whack, you usually won't have to change much to see a noticeable difference. Color Figure 30 shows the change in my mage.

 Make sure that the Preview button is checked, so that you can see what the changes will look like as you make them. This is true for many of the dialog boxes and control panels in Photoshop.

Experiment with adding and subtracting colors from the other Channels by moving each of the sliders left and right. You can have some pretty whacked-out results! When you're through, click OK to accept the changes.

Creating a Spot Color

Spot Color refers to colors on an image that stand alone. In other words, they don't mix with other colors in your image. In older versions of Photoshop, designers who used spot colors either placed the color in a page layout program such as Quark or PageMaker, or placed the spot color in cyan, yellow or magenta, then later told the printer what PMS ink to substitute in its place.

Photoshop 5 had made life easier for the two- and three-color designer with the inclusion of Spot Channels. These are Channels that hold color information strictly for PMS colors. Spot Channels are particularly useful when a client has a specific PMS color for a logo that would otherwise be difficult to recreate.

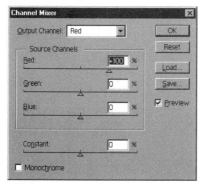

Figure 6–37: The Channel Mixer dialog box.

Working in Photoshop: Creating a Spot Color Channel

To create a two-color image with a Spot Color Channel:

1. Open a Grayscale image or a color image and convert it to grayscale by choosing Image -> Mode -> Grayscale. Hit OK when Photoshop asks whether you want to remove the color information. For this example, I am just using a Grayscale version of the image that I used in the last example. Open the Channels Palette by choosing View -> Show Channels.

2. There should be one Channel in the Palette, Black, indicating that this is currently a Grayscale image. From the Palette pull-down menu, choose New Spot Channel. The New Spot Channel dialog box will appear, as shown in Figure 6–38. Click on the color box to access the Custom Color dialog box.

3. From the Book pull-down menu, choose Pantone Coated (one of the more common premixed spectrums) and type in your desired PMS color. Type it quickly to make sure you get the color you want (Photoshop apparently thought it'd be more fun to make us poor typists try to get the number right in a hurry, rather than to provide a text area and <Enter> button). When your color is selected, hit OK.

4. Back in the New Spot Channel dialog box, fill in 100 for the Solidity percentage. The percentage you fill in will affect only the way the image appears on screen, not the way it will print. Click OK.

5. Notice that the Channels Palette now has two Channels—the original Black Channel, and a new Channel, named whatever Pantone number you selected. With the Black Channel active, select the portion of your image that you want to apply the spot color to. Cut this image by choosing Edit -> Cut. For the sake of this example, I made a selection of the two women in the forefront of the picture, then inverted the selection, feathered the selection for a more realistic cut and cut away the background.

6. Make your new Pantone Channel active by clicking on it. Choose Edit -> Paste to paste the selection from your pasteboard into this Channel. You'll notice that the color you chose is now applied to the portion of your image that you pasted. Notice, too, that, unlike most instances when you paste an object into Photoshop, a new Layer is not automatically created in the Layers Palette. In fact, you'll even notice that the shading on the active Layer is now grayed out, and the Palette is rendered temporarily inactive until you leave the Spot Channel.

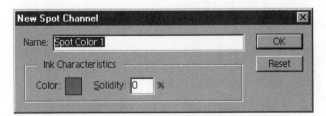

Figure 6–38: The Spot Channel dialog box.

You can create shades of your PMS color by reducing the color value percentage in the Color Palette, then filling in a selection while in the Pantone Channel.

A Few Last Notes about Channels

There are a couple of other options that you may see and wonder about when it comes to Channels.

Image -> Apply Image

Later on in this book, you'll see how to use Layer Masks to create collages. Apply Image can help you create pretty cool composite collages also, but in a different way. The Apply Image dialog box is shown in Figure 6–39.

Apply Images mixes the Channel information of one image with another image. As you can see by Figure 6–39, the *Target* image, which is where the change will occur, remains fixed—you can't change it. The Target image is always the image in the active window (it must be open). The *Source* image, which is where the Channel information will be derived from, can be changed by selecting an image from the pull-down menu. In order for an image to appear in the Source pull-down menu, it must be open and must be exactly the same size (physical size and resolution) as the Target image. Use the Crop Tool or the Image Size dialog box to alter the image size of the Source, if necessary.

Once you select the source, you then select which Layer of the Source you want to pull color information from. You then select which specific Channel you wish to mix with the Target—you can choose just one individual Channel, or the RGB (or CMYK) composite.

Use the Blending mode pull-down menu to decide how you want the Source colors to interact with the Target colors.

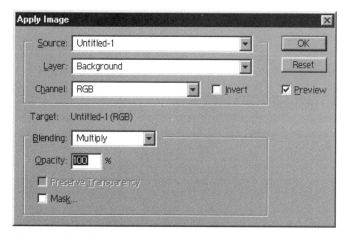

Figure 6–39: The Apply Image dialog box.

Blending modes as shown and described later in this chapter.

After your selections have been made, click OK, and Apply Channel will take the chosen Channels from the Source, mix them with the Channels from the Target, and show the results within the Target image.

> **The effect the Source Channels has on the Target image depends on the state of the Target image. All effects will happen to the active Layer, as well as to any specific selection that has been made.**

Duplicate Channels

Pretty boring stuff with this one—you can duplicate any Channel (one at a time—this option will be grayed out if you are in composite mode) into either a different image or canvas or into the image that you are currently working on. You can find this option in the Channels Palette submenu. The only real reason to use this is if you want to work on a Channel specifically without ruining the original Channel but, with the History Palette giving you multiple undos, there's little reason for that.

Split Channels

Choose Split Channels from the Channels Palette pull-down menu. This will turn each Channel of an RGB and CMYK picture into its own individual Grayscale canvas. This can be helpful if you want to quickly make a one-color image from any particular Channel or when you want to use the Merge Channels feature, which we'll look at in the next section.

Merge Channels

Choosing Merge Channels from the Channels Palette submenu can create some pretty cool results. Basically, if you have Channels that are already separated into their canvases, such as the result of Splitting Channels as we saw in the last section, or if you have individual Grayscale images, you can use the Merge Channels command to turn them all into one image. It's a finicky command—all of the images that you merge have to be the exact same size and resolution, but there can be some funky outcomes.

From the dialog box, choose either RGB or CMYK, and, in the subsequent dialog box, choose which image should be designated to which Channel (if you have only three Grayscale images to use, CMYK won't be an option). Choosing MultiChannel will allow you to place all of the available images into one canvas (more than four), although you won't be able to see a composite of the image (as you can with RGB or CMYK), so this is a pretty uninteresting choice.

BLEND MODES

Practically everywhere you look in Photoshop, you have the option to blend colors. Blend Mode pull-down menus can be found on the Layers Palette, as well as the Options Palettes for each of the painting tools. These can be somewhat confusing, and, at first, it's pretty tempting just to ignore the fact that these pull-down menus are there at all. But once you get the hang of them, they can serve as pretty cool special effects.

Blend Modes work on the premise that two colors will somehow be mixed together. Whether that means painting one color on top of another or making one Layer interact with an underlying Layer, the color modes work their magic based on unique mathematical formulas to determine the results.

To understand this better, Color Figure 31 and Figure 6–40 show two images to illustrate the fundamentals of each concept, as well as using this as the model for describing each individual blend mode option. The image in Layer 1 provides the *base color*—the underlying color. The image in Layer 2 provides the *blend color*—the colored pixels that will blend with the base colors.

Any Layer that provides the blend color will blend with the Layer that lies directly below it. If that Layer is only partially filled or at an opacity of less than 100%, the Layers below that will be affected too, and will also provide base color.

Figure 6–40: The images that I'll be using to describe the Blend Mode. I'll show the result with both the toast on top (in the Layers Palette) and the computer on top.

The *blend color* does not have to be supplied by a different Layer. You can set the Blend Mode to any of the painting tools and paint directly onto a Layer. The color that you paint with becomes the blend color, while the image that you paint onto provides the base color.

Anyway, when the *blend color* mixes with the *base color*, you get the *result color*. Simple enough.

The following describes and provides samples for each of the color mode options. Each figure will show the result with Layer 1 in front and Layer 2 in front, to see how they would differ and affect one another. In each case where applicable, the image on the left will be the result with the toast picture on top, and the image on the right will be the result with the computer picture on top. For each of the modes, the result is shown in Color Figures 32–35 except where indicated that the figure is shown here, instead.

Normal (Default)

No need to waste valuable printing inks with this. Normal Mode simply displays your color pixels as they should appear, with no special effects. In other words, don't touch the Blending Mode pull-down menu, and look at your screen. You have achieved Normalcy.

Dissolve

Dissolve is kind of the same as Normal, except that it will randomly replace some of the pixels in the blend color for the pixels in the base color. This typically wouldn't have a very visible effect for the images in our example, but Color Figure 32 shows the result when we choose Dissolve from the Paintbrush Options Palette and paint with a large brush. The areas of heavy color concentration remain largely unaffected, while the fringe areas seem to break up, or dissolve. This Blend Mode can be a good tool to use when creating the tail of a comet.

Behind (Available for Paint Tools Only)

This is actually pretty cool. You won't find it listed in the Blending Mode options in the Layers Palette, but it is available for any of the painting tools. Behind works only on the transparent portions of a Layer (if the Layer does not have the Preserve Transparency box checked) and seems to be applying color *behind* the exiting pixels. Check out Chapter 5 for a more in-depth look at this option.

Multiply

Now we start getting into some of the math. The Multiply option is figured with the following equation:

```
(Base Color) x (Blend Color) = Result Color
```

The resulting color in Multiply Mode is always going to be darker. If you Multiply a color with black, the result will be black, and if you Multiply a color with white, the result won't show any difference to the color at all. If you're painting with a color in Multiply Mode and you continue to paint over the same pixels, those pixels will get progressively darker.

As you'll see in Chapter 8, when we deal with filters, Multiply is one of the modes that we'll choose when we want to "trick" Photoshop into thinking that there is mass on a Layer when there really isn't.

Screen

The Screen Mode is uses the following equation:

```
(Inverse of Base Color) x (Inverse of Blend Color) = Result Color
```

If you remember your grade school math classes at all, you'll probably be able to figure out that the resulting color of choosing Screen will always be lighter. If you Screen a color with white, the result is white, and if you Screen a color with black, the result is that the color remains unchanged.

Just like Multiply, Chapter 8 will show that Screen is used for creating content-filled blank Layers for certain filters.

Overlay

Overlay will both Multiply and Screen the color in your image, based on brightness value of the base color. By Multiplying the areas in the base that contain darker pixels and Screening the areas in the base that contain lighter pixels, Overlay will usually emphasize the base's shadows and highlights, while mixing the remaining pixels.

Painting with black or white does not result in black or white but will make your resulting color darker or lighter, respectively. It's almost like burning or dodging, but in a more discriminating way.

Soft Light

Of its two cousins, Overlay and Hard Light, Soft Light is the dullest, darkening the dark pixels of the blend color and lightening the light pixels of the blend color, but to a lesser degree than Hard Light will do. Soft Light has largely the same effect that burning or dodging might have.

Painting with black or white has pretty much the same effect as it does when you paint with black or white in Overlay mode.

Hard Light

Hard light pretty much does what Overlay does but relies on the blend colors for pixel information, rather than the base colors. The result will be the opposite of the result you'll achieve using Overlay. Darker areas on the blend color are Multiplied, while lighter areas are Screened.

Hard Light is a good one for enhancing the shadows or highlights of a blending image. Painting with black or white will result in black or white.

Color Dodge

Imagine that the whole world just went neon. That's pretty much the result you'll see when you use the Color Dodge Blending Mode. The pixels in the base color are brightened to emulate the blend colors. Therefore, your result will always be significantly brighter.

Painting with black has no effect, while painting with white will eventually result in pure white. Try to paint with a 50% opacity or less, using a large, soft-edged brush to really get some nice effects or to help eliminate an abundance of shadows.

Color Burn

The opposite of Color Dodge, Color Burn darkens the pixels in the base color to emulate the darker pixels in the blend color. The result is always darker. Lighter pixels in the blend color have no effect on the result.

Painting with white has no effect, while tentatively painting with black can really enhance some shadows very nicely.

Darken

Darken will replace one pixel for another, from either the base color or the blend color, depending on which is darker. In other words, the result is a composite comprised of the darkest pixels available between both the base and blend colors.

The resulting color could have some surprising color shifts. As with certain other blending mode options, Photoshop will judge brightness based on a value provided to each pixel within each color Channel. So, if the pixels in the cyan Channel of the blend color is lighter than the pixels in the cyan Channel of the base color, but the reverse is true for the magenta and yellow Channels, you might see a bizarre shift in color to a darker orangey/purple, as Photoshop ignores the cyan, but replaces the original magenta and yellow values with the darker blend color counterparts.

Painting with white has no effect, while painting with black results in black.

Lighten

Lighten produces the opposite result of the Darken option, replacing lighter pixels from the base color with lighter pixels from the blend colors. The result is a composite made up of all the lightest pixels that the blend and base colors have to offer. As with the Darken option, watch for odd color shifts.

Painting with white results in pure white, while painting with black has no effect.

Difference

You can expect to see some pretty wild and dramatic color shifts using Difference (actually, you might notice that, as you move lower on the pull-down Blending Mode list, the options are increasingly wilder and more useful for effect than for color enhancement or correction). Difference will, on a Channel-by-Channel basis, calculate the brightness value for each pixel. Depending on which has the greater brightness value, it will subtract either the blend color from the base or the base color from the blend.

Painting with black has no effect, but painting with white inverts the pixels, making edited pixels look like a photo negative.

Exclusion

Let's play SAT for a second: Exclusion is to Difference as Soft Light is to Hard Light. By working off the same model but substituting medium colors to gray, it creates an effect that is similar to Difference but less drastic in contrast.

Painting with black still has no effect, while painting with white still inverts the base color.

Hue

No longer translating the pixels into grayscale and assigning them a brightness value (remaining options on the list are unavailable for Grayscale images), Hue and the remaining options will create a result based on the HSL color model. With the Hue option, Photoshop will use the Hue of the blend color, with the saturation and luminance of the base color. The result will often leave you with an image that alters the colors unpredictably but that no longer leaves even a recognizable semblance of the original blending image.

Saturation

You'll probably start to notice a vicious circle here…. The result is comprised of the Saturation of the blend color with the Hue and Luminance of the base.

Luminosity

The resulting color is a combination of the Luminance of the blend color with the Hue and Saturation of the base color.

Color

Skip this one for a second and read "Luminosity." Then come back to this one. (I'm reviewing these in the order they're provided in the pull-down menus, but I think it would make more sense with Luminosity before Color.)

Okay, are you back? Color is the opposite of Luminance—the result is a combination of the Luminance of the base color with the Hue and Saturation of the blend color, as Figure 6–45 illustrates.

The Info Palette and Eyedropper Tools

The Info Palette has so many good uses, including measurement information to determine precise spacing and measurements of image areas. But probably the best use of the Info Palette is to know the exact composition and color breakdown of any pixel, just by rolling the cursor over it.

You can access the Info Palette by choosing Windows -> Show Info. The Palette is shown in Figure 6–41.

◆   Color Information: The upper portion of the Info Palette provides the color information in both RGB (left) or CMYK (right). As you roll over different colored pixels within the image with your cursor, you'll see the numeric values for each color change in the Info Palette. The numeric values equate to the percentage of each color component (RGB or CMYK) needed to create the color of the pixel in question. Figure 6–42 shows the Info Palette next to the Color Picker, to illustrate how the values in the Info Palette relate to different color mixtures.

If your image is currently in RGB mode, you may notice something odd about the CMYK values as they're presented in the Info Palette. As Figure 6–41 shows, some portions of my RGB image cause an exclamation point (!) to appear after the CMYK values. This means that that particular color is out of gamut. In other words, it's out of the range of printable colors, and if you were to print it, the closest you would get would be the mixtures of the percentage values that appear in the Info Palette. Or, to be more clear about this point, the color that appears on your screen will look a good deal different when it comes off the printer.

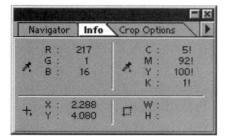

Figure 6–41: The Info Palette.

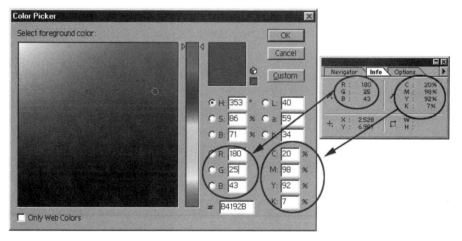

Figure 6–42: How the Info Palette and the Color Picker relate.

 If you find that your colors are out of gamut in certain areas, use one of the selection methods to isolate the areas in question and feather the selections so that the edges are not so harsh. Then apply any of the color manipulation tools discussed earlier in this chapter, especially trying to desaturate the color or change the brightness.

◆ Measurement Information: The lower portion of the Info Palette deals with the measurements of your image. As you move your cursor around your canvas, the numbers on the bottom left will indicate your exact position on both the X and Y axes, in whatever unit of measure that is currently being used. The Width (W) and Height (H) values in the lower right quadrant of the Info Palette provide you with the Width and Height measurements of any selection that you are making.

◆   Changing Units of Measure: Are you currently working in inches but need to measure something in pixels? You can quickly change the units of measure from within the Info Palette. Simply click and hold your cursor on the crosshair icon in the lower left quadrant to access a pull-down menu of various measurement units. You'll see the rulers (if they're open) change to whatever measurement unit that you choose.

Going hand in hand with the Info Palette is the Color Sampler Tool, found underneath the Eyedropper Tool in the Toolbar. The benefit with this tool is that it allows you to compare and contrast up to 4 separate points within your image, by placing markers. Markers are left simply by clicking on a desired location. Figure 6–43, for example, shows an image upon which I have left four markers (four is the maximum allowed) and how the Info Palette expands to provide information on all these separate places.

These are helpful so that, as you adjust your colors through any of the adjustment methods discussed earlier, you can see how the areas that you pointed are being affected.

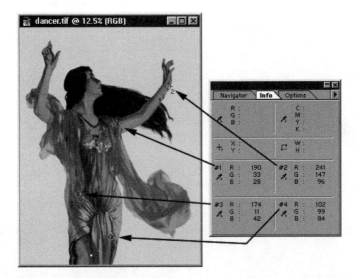

Figure 6–43: The Color Sampler Tool can be helpful in tweaking colors.

IT AIN'T EASY BEING GREEN (IN A CMYK WORLD): A FEW RANDOM THOUGHTS ABOUT COLOR

If you were one of the 11 people who bought and read my second book, *Digital Publishing To Go*, then you may remember me using that title once before. But, considering that book didn't exactly fly off the shelves, I thought I would try to salvage it.

Over the last few years, I've had the opportunity to make mental notes about color and color usage as it relates to people, companies and projects. So, for the sake of making your life easier (and fulfilling a last-minute requirement for one extra section in this book), I give you a few random, personal observations on the topic of color:

◆ When you're printing a solid black, don't overdue the black level of the CMYK mixture. A really strong printing black should have a breakdown of around 65% Cyan, 52% Magenta, 52% Yellow and no more than 93% Black. On screen it'll look more like a very dark, muddy brown than a pure black, but off the commercial press it will print a nice, deep color. If you use more than this amount, the ink will come off the press very over-saturated, may stain the other colors and take a very long time to dry.

◆ When you're developing something for advertising purposes, it's been shown in studies that red is the color that attracts the most attention, although by far blue tends to be the colors most corporations use.

◆ When you're building a web site, it's easier for people to read black text on a white background, and reds and yellows appear fine. However, if you are designing graphics for video, or expect that your Web site might be viewed on television, it's the opposite: text is read more easily when it's white text on a black background, and reds and yellows tend to bleed and not come off as well.

◆ Often times, a color that you really like in RGB will be out of gamut (not printable) and the closest color that Photoshop will recommend will just be, well...gross. You can usually get a closer color to what you want just by reducing the black or white amounts in the color (by using the lower slide bar in the Levels dialog box).

◆ If you're doing graphic work for a client, the chances are that most smaller to medium clients are more interested in speed of project completion and will never notice or care about a few shades of color either way. Unfortunately, time most often takes precedent over quality of color, and many people don't even know how to be discriminating when it comes to color on their projects. So, although it's not always the case, and it seems like poor advice, the reality is you're often better to sacrifice pure color condition for speed of output.

Well, there are, or course, millions of small nuances that you'll pick up as you work with color over time. It can be a tricky science, and lot more complicated to really get the hang of than selection techniques. This is mostly due to the fact that color is not just a function of Photoshop, but a function of nature.

SUMMARY

Ah, if life were one big box of Lucky Charms, with rainbows and colors and magic symbols (especially marshmallow magic symbols). Well, unfortunately, the world is not made of marshmallows, but there is no denying that color, while often taken for granted, is what helps make each and everything in our world distinguishable from one another. While we may take little notice of this in our everyday life, as designers we have no choice but to pay strict attention to color issues, and how they affect our work. From using RGB for Web sites, to CMYK for print and all the other issues in between, understanding color will make all the difference between your design being a work of art, or just a complete mess.

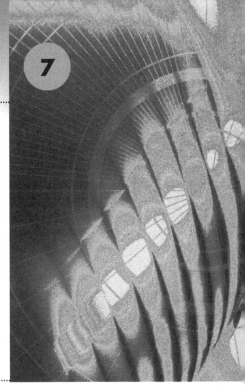

CONCERNING
PRINT AND
DIGITAL

ONE PROGRAM, SO MANY PROJECTS

Photoshop's basic "reason for being" is as a graphic design tool. But the term *graphic design* is broad, and the end product can drastically effect the way in which you might set about designing. Digital project development (including Web, CD-ROM and DVD design) in many aspects takes a completely different set of talent and understanding than print design does. While many people can do both, there is a growing trend in design agencies to segment artists into one category or another. The aesthetic differences between the two—what looks good on the Web versus what looks good in print—is something that I can't help you with. An artistic eye isn't something that can be taught. But understanding some of the more important specifics of each medium is, and that's what we'll review in this chapter.

RESOLUTION ISSUES

In Chapter 1, we learned about resolution, including how to change it, what effect it has on file size and how it may alter the way an image looks (such as how it becomes pixilated when made larger). We also discussed different types of resolution that you'll concern yourself with, such as the physical size of an image, the ppi, dpi and lpi. But understanding what each of these means doesn't help out much in understanding what resolutions to use for certain projects.

What Resolutions to Use

The resolution that you will need for your image will largely depend on the type of project that you're working on. If you are working on a Web site or CD-ROM interface, for example, 72 ppi is high enough—one image pixel for every pixel that your monitor displays. This pretty much holds true for any project that will be viewed on a monitor-based display vehicle.

For print projects, you're going to need to increase the resolution. The more pixels you allocate to your image per inch, the more clarity and color will be available for printing. With printing, however, it gets a little more complicated, since the resolution will largely depend on what you are printing. Presses work with various paper types differently, as the way some paper types treat ink can have a wide range. A couple of general rules you could follow, however, would be the following:

♦ The general industry standard is to establish a resolution between 150% and 200% (1.5—2.0 times) the screen frequency (lpi) used by your printer. You'll have to ask your printer what screen frequency is used (commonly between 120—150 lpi). If, for example, the printer prints at 133 lpi, your image resolution should be set between 200 and 266 ppi.

♦ Personally, in my experience, I usually keep nearly all my print images at a resolution of 300 ppi. That seems to ensure a high enough quality of print for superior detail.

Table 7–1 gives a quick glimpse of what resolutions to use with various types of projects, and which projects require that you pay attention to which resolutions at all.

Table 7–1: Resolution at a Glance

Type of Project	Image Size	ppi	lpi
Images meant for monitors only Web sites, CD-ROMs, kiosks, etc.	Depends on the resolution of the monitor it will be viewed on. For general audiences, assume 800 x 600 pixel resolution	Almost always at 72	Don't worry about it
Print pieces:			
Newsletters, flyers, coupons	Doesn't matter—bigger images just mean bigger paper (and more expensive projects)	97.5–130	65
Newspapers	Doesn't matter—bigger images just mean bigger paper (and more expensive projects)	127.5–170	85
Magazines, brochures, catalogs	Doesn't matter—bigger images just mean bigger paper (and more expensive projects)	199.5–266	133
Annual reports and coffee-table books	Doesn't matter—bigger images just mean bigger paper (and more expensive projects)	265.5–354	177

PRINTED PIECES

For a long while, print was the primary objective of most Photoshop work. But even though some focus has shifted a bit to creating Web sites (the upgrade to version 5.5 was almost strictly for Web designers), the print medium is far from dead. In fact, even though the Internet is getting all the press these days, print is enjoying somewhat of a renaissance. From magazines to brochures, print ads, posters and flyers, there is dramatic demand for quality print designers.

Dealing with Print Work— Preparation in the Photoshop Stage

Although there is nothing in the design world that would impede your creativity, there are limitations in the real world when it comes to print. Understanding these limitations and the specific nature of dealing with print graphics will help you not only to get the most out of your work, but also to avoid making potentially costly mistakes down the road. Understanding issues such as bleed space, color preparation and image integration with a page layout program will make your work that much better.

Through this section, I'll be referring to QuarkXPress when I talk about page layout programs. Even though others exist, such as Adobe PageMaker and Adobe InDesign, there really isn't any page layout product on the market yet which can compare with XPress.

Establish Bleed Space

When an image is printed to the very edge of the paper, it's said to "bleed" off the page. Figure 7–1 shows examples of bleeds—from one bleed (images that are printed only to one edge of the paper), to full bleed (images that are printed to every edge of the paper).

When you send a piece to be output by a commercial printer, they will be printing many copies of your piece on very large pieces of paper, then trimming each page to create individual units. Trimming pages that bleed to one or more edges is a trickier job than trimming pages that don't bleed at all.

In this section, when I use the term *printer*, I'm referring to a commercial printer, who outputs large quantities of units—not your desktop printer.

To ensure the best quality of a printed page that bleeds, you need to work with a page size that is larger than the anticipated size of the final printed piece. For example, let's assume that you are going to be printing large quantities of a one-page flyer, 8.5" x 11." If your flyer will look like the image on the left of Figure 7–2, then starting your new document in Photoshop at 8.5" x 11" would be just fine. That's because, in that example, the printing isn't touching the edge of the paper on any side—there is no bleed.

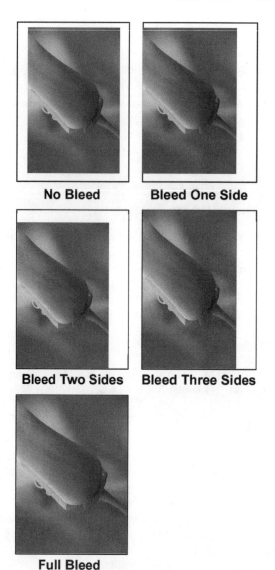

No Bleed   **Bleed One Side**

Bleed Two Sides   **Bleed Three Sides**

Full Bleed

Figure 7–1: Examples of bleeds. More bleeds could mean a higher cost for your print job.

However, if you are going to be designing your flyer to look like the image on the right of Figure 7–2, your initial new document will need to be larger than 8.5" x 11". There is full bleed in this flyer and, to ensure that the ink actually makes it to the very edge of the page, you'll need to create excess imagery to begin with. Figure 7–3 and

Figure 7–2: Designing a flyer without bleeds (like the one on the left) can be a bit simpler. Full-bleed images (like the one on the right) need special treatment.

Color Figure 36 show how the flyer with full bleed was originally created in Photoshop. Notice that the actual page size is 9" x 11.5". I've created my document with 0.25" of extra space around each edge of the canvas, and I've designed my imagery to allow extra ink to exist in those margins, even though those margins will get trimmed off by the printer.

The reason for making the initial document larger to begin with is that printer's trimming machines aren't perfect. Without leaving extra space along the edges, you are likely to end up with a very slight white border around some edges of a piece that is supposed to bleed if the printer is even a fraction of an inch off when trimming.

Typically, printers prefer designers to leave anywhere between 1/8" and 1/4" on any side of an image that bleeds. You could technically get away with 1/16", but that's kind of cutting it close (no pun intended).

If you forget to allow for bleed in the original Photoshop document, don't cheese out and try to stretch the document when you do your page layout in QuarkXPress or InDesign. It won't work. All that you'll accomplish is running the risk of blurring your image by making it unnaturally larger, and maybe even causing important imagery or text that falls close to the edge to get unexpectedly cut off when it goes to the trimmer.

Figure 7–3: The Photoshop document for creating a flyer with full bleed. Excess image beyond the edges is necessary for trimming.

To let the printer know where to cut a page that will bleed to the edge, set crop marks in your page layout program, similar to what was shown in Figure 7–4. Establish your page size to the final dimensions of your printed piece, and then import your image onto that canvas so that the bleed space in your Photoshop-created file runs off the XPress canvas.

Check with your printer and your service bureau as to the cost of bleeds. Depending on who you use and how often you use them, bleeding to one or more edges could potentially bump up the price of producing any piece.

Choose the Right Color Mode

Use CMYK for printer pieces. If you have the RAM, design them in CMYK originally, so that you don't get excited about colors that appear in RGB but will never print on paper. And don't, under any circumstances, allow a client to approve an RGB image that he sees on your monitor and expect that that client won't sue you when his actual piece arrives at his doorstep looking significantly worse than what he saw on your screen.

Figure 7–4: Crop marks in this QuarkXPress layout tell the printer where to trim your image.

It is okay, though, to work in RGB mode while you are creating your printed piece but to continuously view your image as it would appear in CMYK mode. To do this, make sure your image is in RGB mode, then chose View -> Preview -> CMYK. Working like this will cat up RAM, so if you don't have enough RAM, you may just want to use this option to check your work from time to time.

But why, if the image needs to be in CMYK anyway, would you want to work in RGB mode? Well, to begin with, the resolution of print pieces is high, so the file size is going to be high, as well. But CMYK images are significantly higher than RGB images in terms of file size. This means that RGB images won't cause such a strain on your RAM resources. Secondly, you'll have more filters available in RGB mode—in fact, all of them are accessible in RGB mode, while many of them are inoperative while in RGB mode.

But no matter what you do, don't forget to change and save your work as a CMYK before importing it into a page layout program and sending it to a service bureau or commercial printer.

Out-of-Gamut Warnings

Working with color can be a lot more precarious in print than on the Web. Not that the Web is necessarily *easier* when dealing with color, but screwing up something on the Web won't cost you thousands of dollars in reprinting, as screwing up a print project will.

Take advantage of the many "out-of-gamut" warnings that Photoshop provides. Out of gamut, if you haven't read in this book already, refers to colors that are outside the CMYK range—in other words, they are colors that you might see in RGB on your monitor but that can't be reproduced on paper using the CMYK mixtures.

Photoshop gives you plenty of ways to know if the colors you are working with fall out of the printable range:

◆ The Color Picker: The small out-of-gamut icon (a triangle with an exclamation mark) appears when a nonprintable color has been chosen. The closest possible color is provided.

◆ If your cursor is on a pixel of your image that contains a nonprintable color, the Info Palette will show the closest CMYK values to that color and put an exclamation mark next to each number. See more about the Info Palette in Chapter 6.

◆ If you're in RGB mode, choose either of the following:

   ◆ View -> Preview -> CMYK to see how your image will appear as a CMYK image. This is helpful if you don't have much RAM, so you need to work in RGB but want a quick peek into the CMYK world for a more realistic presentation of your image.

   ◆ View -> Out-of-Gamut to turn all of your nonprintable colors gray.

Make sure that, no matter what you do, you change your image to CMYK mode before bringing it to the service bureau for outputting it to film. If you don't, you can get some unexpected results, and, equally as annoying, some service bureaus will actually charge you extra for having to convert an image to CMYK for you.

My Suggestion for Working with Two Colors

Once in awhile, for aesthetic or cost reasons, you're going to design something to be printed in just two colors. Usually, one of those colors is black, and the other is a PMS (Pantone Matching System) color, designated by a code found either in Photoshop or in the PMS swatch book.

In Chapter 6, we reviewed how to create a spot color in Photoshop—something new as of version 5.0. We also learned how to create a Duotone, in which two colors are mixed together. But in my experience, I've found that, for two-color printing, you're better off avoiding both of these options and creating your image in the CMYK color mode. The idea, in the end, is to create a CMYK image that has color information in only two Channels, so that only two pieces of film are created.

To do this, let's say that you want to create a two-color piece in which one of the colors is going to be black, and the other color is going to be PMS 3268, which is sort of in the green family. What I would recommend is to work in CMYK mode and choose Image -> Adjust -> Selective Color, to access the dialog box shown in Figure 7–5. Go through all the colors in the pull-down menu, and reduce the percentage of colors in the sliders to –100%, except for the Cyan slider—increase that one to +100%, and leave the Black slider alone.

The reason, in this case, that we are increasing the cyan instead of any other color is that the PMS color that we are using is greenish. If it were more toward red, we'd be increasing the magenta color instead. It's not necessary to keep the colors in the same family, but it helps.

When you are done, click OK, and open the Channels Palette. Click on the Magenta Channel and select all. Then delete everything on the canvas, which will clear the color information that may be left on that Channel. Do the same for the Yellow Channel. When you bring the image to your service bureau, only two pieces of film will be output. Give these to your printer, and instruct the printer to use the cyan plate for the PMS color.

Alpha Channels, TIFFs and the Hidden QuarkXPress Function

Depending on the type of piece you're designing, it may be necessary to import an image into QuarkXPress by itself—without the background of the image interfering.

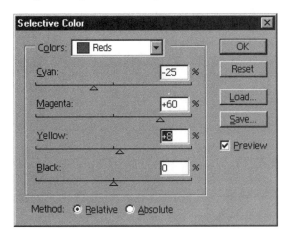

Figure 7–5: The Selective Color Dialog box.

Not too long ago, in older versions of XPress, the best way to do this was to create a path in Photoshop (using the Pen Tool, usually, which is covered later this chapter) and save your image as an EPS (a format which retains path information).

This is still a perfectly acceptable way of doing things. But there are those (myself included—and, by the way, if I use one more parenthetical notation in this section, please shoot me) who would rather use TIFFs for print work whenever possible. In my opinion, TIFFs retain color and detail as well as EPSs do, but because of the LZW compression scheme, the file sizes are a lot smaller, making heavy images more manageable and easier to deal with.

The problem in the past, though, was that TIFFs don't retain paths, so that any image that you needed to import sans the background was pretty much limited to EPS. But a new change in a recent QuarkXPress upgrade has changed that and has changed the way print designers work in Photoshop.

To use a TIFF image in QuarkXPress that will extract a background, simply do the following:

1. Create a selection around the image that you want to bring into your XPress layout (the area outside of the selection will be the background that you don't want to appear in your layout).

2. Save your selection as a Channel. You want to name your Channel.

3. Make sure your image is flattened, and choose File -> Save As. From the dialog box, select TIFF as your desired format. Figure 7–6 shows the image that I have saved, with the selection and Channels Palette.

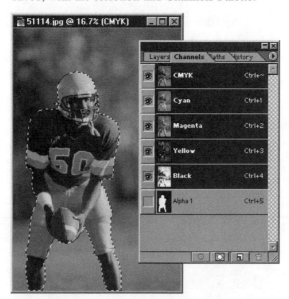

Figure 7–6: The selection around the image I want to have extracted from the background is saved as an Alpha Channel.

4. In QuarkXPress, import your TIFF image into your page layout, as shown in Figure 7–7.

5. With the Move Tool selected (in QuarkXPress, not Photoshop), double-click on the image, and choose Clipping from the upper tabs in the dialog box that appears. Figure 7–8 shows a screen shot of the dialog box.

6. From the Type pull-down menu, select Alpha Channel. Use the Alpha pull-down menu to select which Channel you want to use (if you have saved more than one Channel). Hit OK when through. Figure 7–9 illustrates how this affects the overall layout.

Some Types of Print Projects

Although there are some universal truths about print work that apply to each project (such as the issues we just reviewed), there are finer details that exist for specific types of projects. The following section will review a couple of the more common types of print projects that designers will work on and some of the issues that exist for each, including some special considerations that are important to remember.

Booklets (Brochures, Catalogs, etc.)

The design of "booklets," a term that I'll use broadly to encompass brochures, catalogs, pamphlets, etc., can be tricky to master. There are too many different types of booklets to go into, but each of them shares a few common qualities:

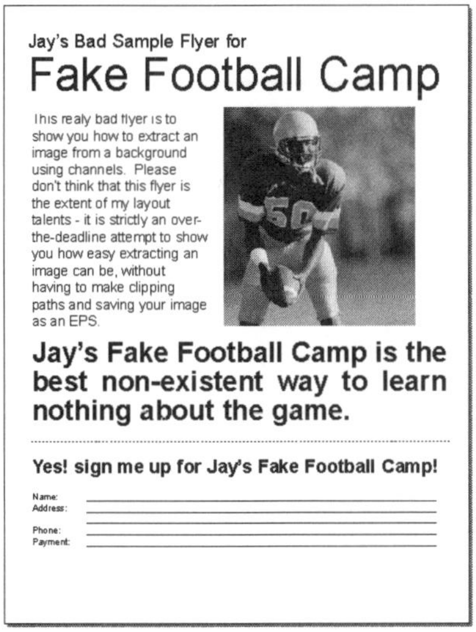

Jay's Bad Sample Flyer for

Fake Football Camp

This realy bad flyer is to show you how to extract an image from a background using channels. Please don't think that this flyer is the extent of my layout talents - it is strictly an over-the-deadline attempt to show you how easy extracting an image can be, without having to make clipping paths and saving your image as an EPS.

Jay's Fake Football Camp is the best non-existent way to learn nothing about the game.

Yes! sign me up for Jay's Fake Football Camp!

Name:
Address:

Phone:
Payment:

Figure 7–7: My page layout in QuarkXPress.

Figure 7–8: The Clipping tab in the modify dialog box.

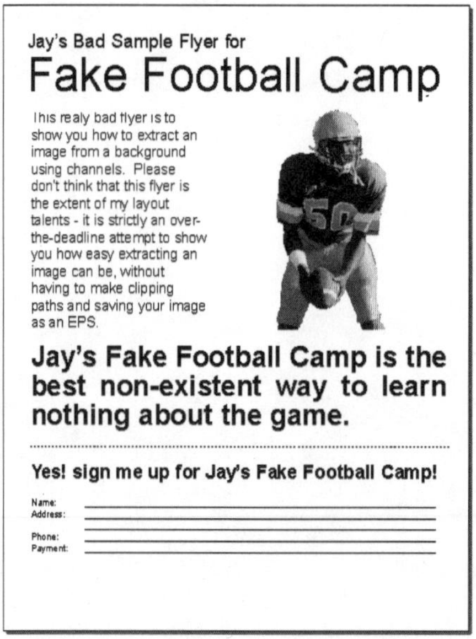

Figure 7–9: My page layout after I have extracted my main image from the unwanted background. If I spent the time to really smooth out my selection, it would appear far smoother in XPress.

◆ **Resolution:** Print pieces will vary in required resolution. Typically, you'll design your pieces to be 1.5–2 times the lpi (ask your printer what line screen will be used). From personal experience, I typically set the resolution to 300 ppi, regardless of the type of project. To date, I've never encountered a problem when I do this. Earlier in this Chapter, Table 7–1 showed the resolutions that are typically needed for various sorts of projects.

◆ **Color:** Use CMYK for four-color printing. If you're low on RAM, you can work in RGB, but make sure that you check the out-of-gamut warnings (in the View menu) once in awhile to make sure you're working with printable colors. And definitely make sure that you convert your image to CMYK before bringing it to the service bureau for output.

◆ **Technology:** Print pieces can be pretty grueling on your computers. To do pretty much anything in print, you're going to need to invest in some serious machinery. Because most service bureaus are on Macintosh computers, and both Photoshop and page layout programs seem to be more fluid on the Mac, I'd recommend getting a G3 or better (preferably, a G4), with a minimum of 164 megs of RAM. Get yourself a 19" monitor or better, so you don't strain your eyes—printing will take some pretty precise, detailed work, and you'll often find yourself working at an incredible magnification level.

◆ **Special Considerations:** There are a few points that present themselves as problems to print designers but that don't apply to everything that you'll print.

  ◆ **Trifold Brochures:** Some print pieces will be harder to design for than others. In particular, creating a trifold brochure sometimes proves to be a tricky process. The name alone is a bit misleading: *trifold* should literally mean that the piece has three folds. But that's not the case. Rather, *trifold* means that the piece will have three panels and only two folds.

  Take the sample piece in Figure 7–10 and Color Figure 37 that we use in my agency as part of our media material. This piece is printed on an 8.5" x 11" piece of paper and is folded in two distinct places to create three panels on each side. Notice that the back of the piece is actually the middle panel and resides next to the cover.

  When you design this type, be careful about where you place the folds, or *gutters*. Too often, designers will make the mistake of setting up their page in Photoshop or QuarkXPress and assuming that all they need to do is divide the 11" of paper width by 3 to get the measurements for each panel. But this error in thinking will almost certainly lead to a costly mistake.

  As Figure 7–10 shows, the cover (the panel on the far right) and the back (the middle panel) are of equal width—each is 3.75" wide. The foldover panel (on the far left) is shorter—it's only 3.5". That's because we have to take into consideration that we will be using a small amount of paper in the actual folding of the piece and need to make that last panel compensate for it.

Figure 7–10: A typical trifold brochure. There are really three panels, not three folds.

The measurements on the other side of the page have to match up. So, in the previous example, the panel on the far left is the shorter panel when we are looking at the side with the cover on it. The inside of the brochure, though, which is on the other side of the page, has the opposite occur—the shorter panel will be the one on the far right.

◆ **MultiPage Spreads:** I'm not sure why, but for some reason, I've had a lot of clients who can't seem to grasp the concept that you simply cannot have a 10-page brochure. Come to think of it, I've encountered more than an acceptable share of designers who can't grasp this concept, either.

Basically, let's say that you need to create a multipage brochure with 5.5" x 8.5" pages, like the one shown in Figure 7–11 and Color Figure 38. To get each panel (or page of the brochure) to measure 5.5" x 8.5" take a standard sheet of 8.5" x 11" copy paper. Fold it in half, along the 11" side. When you do this, you'll see that you now have a small booklet, with four panels, or pages, each measuring 5.5" x 8.5".

Now, take a second sheet of copy paper and fold that one same way. Put one sheet inside of the other sheet, so that the folds of each are together, as illustrated in Figure 7–12, and staple them at the folds. The outside front panel

Figure 7–11: This eight-page brochure was made by folding two pieces of paper into one another.

is the cover, and the outside back panel is the back cover. If you count each page from front to back, you'll see that there are a total of eight pages—two pieces of paper, each with four panels. Therefore, it is impossible to have a booklet in this style with any number of pages. Booklets made from multiple pages stapled together like this are called saddle-stitched.

The other form of binding, called *perfect binding,* is used for longer pieces, such as this book. In pieces that are perfectly bound, the pages are glued to the binding in groups of folded pages called *signatures.* Each signature is printed and glued separately.

Now comes the second part that's tough to grasp. Let's assume that the publication is twenty-four pages (six 11" x 17" spreads, folded into 24 8.5" x 11" panels). Carefully take the staples out of the binding. With all the spreads now independent of each other, find the panel for page one. Lay it flat, and you'll see that page one, the first page, is on the same spread as page 24, the last page. Turn it over, and you'll see that page 2 is on the same spread as page 23. You'll see this same thing on every spread that was in the publication.

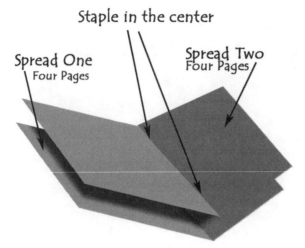

Figure 7–12: When folded, each piece of paper has four panels, so two pieces of paper, times four panels = (2 x 4) = 8 panels, or eight pages.

So what does all this mean to you? Well, if you're working on a 24-page book that is to be saddle-stitched, you will most likely want to lay it out in *readers spreads*—the same order that you would read the publication. Figure 7–13 shows an example of a Quark document laid out in readers spreads. However, although you'll need to do this to understand the logistics and order of the piece, you can't deliver it to a printer like this. Instead, you'll have to tear it apart and relay the project out in *printers spreads*, as shown in Figure 7–14. This will ensure that, when your project is printed and bound, it will make sense to the reader.

Why, you might ask, is this droning monologue about laying pages in QuarkXPress taking up so much space in your Photoshop book? The answer is twofold: First, if you plan on doing any print work, it's important that you understand the marriage between Photoshop and a page layout program, and that Photoshop has little value as an island. Second, setting up pages in printers spreads can be a difficult task, and messing up even by a fraction of an inch can be a costly error. If you're not seasoned at it, you may want to limit your risk of error while designing your Photoshop elements. Printers spreads are a challenge only when there are graphics that continue from one page onto another, such as large backgrounds. Reduce the occurrences of images like this, and you'll reduce your headaches and risk.

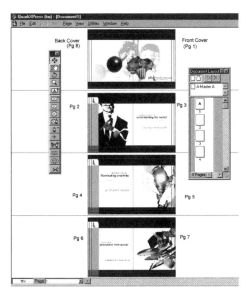

Figure 7–13: This QuarkXPress layout shows my eight-page brochure in readers spreads—the way a reader will view them. I've put each page's respective numbers alongside each panel, with the front cover being page 1, and the back cover being page 8.

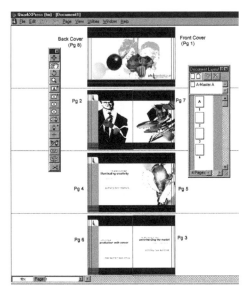

Figure 7–14: The layout in printers spreads is necessary for the pages to line up properly when they are bound after printing. Notice that only the inside and outside spreads of this eight-page piece are affected—the cover and center spreads remained the same as they did in the readers spreads.

◆ **Other Programs:** As you might expect, you're probably going to need more than just Photoshop to complete a printed piece. The most likely programs that you'll have to get to know are:

◆ **Adobe Illustrator:** Illustrator is the most powerful tool on the market when it comes to creating computer line art or illustrations. Illustrator is a vector-based program, which both contrasts and complements Photoshop in a variety of ways. Photoshop is a bitmap program, with higher file size for higher resolution images, and while Illustrator uses a mathematical formula for creating graphics, resulting in a much larger file. Smooth, photographic quality color transitions don't happen in (Illustrator without significant talent and work) so images often have a cartoonish or illustrative quality.

◆ **QuarkXPress (or Adobe PageMaker or InDesign):** Once you create your graphics, you're going to need to lay them out in a page layout program. At the time of this writing, the leading program in the industry is QuarkXPress. These programs will allow you to place images and copy onto multiple pages, and prepare them to be printed.

Large Format

Large-format printing can include any type of project that is significantly larger than a standard-sized piece. These would include posters, banners, or even billboards. Some of these projects, such as movie posters, would be printed by a commercial press, and, therefore designed in a similar fashion as a smaller piece. But there are times when you need a poster or large piece that is either too large for a standard commercial press, or you simply don't require a high enough print run to warrant the expense. This is when you turn to the large-format printer.

Large-format printers are actually quite a bit like your standard desktop color printer, but they can range up to 60" wide, and, because they work off a roll of paper, they have very few limitations on length. Figure 7–15 shows a sample of a bus-side advertisement that my agency printed on a large-format printer.

There are two nice qualities about large-format printing. The first is that they are rarely, if ever, viewed up close, meaning that precise detail can be forgiven. The second is that most large-format printers usually print at only 150 dpi, which means that what might ordinarily be a huge file size (imagine a 60" x 72" poster in CMYK at 300 ppi!) won't really be so bad. In fact, my agency has done quite a few large-format pieces very successfully, without overburdening our systems due to enormous file sizes. For that same piece, 60" x 72", we would create the whole piece instead at 50% size, or 30" x 36", 150-ppi resolution, and instruct the large-format printer to print it at 200%.

And Finally...

There is a hidden but useful command that can be helpful to anybody, but especially to photographers and people who work with higher resolution images, so I'll put this in the print area.

Figure 7–15: This bus-side poster was a large-format print, over 56" wide.

Picture Package

Picture Package is new to version 5.5, and for something that is just tucked away and likely programmed to be just a cute extra in an otherwise intense upgrade, it's really pretty cool.

Remember "picture day" in grammar school? The one day that all the little public school kids didn't come in dressed like slobs and actually combed their hair in the morning? You sat in your seat, flashed your best smile for the camera, and presented the grandparents and obscure relatives from every corner of the nation with their choice of wallet size or 5" x 7" copy of the precious photo. When your pictures arrived from the photo lab, ready to be distributed to the family, they probably looked a lot like the photo page in Figure 7–16.

Well, now Photoshop lets you arrange pictures in this and similar types of layouts through a simple dialog box. To use the Picture Package:

1. Choose File -> Automate -> Picture Package to access the dialog box shown in Figure 7–17.

2. In the Source Image area toward the top of the dialog box, you can decide which image you want to use in your page layout. You don't necessarily have to have your desired image open to turn it into a Picture Package. If it is open, and it's in the active canvas, simply check the box marked *Use Frontmost Document*. If it's not the active canvas, or if your desired image isn't even open, push the Choose button, and navigate through your computer to find the image you want to use.

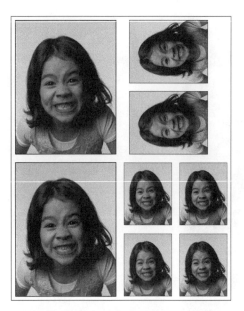

Figure 7–16: One of the many Picture Package layouts.

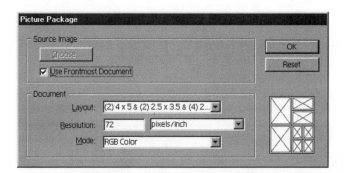

Figure 7–17: The Picture Package dialog box.

3. Select your layout from the Layout pull-down menu in the document area. You'll see that you have a wide selection of layout options to choose from. A graphics image of your selected layout will appear on the right side of the dialog box.

4. Select the resolution of your page. Keep in mind that if you choose a resolution higher or lower than the native image that you are packaging, you'll likely alter your image in unexpected ways (for example, setting the resolution significantly higher than the image you are packaging will likely make it pixilated and blurry).

5. Last, choose the color mode you want for your Picture Package. If you plan to print this off your color desktop printer (or any other color output device), you should select CMYK for your mode selection. Push OK when through.

This is a great tool for the photography and/or desktop publishing hobbyist. If that's you, and you plan to print these type of things from your color desktop, the paper you choose will make as much of an impression as the image itself. I would recommend some of the glossy, photographic-quality paper. This type of paper is usually more expensive, but it's worth the extra cost.

The only drawback of the Picture Package feature is that you can package only one image per page. It would be really cool if you could use multiple images on any one of the available layouts. So, if anybody over at Adobe is reading this book, please rip this page out and put it in the Suggestion Box. Thanks.

DIGITAL DESIGN

When you talk about digital design, or "new media" work, most people automatically think about the Web. This won't come as a surprise to anyone, considering how much press the Web has had in recent years and how much of an effect it has on the economy. The demand for good Web designers was so great, in fact, that the Photoshop released version 5.5 almost strictly to help designers in their Web development work.

It's no secret that the Web has changed a lot of worlds—the commerce world, the investment world, and even the design world. At my agency, of 35 projects we are currently involved in, all but four of them involve a Web site in one way or another. The Web has become such an important means of communication that Adobe gave Web designers their own upgrade with version 5.5. And I have dedicated a whole chapter to it in this book, as well as entire book titled *PhotoShop 6 for the Web To Go*.

But while the Web might be the predominant force or at least the headline grabber, there are other important projects, such as CD-ROMs and DVDs, that also require strong Photoshop skills. This section will review each of these, with particular attention paid to the Web.

WEB SITES

As with print, there are many universal things you'll need to know when it comes to developing Web sites. But there are also specific tools and features within Photoshop that will help not only to make designing more streamlined, but also to make the end result more interesting.

Universal Web Issues

Designing for the Web is a different art form than designing for print. It takes a different set of talent, a different technological understanding, and an ability to think outside the limitations of a linear print piece.

◆ **Resolution:** Resolution issues for Web sites are very simple to understand. Basically, the only resolution you need to work with and create images in is 72 ppi. Since the images will be appearing only on monitors, which display images at 72 ppi, you need to create only one pixel of your image for every pixel of your monitor (a 1:1 ratio).

If you are freelancing or in any position that forces you to do sales, you can use the graphics for any site you create to increase your overall dollars. In a good percentage of the sites you'll create for clients, a print brochure will be needed at some point to accompany the site. Mention this to your clients and offer to create the initial graphics for the site at a higher resolution and to archive them for later print use. You can charge extra for this service, as well as plant a seed for the development of a printed piece in the client's head. Consistency between media vehicles is important—you'll be surprised by the extra money you'll earn by offering this service.

◆ **Color:** Again, since Web imagery will be seen only on a monitor, which works by shooting red, green and blue light into your eyes, you can take full advantage of the RGB gamut and design in this color mode. You can leave your images in RGB if you save your image as a JPEG file. If you're going to save your image as a GIF, though, the color mode will need to be changed to Index Color. You probably won't need to worry about this, though—as you'll read later in this chapter. Photoshop 5.5 introduced the Save for Web dialog box, which basically handles any color mode changes for you.

◆ **Technology:** Fortunately, if you plan on doing only Web-based Photoshop design without dabbling in print at all, you can get away with a relatively weaker computer. The RGB color mode and low-resolution requirements mean that file sizes will also stay quite small—in fact, if you're designing for an audience that will primarily be using 28.8 bps modems, no page should wander much over 100 k in file size anyway.

These lightweight graphics mean that you can get away with a less expensive computer. Although some loyalists would disagree with me, if you can stand to work on a Windows-based PC for Web graphics, I'd recommend it. This is because of ugly color shifts that occur between Macintoshes and PCs (colors tend to look a good deal darker on a PC). Since the majority of the world still views the Web on a PC, you'd be better off designing on one as well, so that you see what your audience will see.

Beyond that, if you're on a tight budget, you can get away with a Pentium II processor with a minimum of 96 megs of RAM. As with print designing, or anything else, really, I'd still recommend a 19" monitor or better to keep from hurting your eyes.

◆ **Special Considerations:** When you print something and watch it come off a press, you know exactly how your audience will be viewing it. They'll see it the same way that you see it. The Web is different, though. How you see the Web on your monitor does not necessarily mean that the rest of the world is seeing it the same way. Keep in mind some of the following points when designing your Web site:

   ◆ **Color:** Even though you'll be designing your site in the same color mode that the rest of the world views it in (RGB), you'll still never be 100% certain as to what they're seeing. Different monitors and different operating systems may cause severe and unwanted shifts in color for many of your images. Although we can assume that, by now, the overwhelming majority of Web viewers have a color monitor, we have no idea of knowing how many colors they can see or how they see them at all.

   Mac users, for example, will see colors lighter than PC users. This means if you're designing on a Mac, try to keep your colors even lighter than you ordinarily would to compensate for the increased darkness PC users will have. Not too long ago, a good portion of monitors could see only 256 colors (8-bit). Even monitors that could see more than that were often left at the factory settings of 256 colors by users who didn't know how to change the settings (or were not even aware that it was an option). This meant that if you include a JPEG photograph with tons of colors, gradients and subtle blends on your Web site, an 8-bit monitor will ignore all but 256 of those colors, likely causing gradients and blends to band and rich color mixtures to become flat.

   Fortunately, times have changed, and the large majority of the Web-viewing public has monitor settings higher than 8-bit. That means that Web developers have more freedom to play with colors and do not have to worry too much about the confines of the user's system.

   ◆ **Download Considerations:** This one is really all over the place. Not too long ago, it was easy to assume that everyone had a 28.8-bps modem. But that's not necessarily the case anymore. With DSL, cable, ISDN, as well as a more simple 56.6-bps modem on the market in wide release, it's hard to know who or how many people have access to high-speed connections. You don't want to create a graphically boring site for people who have high-speed connectivity, but at the same time, you don't want to lose the million ADD sufferers who can't wait longer than a minute for images to download with their 28.8-bps connection.

   For the most part, connection speeds have increased across the board over the last couple of years. This is especially true in the workplace, in which high-bandwidth connectivity has infiltrated rather quickly. Homes have been slower to adapt to connections such as cable or DSL, mostly due to the fact that connection companies have been slower in offering them in all areas. However, 28.8 modem speeds aren't the norm any longer, and you can design for 36.6 or better, in most cases. This provides at least a little leniency for heavier design. While the standard a few years ago was to keep all pages under 150 k, designers now push the limits to 150 k or higher, depending on the audience.

♦ **Pixel Resolution:** We've already established numerous times in this book that, when you're designing for the Web, you can keep the image resolution down to 72 ppi. But as you may or may not know, different monitors provide different resolution displays, or even a choice. Typically, when a monitor comes out of the box, by default it's set to 640 x 480, which means that it will show 640 pixels horizontally across the screen and 480 pixels vertically. Icons, text and other objects, then, will seem rather large.

People can change their monitor resolutions, though. 800 x 600 is arguably the most common setting, as more monitors are increasingly being shipped with this as their default resolution, instead of 640 x 480. Still others (myself included), view the world at 1024 x 768. By comparison, as you increase the resolution of your monitor, the images on the monitor become smaller. Figure 7–18 shows you my desktop at different monitor resolutions.

If you're designing for a general audience, like most of the sites that my agency creates, you'll probably want to design for 800 x 600. This means that some people who have 640-pixel monitors will have to scroll horizontally to see some of the information that falls outside their 640-pixel right-side boundary.

640 x 480   800 x 600   1024 x 768

Figure 7–18: Different monitor resolution settings. The higher the resolution, the lower the objects appear on screen.

Except in very specific cases, you'll usually have to worry only about the horizontal monitor resolution. The object is to keep as few people as possible from having to scroll left and right. Most people on the Web are accustomed to scrolling up and down, so there's little point in concerning yourself with the vertical resolution.

After you decide which resolution you will design for, don't expect to begin your first image on a canvas of equal horizontal width. In other words, if you have decided that you will design your site for an 800-pixel horizontal resolution monitor, don't open a canvas to start your designs that is 800 pixels wide. You have to take into consideration that the vertical scroll bar that may appear on the right side of your browser is about 40 pixels, and each side of the browser itself is a few pixels each, and, finally, that most of your images will automatically be placed with a buffer of at least 5–10 pixels between it and the browser frame. So, if you want to avoid left and right scrolling on an 800-pixel horizontal monitor, you shouldn't build any graphic to be wider than 740–750 pixels.

◆ **Other Programs:** While you can do all of your primary layout in Photoshop, and all of your individual graphics there, as well, you're going to need a little more than Photoshop to build your site.

　　◆ **ImageReady:** Since the release of Photoshop version 5.5, ImageReady has been bundled and packaged with Photoshop. This is a terrific program that works seamlessly with Photoshop to help slice apart graphics and create Java rollovers and even animation. What's even better about it is that it will generate HTML script for you and allow for easy updates to the HTML script if you make any changes.

　　◆ **Macromedia DreamWeaver:** I'm adding this program under protest. Personally, I like very clean HTML—scripts that are hard-coded by hand, not dropped and dragged in some pretty but generic GUI third-party program. But the designers in my agency, who have developed some really complex and highly functional static and e-commerce Web sites, swear by it. After looking at it, I have to say that it does seem easy, and of all the third-party GUI that I've seen, DreamWeaver seems to provide the most flexibility.

　　◆ **Any Simple Text Editor:** No matter how easy DreamWeaver or Web construction set might be, you'll always need to do at least *some* coding or editing by hand. If you own a computer, you already have SimpleText (Macintosh), NotePad or WordPad (Windows). Any of these will do for opening simple documents and doing your own editing.

◆   **Any FTP uploading program:** Once you have a host for your Web site, you're going to need to get your files and images on to it. FTP programs can be found on the Web as free downloads. The best that I've seen are Fetch (Macintosh) or WS_FTP (Windows). Both are simple to use and typically hassle free.

Photoshop Specifics

For each Web site that you put together, there are ways that Photoshop can be a valuable resource over and above the standard design tools that it offers. Special transparency tools, image optimizing/saving features and the inclusion of ImageReady for more dynamic add-ons are important aspects of Photoshop for Web designers.

Transparency Made Easy

Transparency can be a big deal when it comes to Web design. Besides being able to shave at least a little off of the file size of some images, it allows for specific images to be extracted from their backgrounds, in a similar way to how we used TIFF formats with Alpha Channels to extract a main image in a printed layout (discussed earlier in this chapter).

Photoshop 5.5 added a few new masking tools that deal directly with transparency. The Magic Eraser, the Background Eraser and the Extract function each help turn portions of your image into transparencies, which can later be translated for direct Web use in the Save for Web dialog box.

The Magic Eraser

The Magic Eraser, shown in Color Figure 1, works just like the Magic Wand Tool, with one distinct difference: Instead of creating a selection of certain pixels, it makes those pixels transparent. Simply click on a pixel of any color you choose, and all contiguous pixels (by default) within a certain shade of that color will become transparent. Figure 7–19 demonstrates this.

The Options Palette for the Magic Eraser Tool, shown in Figure 7–20, allows you to manipulate how the Eraser Tool works. Access the Options Palette as you would for any other tool by double-clicking on that tool or simply selecting the tool and hitting the <Return> key (<Enter> in Windows). Click on the Contiguous checkbox to the "on" position to keep the erased pixels contiguous to the selected pixel. Click it off to allow noncontiguous pixels of the same or similar shades to be erased.

You can also manipulate how many shades of the selected color will be affected. Set the Tolerance by manually entering a value in the Options Palette to make your transparency smaller or larger. A small value, say, 10, in the Tolerance area will mean that when any pixel is clicked on, the only pixels that will become transparent will be those that fall within 10 shades of that particular color. A higher number will allow more pixels to be affected.

Figure 7–19: The sky was made transparent by the Magic Eraser Tool.

Figure 7–20: The Magic Eraser Options Palette.

 Even though this is an Eraser Tool, you do not need to worry about a brush size—this is a point-and-click tool, and you will be clicking on only one pixel at a time.

The Background Eraser

The Background Eraser, also new in version 5.5 and shown in Figure 7–21, works much like the Magic Eraser if it were crossed with the Airbrush Tool. To make an area of your image become transparent with the Background Eraser, simply select your desired brush size and drag your mouse over the areas of your image that you wish to make transparent. It's just as simple as that, really. There is a cool twist, though—a small center point in the middle of your Background Eraser brush will determine the color of the pixel you click on. As you drag around your image, pixels of that same color will also become transparent.

The Option Palette for the Background Eraser, shown in Figure 7–22, allows you to choose which type of eraser you want to use:

◆   Find Edges will help maintain the integrity of edges of an object, while erasing
    contiguous areas of the same color.

◆   Contiguous will erase all areas in an image that contain the selected colors that are
    next to each other.

◆   Discontiguous erases all areas in an image that contain the selected colors. These
    areas do not have to be next to each other or touching.

The Tolerance slider works the same as it does in the Magic Wand Tool. The higher the
tolerance, the more color tones will be eliminated, based on the selected color.

You can also choose Protect Foreground to make sure that any areas in your image
that contain the Foreground color will not be erased.

Figure 7–23 shows the result of using the Background Eraser Tool.

Figure 7–21: The Tool Palette, with the Background Eraser pointed out.

Figure 7–22: The Background Eraser Options Palette.

Figure 7–23: The Background Eraser at work.

Extract Image

This feature was initially premiered in Photoshop 5.5 and is an excellent resource for creating transparencies around objects that have hard-to-select elements about them, such as fur or wispy hair. While not the perfect feature—it has a few problems—it's still very helpful, and many of the problems have been solved with the addition of two new tools in Photoshop 6.0.

To use the Extract Image command, follow these steps:

1. With your file open, choose Image -> Extract to access the dialog box shown in Figure 7–24.

2. Make the Edge Highlighter Tool active by clicking on it. The Edge Highlighter Tool works just like the Paintbrush Tool—just drag your cursor to create a stroke. However, with this tool, you're not as much applying paint as you are isolating an edge.

3. Create an edge around the object you want to extract—remember, everything outside your edge will become transparent. If necessary, you can increase or decrease your brush size by adjusting the Brush Size slider on the right (sorry—no Brushes Palette here!).

For very hard to define edges, such as shown in the Figures for this example, select a decent size brush, and create your edge outline so that the highlight color overlaps both the image that you want to extract, and the background that you want to make transparent.

If you need help with making your highlighted edge, click the checkbox marked *Smart Highlighting* on the far right of the dialog box. This works in a similar way as the Magnetic Lasso and will create an edge based on the color differential of your image.

4. You can change the color of your highlight by selecting from the Highlight pull-down menu. Red, green and blue are available as presets, or you can access the Color Picker by choosing Other. Once you have created a highlight around the entire edge, activate the Fill Tool (the same paintbucket icon that appears in the regular toolbar). Fill the inside of your edge selection by clicking on it. Make sure that the edge is completely closed before you click or you will fill your entire canvas.

You can edit either the fill or the edge highlight by using the Eraser Tool. You can start over from scratch, too, by holding the <Option> (<Alt> in Windows) key and pushing the Reset button (former <Cancel> button).

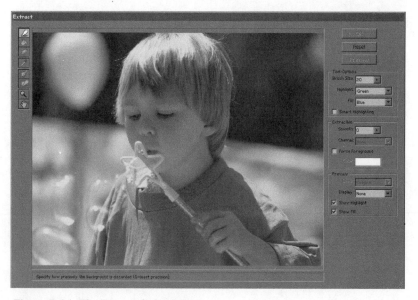

Figure 7–24: The Extract dialog box.

5. You can change the fill color by using the Fill pull-down menu. Figure 7–25 shows what the preview window should look like at this point. Decide how precise you would like your extraction by changing the Smooth slider in the extraction area. Choose a lower number for less precision and a higher number for greater precision (although this will take a few moments longer to complete).

6. Click the Preview button to see your extracted piece. Cool, huh? Figure 7–26 shows a sample of what this should look like.

You might notice that the Preview button is grayed out and not available until you fill your selection. If you would like to make an extraction of just the highlighted area (I'm sure that with 6 billion people in the world, *somebody* will find a reason to do this), click the Force Foreground button. The color that is chosen in the accompanying color display will be the color in the highlight that is retained. Click this display to access the Color Picker or make a direct selection using the Eyedropper Tool and selecting a color from your image.

7. When Photoshop 5.5 introduced the Extract feature, many Web designers applauded the idea, but had some trouble with the execution and the result—it didn't always work without a few problems. As you can see, we have a few problems ourselves with the image that we just extracted. Although the hair looks good, with only a few problems, the boy's shirt seems as though it's been through a war. To fix this, use the Clean-Up Tool, which largely works as an eraser, or the Edge Touchup Tool, which will add to or subtract from an edge to help make it smoother.

Hold down the <Command> key (<Ctrl> in Windows) to move the edge highlight outward, returning some of the image pixels that were made transparent.

8. To see your edge highlight and fill again, click the appropriate checkboxes to make each appear. Re-edit if necessary.

9. By default, the transparent areas will appear as a checkerboard. You can change this by selecting a Matte color from the Show pull-down menu (customize your color in the Color Picker by choosing Other, or see your results as they would be represented in a Channel by choosing Mask).

10. To go back to your original image, Choose Original from the View pull-down menu. Return to the extraction by selecting Extracted from the same menu.

Figure 7–25: The Extract dialog box with the highlight and fill applied to the areas to be extracted.

Figure 7–26: The image has been extracted from the background. Notice how the whisps in the hair have survived, although there were a few minor problems, especially in the shirt area.

11. If you already have a selection saved as an Alpha Channel, you can use this as a starting point by loading it in from the Load Highlight pull-down menu.

12. Click OK when you are happy with your extraction. Figure 7–27 shows the result.

Saving Images

Photoshop 5.5 introduced us to the Save for Web feature shown in Figure 7–28. Accessed by choosing File -> Save for Web, this function has helped trim down a tremendous amount of time that used to be spent on trial-and-error style optimization.

Divided into one, two or four preview windows, Save for Web allows you to compare and contrast up to three images optimized at different settings against the original. As the figure shows, each preview window provides you with not only a review of the variables that you've set (or that Photoshop chose for you by default), but also the file size associated with the image and how long that image would take to download at different speeds of modems.

To use the Save for Web dialog box, click on any of the preview windows except the window in the upper left that shows the original. (This is assuming that you are working in 4-up mode. The various modes are provided in tabs along the top of the dialog box.) A dark outline shows you which preview window is currently active.

In the command area on the far right, you have the ability to set the parameters that you wish, starting with choosing either GIF or JPEG as the desired format.

Figure 7–27: The extracted image after it has been touched up and has had the edge highlights extended.

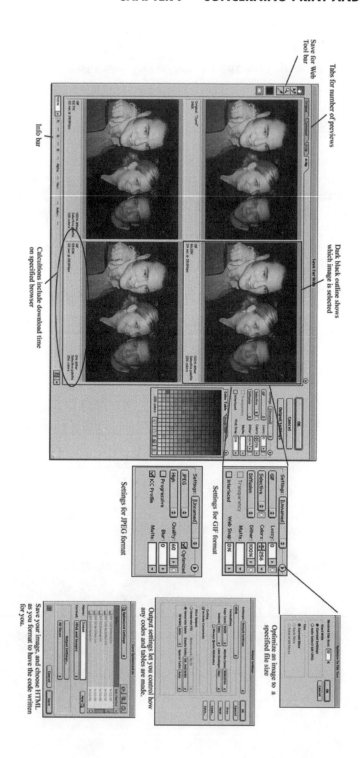

Figure 7–28: The Save for Web dialog box.

You have the option of choosing .PNG as the desired format, as well, but as .PNG is so rarely used, we won't review it in this explanation.

The following is a quick list of the options that come with each desired format and a brief explanation of what each means and allows you to do. The first pull-down menu in the upper left of the control area columns allows you to select the desired file format. For a more complete explanation, check out my other book, *Web Photoshop 6 Primer*.

Options for Saving GIF Images

The GIF format is usually chosen for images that have flat colors without many smooth color transitions. This keeps the file size down as fewer colors are needed. GIFs are also popular because they support transparency and allow for animation.

As shown earlier in Figure 7–28, there are many options associated with saving your image as a GIF, which include the following (Each is listed as they appear in the Save for Web Dialog box, starting below the format selection pull-down menu and moving downward through the first column of options. The titles that appear in this list do not appear in the dialog box unless you move your cursor over the pull-down menu and leave it there for a couple of seconds.):

◆ Color Reduction Algorithm: Choose from a number of different color palettes for your image. Different palettes will structure the colors in your image differently and can have an effect not only on file size but also on how the image appears on screen.

◆ Dithering Algorithm: Dithering affects the ways in which the colors work together and potentially overlap to create the appearance of colors that don't actually exist in the image. Choose a dithering type or not to dither at all.

◆ Transparency: If a portion of your image has been made transparent, check this box to turn the transparency on.

◆ Interlaced: Check this box to allow your image to load all at once, but very blurry. It will become more clear in a series of "steps." Leave it off to have the image download more slowly from top to bottom, one at a time.

◆ Lossy: Use this slider to compress your GIFs further by reducing unnecessary colors. More compression will mean lower files sizes but will also deteriorate the quality of your images.

◆ Colors: Similar to the Lossy slider, use this value area to determine the number of colors that will exist in your image. The lower the number of colors, the lower the file size, but the worse your image may look.

◆ Dither: If you chose Diffusion as your Dithering algorithm (discussed earlier), you'll be able to use this slider to set the level of diffusion in your image.

◆ Matte: The Matte color will replace the transparent areas of an image if the Transparency button is turned off. If the Transparency button is on, the Matte color will place a thin line around the image to create an easier transition to the browser background. Choose a color or turn Matte off completely.

◆ Web Snap: Use this to determine how many of the existing colors will snap to the nearest Web-safe color. "Web-safe" colors are colors that will look the same on both Mac and PC monitors and were more important to worry about when more people had 8-bit monitors (discussed earlier in this chapter).

Options for Saving JPEG Images

Designers will more often choose the JPEG format because it allows for millions of colors and creates smaller file sizes for photographic images that have lots of color transitions.

The following are the options that you'll have when you select JPEG for your image format:

◆ Compression Quality: Four basic, self-explanatory choices here, the higher the quality selected, the better the image will look, but the higher the file size will be.

◆ Progressive: Similar to the Interlacing of GIF images, turning Progressive on will change the way your image appears as it downloads. It will also increase the file size, and a few older browsers may not recognize a progressive JPEG.

◆ ICC Profile: If you set up the ICC profile as discussed in Chapter 1, you can embed the profile with the image to ensure that the colors look as close to the original as possible, regardless of where the image is viewed.

◆ Optimized: This box will help reduce the file size even further, particularly if the Compression Quality is set to "high." But not every browser will recognize an Optimized JPEG.

◆ Quality: Where the Compression Quality selection gave you four choices, the Quality slider lets you be more specific. Use the slider for more discrimination in the exact quality of your image.

◆ Blur: Blurring your image will reduce the colors and, therefore, reduce the file size. Use this slider to blur your image slightly in an attempt to make the file size smaller. You're better off blurring your image with one of the Blur filters before you open the Save for Web dialog box, though.

◆ Matte: Since JPEGs don't support transparency, choose the Matte color that will replace any portion of your image that may be transparent.

As you make your selections and set each variable, the active preview will change to show what the image will look like in a browser, as will the file size readings and the download time required for certain modem speeds. When you click OK, the image in the active preview window will save under a file name that you supply.

Web Photo Gallery

Another nice feature will particularly appeal to Web designers who put up galleries of images on their sites. The new Web Photo Gallery is located in the Automation menu and, by your direction, will take the contents of any folder and create thumbnails of all the images the folder contains. Even better, it will write the HTML code for you to arrange the icons on the page, as well as link them to a larger version of each! Cool, useful, and easy—what more would you want?

To set up the Web Photo Gallery:

1. Select File -> Automate -> Web Photo Gallery to access the dialog box shown in Figure 7–29.

2. In the Files section, use the Choose buttons to select both the source and destination folders for your images. Click the Include All Subdirectories checkbox if you want to include images that may be in subdirectories of the one you have chosen.

3. Fill in any note information about yourself, the site and the date in the Site section.

4. Select the size you would desire for your thumbnails in the only pull-down menu of the Thumbnails category. If the available options (Small, Medium and Large) strike you as somewhat vague, that's because they are somewhat vague.

5. Click the Resize Gallery Images checkbox to activate this section and allow your users to view larger versions of all icons. Use the corresponding Size and Quality areas to determine how large, small, detailed or not detailed your images should be.

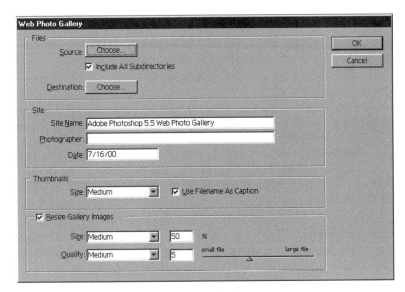

Figure 7–29: The Web Photo Gallery dialog box.

Remember, you have no idea of how large the finished file size will be, nor will you know the image quality or how long it will take for a user to download. Don't do this completely in the dark. I would recommend testing a few of the images that you want to include in your gallery by going through this process with just one or two images in your folder first. That way you can test it without wasting valuable time creating a large gallery that you may not end up using, due to high file size or poor quality.

Click OK when through. The HTML text will be placed in the same folder as your images. Just cut and paste this into your existing HTML text.

The ImageReady Addition

Once a stand-alone program, ImageReady became a bundled part of Photoshop with the release of Photoshop 5.5. A strictly Web-based application, ImageReady allows for the easy creation of rollovers and animation. While a full description of each of these falls outside the scope of this book, it is important to understand how ImageReady works with Photoshop, and what is probably the most important feature in ImageReady—the ability to slice images.

ImageReady And Photoshop: How They Differ, How They Work Together

One of the nicest things about most of the Adobe products (I haven't seen them all, so I'll protect myself with use of the word *most*) is that they all utilize a standard interface and production layout. This allows you, the designer, to find your way around a variety of programs quickly, so that even if you don't know the details, you're already at home with the generalities. Even Illustrator 9, which works with vector images, as opposed to Photoshop's bitmap pictures (Photoshop is still a bitmap program, even with the few vector additions of the Shape Tool and new Type Tool), looks remarkably similar to Photoshop, even though their methods of creating and manipulating graphics are technically quite different.

The same holds true for Photoshop and ImageReady. In fact, the interface between the two programs looks so much alike that I sometimes find myself having to look at the icon at the top of the Tool Palette, just to see which program I'm currently in. Unlike Illustrator, however, which is purely a stand-alone program and can work with Photoshop with a mutual diplomacy, ImageReady has been engineered to be more of an extension of Photoshop. Much of the tools are the same, as are the ways in which you may go about applying color corrections, working with layers, etc.

But for there to be a need for each program to exist independently from each other, they each have to do things that the other doesn't. In general, you'll be working most efficiently if you do the majority of your creating, manipulating, selecting, correcting and retouching in Photoshop, and leave minor touch-up work to ImageReady for last-minute changes. ImageReady's main function will be the special Web effects that Photoshop can't come close to accomplishing: creating slices, animations and rollovers for your Web site.

Quantum Leap: Jumping Between Programs

Adobe has made this very simple. Instead of the annoyance one might expect by having to save an image in one program and reopen it in another Adobe has added a simple feature to the bottom of the Tool Palette of each program. Shown in Color Figure 1, the Jump To button gives you easy access to either program, with virtually no hassles. To use the button, simply press the button (or choose File -> Jump To -> ImageReady).

Slicing Images

One of the most effective methods of ensuring that a large image or an image that contains multiple animations will download quickly on a Web site is to cut the image into pieces and put them back together in an HTML table.

The process of Image Slicing in older versions of Photoshop, before 5.5 bundled ImageReady in with the Photoshop package, was long and tedious. Once your image was complete, you needed to set all of your guides to mark the areas you wanted to slice. Then, with the Marquee Tool, each piece had to be individually selected, made into a unique file, and saved individually. Because different segments would be optimized differently and the size of each will undoubtedly vary, setting an Action would usually be of little help. Then came the really boring part—creating the intricate table in your HTML text and testing it in your browser, just to find that you were one pixel off when creating one segment, and you had to start all over again from scratch.

Every Web developer has had to deal with this misadventure at some point, to the tune of endless frustration. But 5.5 changed that a bit, by giving us ImageReady and the Slice Tool. When I sat in the production room of my agency, teaching our developers how to create slices using ImageReady, their eyes widened as if they had just seen the most amazing invention ever created. Literally hours could be saved, and the new process was so easy to learn!

In Photoshop 6.0, you'll probably notice that the Slice Tool and the Slice Select Tool have migrated over to the Photoshop side. But I would recommend that you still create your slices in ImageReady instead, where the process is more functional and streamlined.

Creating slices merely comes down to mastering one tool—the Slice Tool, shown in Color Figure 1. If you know how to use the Rectangular Marquee Tool, then you know how to use the Slice Tool. There are, however, a lot of options and nuances that you need to learn to take full advantage of the slice function, so without further babbling…

1. In the toolbar, make the Slice Tool active by clicking on it. You'll see a slight change in your image, as a gray outline with symbols in the upper left corner suddenly appears. ImageReady places this there automatically to indicate that the original slice is the image itself.

2. With the Slice Tool, drag with your cursor to select the area where you want to make your first slice. This will feel much like using the Rectangular Marquee Tool, and much of the controls are exactly the same. For example, dragging while holding the <Shift> key will constrain the proportions, holding the <Option> key (<Alt> in Windows) will allow you to drag from the middle instead of the corner, etc.

3. For the sake of this example, let's suppose that you create your first slice from the upper left corner of your image. The result would look similar to Figure 7–30. Notice, however, that two other slices suddenly accompany the slice you just created.

Figure 7–30: Slicing up an image.

4. If you are familiar with how HTML tables are created, you will easily understand that the other slices are necessary to properly assemble your image in HTML. These slices, generated by Photoshop, are called *auto-slices*. Auto-slices differ in quality from the slice you created, otherwise known as a *user-slice*. User-slices have more functionality to them and are displayed with the full color of your image, as opposed to the slightly washed-out look which delineates the auto-slices (both auto-slices and user-slices are reviewed in full in my other book, *Web Photoshop 6 Primer*).

5. Continue using the Slice Tool to make further slices to your image. As you create more user-slices, more auto-slices are also created to fill your entire image, until such a time as you have filled your image with auto-slices.

6. As you create slices, you will notice that each individual slice is numbered. Slices are numbered from left to right, with slice number 1 residing in the upper-left portion of your image.

If you are more comfortable creating slices from guides you have set, you can do this, as well. Simply place the guides in such a way that they break up your image as desired. Then choose Slice -> Create Slice from Guides. All slices created will be user-slices and will be created in place of any slices that already exist.

7. When you are through creating your slices, you can make each one into a separate link by selecting a slice and filling in the hyperlink address in the URL area of the Slice Palette (Window -> Show Slice).

8. Save your file by choosing File -> Save Optimized As. ImageReady will place all of the sliced images into a separate folder and supply you with the HTML text that you need to assemble them in a browser.

CD-ROM AND DVD INTERFACE DESIGN

With the renaissance that print is experiencing and the hype that the Web generates on a constant basis, CD-ROM and DVDs get little press. This is a bit surprising, considering that the demand from companies for either of these items as sales and promotional tools has been steadily on the rise. With the coming boom of "cyber cards" (you heard the prediction here first, folks), the demand for CD-ROM and DVD interface artists and programmers will increase even more.

A "cyber card" is a CD-ROM on the back of what looks like a standard business-card. They're generally business-card size, if not 1/16" larger and fit snugly into the CD-ROM drive of any computer. The best I've seen so far hold up to 40 megs of info, which can include graphics, inter-activity, voice and music overlays or even small video clips.

In my opinion, designing CD-ROM interfaces can be one of the more enjoyable Photoshop art forms that an artist can get involved in. They're as easy to create as Web images, but without the download or scrolling concerns that you have to worry about on the Web. The resolution, color and technology issues are pretty much the same as they are for the Web (described earlier in this chapter), and the special considerations aren't nearly as complex. At least, not for the designer's job, anyway. You'll still want to take into consideration any color shifts that may occur between Macs and PCs, although most corporate CD-ROM or DVD developers will usually know their audience (there is a finite amount of CD-ROMs or DVDs that will be pressed and distributed) and, in my experience, that audience is typically PC-based.

Once you know the monitor resolution you will be designing for (likely to be 800 x 600), you can open a canvas of that size and have a wide-open canvas to be creative with. Because it's playing locally, instead of being downloaded from the Web, there won't be any file size issues to deal with, and it's very rare that a CD-ROM or DVD would ever scroll for more information, unless it was specifically designed to do so.

Figure 7–31 and Color Figure 39 show a few examples of CD-ROM and DVD interfaces that my agency has developed in Photoshop. You can see that this can be a very fun, very imaginative medium to design for.

Figure 7–31: A random collection of CD-ROM and DVD interfaces that were created in Photoshop.

SUMMARY

Even with the fluctuations in the markets, the demand for graphic designers remains high. While the first step is to understand Photoshop as a general tool, breaking into the design field and being a useful member of a team will involve having a more intense knowledge of specific fields, such as print or Web development. Fortunately, Photoshop plays a major role in both, and combines well with other programs to enhance your abilities as a designer to produce quality work.

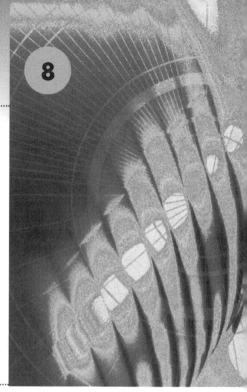

chapter 8

AUTOMATION, FILTERS AND ADVANCED IMAGERY

Once you have all of the tools and commands down, and understand how they can work and work together, you can put all the pieces in place and create some great effects. Filters, which are some of the more fun commands in Photoshop, allow you to really unleash your imagination.

This final chapter will discuss filters in general, review some of the more useful ones (the ones that you need for actual work, and not just for effect) and describe how to combine their use for a composite effect. Some of the examples in this chapter don't use filters at all—but they're provided because they're still useful effects.

But before we get to that, we need to look at the one final feature that allows us to automate our work a bit and make creating any effect even easier.

THE ACTIONS PALETTE

The Photoshop version of creating "macros," the Actions Palette helps to streamline your work and saves you loads of valuable time. By recording actions, you can perform a complex set of functions that can replay repeatedly through any number of images. The Action Palette is shown and described in Figure 8–1.

As an example of a simple Action, let's say that you are going to be arranging a number of images for a brochure that you are designing. All of the images are going to be the same size (2.5" x 1.5"), with the same treatment (an inner bevel). Figure 8–2 shows the images which have already been scanned in. You won't be able to tell, but take my word for it: they are each in RGB color and are twice the size of what is needed (5" x 3"). We want them to be 50% smaller, changed to CMYK mode and treated with the bevel effects.

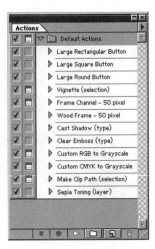

Figure 8–1: The Actions Palette has made tedious work quicker and easier.

Figure 8–2: These images need to be uniform.

To make the preceding into an Action, we do the following steps on one of the open images:

1. In the Action menu options (accessed through the arrow in the upper right of the palette) choose New Action. The dialog box in Figure 8–3 appears. I recommend

giving New Actions a name. For this example, I've named my Action *CMYK, 50%sm, bevel* to remember later what this action does. I also allocated a keyboard command for the action by selecting the function key <F2 + Shift>, which I knew was available. Hit OK.

I knew this command was available because the portion of the New Action dialog box that allows you to create keyboard shortcuts will allow shortcuts only if the key combination is not already used.

2. Notice on the Action Palette that the "Record" icon (the classic red circle) is highlighted to show that it is recording.

3. Choose Image -> Mode -> CMYK to change the color mode for printing (this is a paper brochure, not a Web-based one).

4. Choose Image -> Image Size and reduce the Print Size width to 50%. As long as the Constrain Proportions box is checked, the height will also reduce by 50%. Hit OK.

5. Select All, and choose Layer -> Layer Via Cut to place the image on another Layer instead of the Background Layer (this is necessary for the Bevel effects, which will be reviewed in Appendix A).

6. From the Layer Effects pop-up menu at the bottom of the Layers Palette, choose Bevel and Emboss. Set your desired inner bevel (again, details on how to do this will be reviewed in Appendix A).

7. Flatten your image by choosing Flatten from the Layers Palette pull-down menu.

8. Push the "Stop" icon (the universal square) at the bottom of the Action Palette to stop recording. You have just finished making your first action.

9. Make a different image active by clicking on it. Play your Action by either pushing the "Play" icon (the universal triangle) at the bottom of the Action Palette or setting a keyboard command, as I did <F1 + Shift>.

The Action plays without you having to go through each tedious step. Figure 8–4 shows the process.

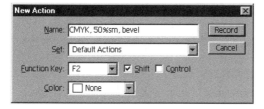

Figure 8–3: The New Action dialog box.

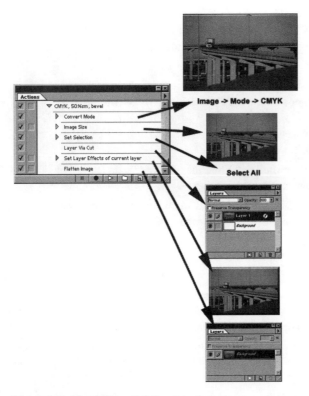

Figure 8–4: The Actions Palette at work.

Batching Actions

What's even easier than having an Action do all the work for you on open images? Having an Action do all the work for you on closed images, of course! (Who knows, by Photoshop 7 or 8, maybe our images will just design themselves...although if Photoshop 6 is any indication, version 7 or 8 may require too much RAM for anybody to actually open it.) Use the Batch option to perform your action on a folder full of images.

1. Simply select your desired Action and choose File -> Automate -> Batch to access the dialog box in Figure 8–5.

2. Select the source where all of the images that you want to run the Action on are located (if they're not located in the same folder, either batch process multiple times—once for each folder—or move all images into one directory before you begin this process.

3. Select your desired folder, sit back and relax.

Figure 8–5: The Batch dialog box makes using Actions even easier. Pretty soon we won't have to do any of our own work at all!

Viewing an Action before Completion

If you create a particularly long and involved Action (or even a short one, for that matter), you can stop it in midstream to judge for yourself the progress of the Action and decide whether you wish the Action to continue. To do this, Choose Insert Stop from the Action Palette menu. Enter any message you wish in the text field and check the box for Allow Continue. When an Action is played and the stop is reached, your message will be displayed and you're given the choice of stopping or continuing. You won't be able to make any changes, but you'll at least be able to judge whether you want the action to complete.

Forcing Menu Items To Work

There may be instances when you try to record a command and you can't, because it's grayed out. You can force the Action Palette to recognize it by choosing the Insert Menu option from the Action Palette pull-down menu. Type in the name of the command and click the Find button. You'll be able to insert functions into your actions that would otherwise be unavailable to you.

Changing the Look of the Palette

Due to the specific nature of the commands placed in each Action, the palette can get to looking somewhat jumbled. One way that you can alleviate this problem is the obvious—close any of the triangles on the side that are open, exposing the Action contents.

The more efficient way to clean up the palette is the convenient ability to turn each Action into a button. To do this, make sure you are not currently recording an Action, and choose Button Mode from the pull-down menu. The benefit of this is in its simplicity: If you've named your Actions well or applied a specific color to them (in the New Action dialog box), each will be easy to find. You also won't need to click on the Play button anymore—just push the button that applies to the Action you want to run.

The downside is that you cannot edit or move an Action while in Button Mode. You also can't create new Actions. If you need to do any of these things, simply choose Button Mode again from the palette pull-down menu.

Creating and Saving Sets

Although this is a relatively simple process, you'll find it useful as you work on images for your Web pages, especially for aspects such as buttons, which often assume the same properties and dimensions. To begin a set, choose New Set from the Action Palette pull-down menu. You can create new Actions within this Set, or you can move already existing Actions by dragging them into the Set folder.

To Save a set, click on the Set name and choose Save Actions from the palette pull-down menu. Place the Set in your desired directory.

The next time you want to use that particular Set, simply choose Load Actions from the palette pull-down menu.

Some Useful Actions—My Personal List

There are any number of combinations of commands you can put together to create an Action. The following constitutes a short list of the Actions that I have found useful in creating content for the Web. I have also tried to assign keyboard commands to as many as possible, also in the name of time saving and convenience. (Isn't it amazing that I have to resort to an actual key to run an Action, instead of using the mouse to push the Play button? A hundred years ago, people still churned their own butter....):

◆ Duplicate	◆ Add Drop Shadow 50%
◆ Duplicate 2x	◆ Add Drop Shadow 75%
◆ Duplicate 4x	◆ Copy & Paste
◆ Add Emboss	◆ Change Hue + 10
◆ Cut & Paste	◆ Change Hue + 30
◆ Create New Layer	◆ RGB: GIF
◆ Duplicate Layer	◆ Save: Close

FILTERS: THE MUSCLE BEHIND THE BRAINS

Yes, Photoshop is a very smart program. Brilliant, even. But if Photoshop's Layers and Channels Palettes are the graphic design equivalent of Albert Einstein, then its Filters menu is a digital Arnold Schwartzenegger. Filters will likely be the power behind many of the truly great works that you create—depending on how you use them. Take it easy with them, use them conservatively, and they'll shine like a candle. Let your imagination run away with you and allow yourself to experiment with various combinations, and the results can be explosive!

Okay, that was a whole lot of analogies for one short paragraph. But I think you get my point. This chapter will introduce you to some of the more important Photoshop filters, as well as a few examples of how some filters can be used together.

A Few Notes about Filters

Before we get into the filters themselves, there are a few things we should go over. We'll quickly take a look at some of these things before diving into the really fun stuff and see what they can each do.

So, What Is a Filter?

Filters are like small programs contained within Photoshop. Each of these small "programs" is focused on accomplishing a specific task that in some way has an effect on your image or selection. These effects can range from giving your image a canvaslike texture, turning it into a watercolor painting, distorting it beyond recognition or even giving it a three-dimensional appearance.

Photoshop comes with a lot of really cool filters already installed in its system. It's very possible to get through life on these alone and not have to look anywhere else. But when you get bored of these, or need to accomplish an effect that simply can't get done or done efficiently with the current Photoshop offerings, there are seemingly endless amounts of other filters on the market to choose from. These "third-party" filters include everything from the way-overused "page curl" to tools for creating spheres, fire, smoke and complex textures. We'll take a look at some third-party filters toward the end of this chapter.

The filters that come with Photoshop are arranged and offered under the Filters menu, in various subcategories. The subcategories give a vague but useful idea as to what the filters contained within will do.

Where Do Filters Come From?

You may have noticed the rapidly changing words on the splash screen that appear every time you launch Photoshop. If you're observant, you may have also noticed that some of these words say *Loading Filters*, and are followed by a very rapidly changing list of all the filters that Photoshop has installed in its system.

So where do these filters reside? All of the filters that come with Photoshop are stored in a Filters folder within the Photoshop folder itself. If you open the Filters folder, you'll see a number of other directories, all of which house some or most of the filters (the two directories marked *Filters* and *Effects* hold the bulk) that you can use in Photoshop.

With the exception of the filters contained in the directory marked *Photoshop Only*, all of the filters contained here will also appear in ImageReady.

The reason you need to know this is because, at some point, you're going to want to add more filters to Photoshop or, in the event of an upgrade, you'll want to move your current filters to your updated version (the upgrade will install with a new, original Filters folder).

If you have purchased third-party filters, simply drag them into the Filters folder in the Photoshop main directory. If Photoshop is currently running when you do this, you'll have to quit and restart the program before you can use your new filters.

If you have installed a newer version of Photoshop (say from 5.5 to 6.0) and your Filters folder is already populated with new, third-party filters, place only these into the upgrade's Filters folder. Don't make the mistake of simply replacing the new Filters folder with the old one—the upgrades often come with new filters that you will lose if you replace the entire directory.

Which Filters Are Offered at What Time?

You won't be able to use all of the filters that Photoshop has to offer any time that you want. Some or all of the filters will be unavailable to you at various times, depending on what you're doing or how your file is set up.

The following list will outline some of the instances in which filters will not be available and what to do to change that:

◆ If you are in CMYK mode, you'll find that many of the filters (and entire filter categories) that you want to use will be unavailable. I'm not really sure why that is, and I'm sure there is a brilliantly sleep-inducing reason behind it, but to tell you the truth, I haven't been interested enough to look into it. To solve this problem, just temporarily change your image into RGB mode by choosing Image -> Mode -> RGB.

◆ No filters will be directly available to you if you have a text Layer active. On some systems, the entire Filters menu is grayed out. On others, Filters are available, but choosing them will tell you that you must render the Layer first, and that proceeding with the filter will cause your text to no longer be editable.

The reason for this is that some filters can really distort the hell out of a graphic. Since text in the newer versions of Photoshop is editable at any point, applying a filter to it would force Photoshop not only to edit the text, but also to apply a filter to the new letters, fonts and sizes at the same time. To avoid this, choose Layer -> Type -> Render Layer. This will cause your text to become a simple graphic, and you won't be able to edit it, but you'll be able to apply any filter that you'd like.

If you're worried about losing editability, consider recording the sequence of filters that you applied as an Action. Then you can go back in your History, edit the text, then reapply all the filters quickly.

◆ As a quick mention, if you apply a filter to a Layer that is linked to another Layer, the filter will affect only the active Layer—not the linked Layers as well.

◆ If you are trying to apply a filter to a transparent area, you could run into one of two problems.

   ◆ The first is that you might be trying to apply a filter that needs to have something to interact with, such as the Charcoal Filter or the Lens Flare filter. For some of these choices, you're going to have to accept the fact that you simply can't apply them to transparency (after all, you need an image to turn into charcoal to see the effect, right?). For others, there is a simple procedure you do take that will "trick" Photoshop into applying the filter anyway (this "trick" is described in detail later in the section).

   ◆ The second problem you might run into when trying to apply a filter to transparent areas of your image is that it simply won't work. Filters such as Clouds, which should fill a Layer or selection with clouds, regardless of whether the area is transparent, may just not work. If this happens, check to make sure that the Preserve Transparency button on your Layers Palette is in the off position.

"Tricking" Photoshop into Making Some Filters Work

As I mentioned earlier, some filters won't work on transparency. The Lens Flare Filter, for example, needs something for the light to reflect off of in order to work. Figure 8–6 shows what happens when I apply the Lens Flare Filter to the active Layer, Layer 4. I want to see what a Lens Flare will look like over the entire image but, unfortunately, the filter affected only the small area of image on Layer 4—it had no effect at all on the transparent regions of that Layer.

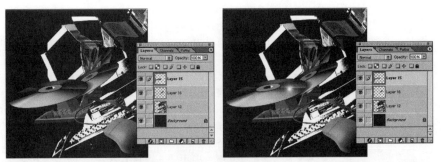

Figure 8–6: The Lens Flare Filter affects only images on a Layer, not the transparent portions, so I can't see how the filter looks over the composite.

Okay, so, I'll create another Layer above the whole image and apply the Lens Flare to that Layer. That way, I can see the Lens Flare over the entire image. But when I select Lens Flare from the Filters menu, I get a message that Photoshop cannot complete the command because my area is empty.

Well, I can always flatten my image and apply the filter…but I don't want to do that yet—I still have a lot more work to do on the image. But there is one thing that I *can* do to see what my image would look like over the unflattened composite:

1. Choose New Layer from the Layer Palette menu to access the New Layer dialog box.

Figure 8–7: Working with the Blend Modes on a new, empty Layer will "trick" Photoshop so that the filter can be applied and shown over a composite.

2. In the Mode pull-down menu, select Screen and check the box marked "Fill with Screen-neutral color (black)."

> **This is good for filters that will apply a light-colored effect, such as Lens Flare. If you are applying a filter that will cause a darker effect, choose Multiply from the Mode pull-down menu and check the box marked "Fill with Multiply-neutral color (white)."**

3. You'll see in your Layers Palette that your new Layer is not transparent as it would ordinarily be, but filled with black, even though your canvas is not filled with black. (Weird, huh?)

4. You can apply the Lens Flare Filter to the entire Layer now, seeing it against the composite, without having to flatten your image. Figure 8–7 and Color Figure 42 illustrate.

A Recommendation

It's easy to fall into one of two traps when it comes to filters: special effect intoxication leading to gross overuse and fear of ruining a piece, which leads to underuse. Or, in simple terms, using it way too much or way too little. My advice is to play. A lot. You're not going to blow the computer up, no matter how many filters you apply, so go ahead and experiment. Use the History Palette often and take multiple snapshots so you won't worry about ruining your work. You might be surprised by the results your experiments will have.

At the same time, don't go overboard, adding different filters to every available space in your image. Nobody wants to see any more pieces with a page curl in the corner, two or three cheesy lens flares, all over a pond-ripple background. It's been done. Over and over again. And it looks obvious. Really successful use of filters become part of the image themselves without standing apart and screaming "Hey, look at me! I'm a filter!"

Most important, if you are going to experiment, have a paper and pen handy. If possible, write down some of combinations and settings that you try. You'll often have what I like to call a "happy accident"—a really good result that was completely unexpected. It's frustrating when that happens and you forgot what you had done to achieve it. Taking notes can keep that from happening.

The "Practical" Filters

The "practical" filters are the ones whose purpose includes both special effects and some useful function for enhancing, correcting or otherwise adjusting your image. While there are others beyond what's listed here, these are some of the ones that you'll likely use in your work on a regular basis.

Gaussian Blur

This is the most powerful way to blur your entire image or portions of it. Much more powerful than the Blur Tool. Figure 8–8 illustrates this.

Motion Blur

As you'll see in other areas of this book, you'll probably be more likely to use Motion Blur Filter in specific ways for special effect purposes, rather than just to blur an image such as in Figure 8–8. Also, notice that the outer edges of the picture don't take to the Motion Blur Filter as well as the middle does—something you should keep in mind when using this filter. Figure 8–9 shows an example.

Figure 8–8: The Gaussian Blur Filter at work.

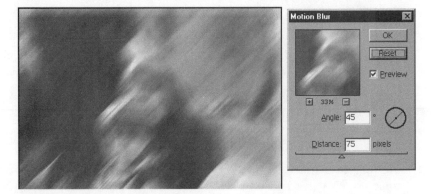

Figure 8–9: The Motion Blur Filter.

Add Noise

Besides being a good filter for graphic effect purposes, try to add some noise to large fields of color when sending an image to print on either a large-format or digital press. It will help keep the color from banding up. Figure 8–10 provides a sample.

Unsharp Mask

A stupid name for a powerful filter. The Unsharp Mask, shown in Figure 8–11, is the best way to sharpen an image—as powerful as all the other sharpen filters combined and significantly more powerful than the Sharpen Tool, which doesn't really work.

Figure 8–10: The Add Noise Filter.

Figure 8–11: The Unsharp Mask shown in an extreme example of use.

COOL EFFECTS

It may sound cliché, but it's true: the amount of effects that you can create in Photoshop is limited only by your imagination and willingness to experiment. There are an infinite amount of combinations that you can devise for putting commands together and with each new combination can come a new look or even a way to develop an old look more easily.

The following are a few random "recipes" you can use to create some interesting effects for yourself. Try each one, then try to take each one a step further on your own—you'll be surprised by the results.

Water Droplets

This one uses a number of filters in addition to some Layer Effects to add realism.

1. Create a new canvas, 5" x 5", 72 ppi, RGB color.

2. With the Background Layer active (I know, I've preached against using the Background Layer to work on, but in this case, we can make an exception), choose Filter -> Noise -> Add Noise to access the dialog box shown in Figure 8–12.

3. Set the Noise amount to 550, with both Uniform and Monochromatic selected. Hit OK.

4. Choose Filter -> Blur -> Gaussian Blur. Set the Radius to 2.6 pixels. Hit OK. Figure 8–13 shows your canvas at this point.

5. Push <Command + L> (<Ctrl> in Windows) to access the Level dialog box. Set the Input Levels to 128, .078 and 145. Hit OK. Figure 8–14 shows your canvas at this point.

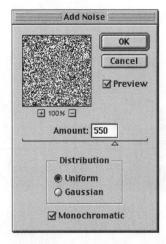

Figure 8–12: The Add Noise dialog box.

Figure 8–13: The Add Noise Filter makes your canvas look like a TV without reception.

Increasing the Shadow levels will make each drop bigger and create more drops. Increasing the Highlights will create fewer, smaller drops. Manipulating the Midtones will affect the thickness and visibility of your drops.

6. Use the Magic Wand Tool to select all the white on your canvas. Set the Tolerance to 1 in the Magic Wand Options Palette.

7. Invert the selection by choosing Select -> Inverse.

8. Create a new Layer by clicking the New Layer icon at the bottom of the Layers Palette.

9. Fill your selection with a light blue or whatever color you feel best represents water drops.

10. Choose Layer -> Effects -> Bevel and Emboss. Set the Style to Inner Bevel, with a Depth of 7. Hit OK. Figure 8–15 shows a sample, and Figure 8–16 and Color Figure 43) show how this sample can be used to make an object look wet.

I changed the blend mode on the droplet Layer to Overlay to give the impression that the drops were really lying on top of the object. I also used the Smudge Tool to make the drops seem to streak down the glass and added a slight drop shadow.

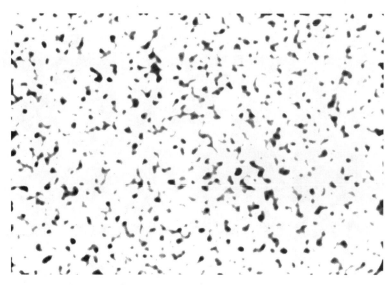

Figure 8–14: By manipulating the Levels on my noise-filled canvas, I've created areas of shapes which resemble water droplets.

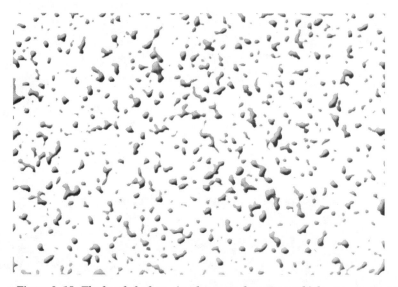

Figure 8–15: The beveled edges give the water drops some thickness.

Creating a Realistic Wave or Flag

Creating a wave or flag is easy enough, once you get used to the Wave Filter. The trick to making it look realistic, however, is in placing the proper shadows. It's not so much of a trick or an effect as it is using your artistic eye.

Figure 8–16: The water droplets, when used with the proper Blend Mode, make my glass and lime appear to be wet.

1. Open a horizontal image, such as the one that I am using in Figure 8–17. Make sure that the image is on its own Layer, not the Background Layer.

2. If your image takes up the entire window, as mine does, give it some extra room by choosing Image -> Canvas size and increasing space on all sides by a few inches (depending on the size and resolution of your original image).

3. Choose Filter -> Distort -> Wave to access the dialog box shown in Figure 8–18.

4. Reduce the Horizontal Scale to 0% (not totally necessary—I just don't like the horizontal wave too much).

5. Keep the Number of Generators low, around 7, and manipulate the Wavelength and Amplitude until you achieve a nice, even wave. Unfortunately, no two waves will be alike, especially considering any size differences between my image and your own. So it would be pointless to tell you what values to use. Click OK when through. The wave on my image is shown in Figure 8–19.

6. Create a selection of your wave by <Command> (<Ctrl> in Windows) + clicking on the Layer that it resides on.

7. Create a new Layer directly above the wave Layer.

8. Use the Airbrush Tool with a large, soft-edged brush to paint the sides of your waves with black. Deselect your selection.

9. Reduce the Opacity of your Layer so that your shadow isn't so intrusive and looks more realistic.

10. Create another Layer below the wave and, once again, use the Airbrush Tool to create a shadow, this time underneath. As the final image in Figure 8–20 and Color Figure 44 shows, it's important to remember that the shadow under the "up" part of the wave will be lighter than the shadow under the "down" part of the wave.

Figure 8–17: I'll use this vertical strip of baseball images to make into a wave.

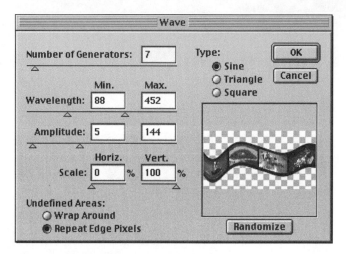

Figure 8–18: The Wave dialog box.

Figure 8–19: The wave created by my filter settings.

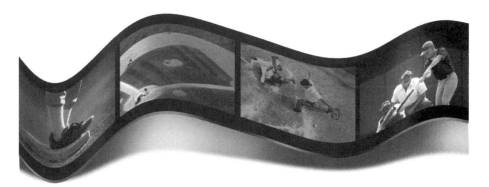

Figure 8–20: After adding the appropriate highlights and shadows, the wave finally looks realistic.

Lighting Effects Bevels

Chapter 4 reviewed some of the Layer Effects and how they can be used to create bevels for any object on a Layer. These have become very popular for all sorts of projects, in particular, as buttons for Web sites. However, there are alternative methods for creating bevels which may provide a different if not more realistic effect. This particular method utilizes the Lighting Effects Filter (try using this in conjunction with the Brushed Metal effect texture described later in this chapter).

1. Create a new canvas, 5" x 5", 72 ppi, RGB color.

2. Set your foreground to a rich shade of blue and your background color to bright red.

3. With the gradient tool, create a diagonal gradient from the top left corner to the bottom right.

4. Choose the Type Mask Tool and type "Text Fun" in a Helvetica or Arial typeface at a font size of 75 points. (This effect tends to look better with san serif font types.) Click OK and center your type selection. Notice that while Photoshop ordinarily places text on its own Layer and preserves the components, this does not hold true for the selection text. Selection text is placed on the active Layer and does not retain information for editing.

5. Choose Select -> Feather and set the feather radius to 3. Hit OK. Your text selection now looks a little round at the edges.

6. Choose Select -> Save Selection to bring up the dialogue box. For Channel, choose New and name it if you'd like. If you don't name it, it will automatically be called *Alpha 1*.

7. Choose Filter -> Render -> Lighting Effects. Figure 8–21 shows the Lighting Effects Filter, one of the most interesting but more complex filters that Photoshop provides for you.

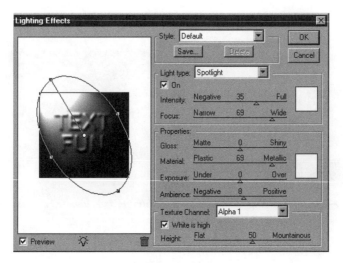

Figure 8–21: The Lighting Effects dialog box.

8. With the Lighting Style set to Default and the Light Type set to Spotlight, choose Alpha 1 as your texture Channel. The preview window will show the emboss effect on your text.

9. Turn the light source so that the spotlight is shining down from a northwesterly direction, giving your text a more universal shadow style. Make sure that the spotlight area is wide enough that none of your text is lost in dark shadows. Click OK.

10. Your image now looks similar to Figure 8–22. For a deeper emboss, go back to step 6, and, immediately after, use the arrow keys to move your selection down about six spaces. The result will be similar to Figure 8–23, and Color Figure 45 adds some dimension to your image.

TEXTURES

Textures are largely used for the creation of backgrounds, particularly those found in Web sites. However, another popular function of the following textures is as bump maps for 3D modeling programs. These textures and others like them make great mountain sides, foreign object texture, or even alien skin!

Rock or Paper Bag Texture (You Decide)

1. Create a new canvas, 5" x 5", 72 ppi, RGB color.

Figure 8–22: The result of the Lighting Effects Filter on a feathered selection saved as a Channel is a realistic bevel.

Figure 8–23: Moving the selection just before running the filter makes the bevel even deeper.

2. With black and white as your Foreground and Background colors, choose Filter -> Clouds. Keep, hitting <Command + F> (<Ctrl + F> in Windows) to redo the filter until you get clouds that have a good amount of contrasting areas, such as in Figure 8–24.

Figure 8–24: The effects of the Clouds Filter.

3. Save your file as a Photoshop format, named *Clouds*.

4. Fill your canvas with a light brown/beige color.

5. Choose Filter -> Texture -> Texturizer to access the dialog box shown in Figure 8–25. Choose Load Texture and select the file named *Clouds*. Set the scaling to 100%, and experiment with the Relief control (depending on how your clouds looked and the exact shade of brown that you chose, the exact amount of relief you'll need will vary). The preview window should show your brown plane as having crinkles in it. Hit OK. Figure 8–26 shows the result.

Wood Texture

1. Create a new canvas, 5" x 5", 72 ppi, RGB color.

2. Choose Filter -> Noise -> Add Noise.

3. Set the Noise Level to 210, with either distribution choice. Click OK, and your canvas looks like a TV with no reception.

4. Choose Filter -> Blur -> Motion Blur, set the angle to zero, the distance to 39 pixels, and hit OK (Figure 8–27).

5. Save your file somewhere you can easily find it as a Photoshop format, with a simple name such as *Noise*. Do not close the canvas.

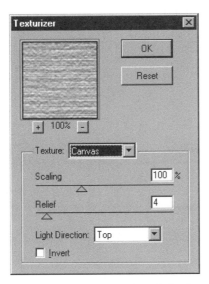

Figure 8–25: The Texturizer dialog box.

Figure 8–26: The result of using the Cloud image we created as a texture.

6. From either the Swatches Palette or the Color Picker, choose a light brown color for your Foreground color.

Figure 8–27: The result of using a Motion Blur Filter on a canvas filled with noise.

7. Fill your canvas with your color, by clicking <Option + Delete> (<Alt + Backspace> in Windows).

8. Choose Filter -> Texture -> Texturizer to access the dialog box. Choose Load Texture from the Texture pull-down menu.

9. Locate the file *Noise* that you saved earlier, and hit Open.

10. Keep the Scaling value at 100%, but experiment with the Relief slider: a higher relief for deeper grooves in the wood, lower for less of an effect. (In this example, I used a Relief of 36). Figure 8–28 shows the canvas. Due to the way the Blur filter works, you may see some discoloration on the sides of your image. If so, use the Crop Tool to cut the sides away.

TEXT EFFECTS

There are a million ways that you can play with text to make it seem to pop off the page. Even though the Photoshop Text Editor is not (and likely never will be) anything to get overly excited about, the following effects will provide your Photoshop text with more life than you thought possible.

Bubbled Text

The 3D Transform Filter is one of the coolest filters added in version 5.0. Although it is a bit clunky (mark my words, future Photoshop versions will undoubtedly add improvements

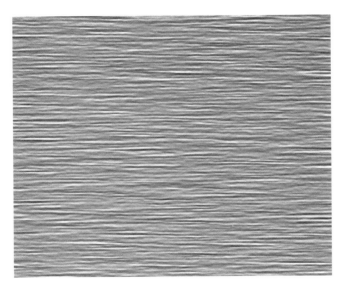

Figure 8–28: My final wood texture.

to this filter), it can still do some pretty amazing things. Mostly meant for changing perspectives of 2D images, such as a picture of a box of cereal or a soup can), this effect can manipulate text in some neat ways, as well.

1. Open a new canvas, 5" x 5", 72 ppi.

2. With a Type Tool, type *Bubble* and center it on your canvas.

3. Choose Layer -> Type -> Render Layer.

4. Select the letters by <Command> (<Ctrl> in Windows) + Clicking on the text Layer in the Layer Palette. Save your selection as a channel.

5. Deselect all and choose Filter -> Render -> 3D Transform to access the palette shown in Figure 8–29.

6. Using the Sphere Tool, create a sphere around part of the letters. Use the Trackball Tool and rotate the sphere upward, just a bit. Hit OK.

7. Erase the bottom of the sphere, as seen in Figure 8–30.

8. Create a new Layer, in between the Background and your text Layer. Load the Alpha Channel you created earlier.

9. Choose Select -> Feather and feather your image by 4 pixels. Fill it with black.

10. Lower the opacity on your Layer to around 30% and move your shadow just a little off center. The final image is shown in Figure 8–31.

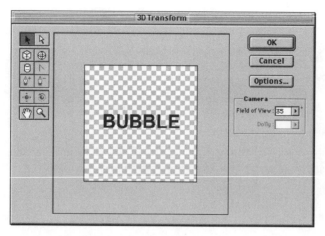

Figure 8–29: The 3D Transform Filter.

Figure 8–30: The result of using the 3D Transform Filter—you'll need to erase the bottom of the sphere.

Figure 8–31: The letters in your text seem to really bubble up when an off-center shadow is placed underneath.

Neon Text

This effect doesn't have to be limited to just text—try it with anything you can create an outline around.

1. Open a new canvas, 5" x 5", 72 ppi.
2. Use the Type Mask Tool to write *NEON*, nice and large.
3. Choose Select -> Feather and set the feather radius to 3 to soften the edges.
4. Fill your selection with black. It will look similar to Figure 8–32. Deselect all.
5. With black and white as your foreground and background color, choose Filter -> Render -> Difference Clouds. Your canvas will look like Figure 8–33.
6. Choose Image -> Adjust -> Invert.
7. Overlay any color (by filling a higher Layer and changing the Blend Mode to Overlay) and your image will look similar to Color Figure 46.

Figure 8–32: My feathered letters filled with black.

Figure 8–33: My canvas after filling it with Difference Clouds. Notice how the word **Neon** *is affected.*

Fire Text

Use this technique when working with a dark background, as it requires white, or at least very light subject matter to create the flames correctly.

1. Open a new file that is 5" x 5", 72 ppi, RGB color.

2. Fill the background with black.

3. Use the type tool to place the word *FIRE* in the center of the canvas. Use white for the letters.

4. Flatten your image and choose Image -> Rotate Canvas -> 90 degrees CW to turn your image 1/4 turn to the right.

5. Choose Filter -> Stylize -> Wind for the dialog box shown in Figure 8–34. Choose Wind for the method and From the Right for the direction. Hit OK.

6. Hit <Command + F> (<Ctrl + F> in Windows) twice to redo the last filter and exaggerate the effect of the filter.

7. Rotate your canvas 90 degrees CCW, back to its original position.

8. Select Filter -> Blur -> Motion Blur. Set the angle to 59 degrees with a Distance of 4 pixels, and hit OK.

9. Choose Filter -> Distort -> Ripple and maintain the default settings. Hit OK. Your canvas will look similar to Figure 8–35.

10. Add a new Layer, and fill it with a bright yellow. Change the Layer Mode to Overlay. Add another Layer and fill it with bright red. Change this Layer's mode also to Overlay. The final image is shown in Figure 8–6.

Figure 8–34: The Wind Filter dialog box.

Figure 8–35: The Motion Blur and Ripple Filters really start to give the fire some shape.

Ice Text

By making just a few changes to the Fire example, we can achieve an effect that is equal in realism, but opposite in subject matter.

1. Open a new file that is 5" x 5", 72 ppi, RGB color.
2. Fill the background with black.
3. Use the Type Tool to place the word *ICE* in the center of the canvas. Choose a sky, icy blue color for the letters.
4. Flatten your image and choose Image -> Rotate Canvas -> 90 degrees CW to turn your image 1/4 turn to the right.
5. Choose Filter -> Stylize -> Wind. Choose Wind for the method, and From the Left for the direction. Hit OK.
6. With the Wind effect, you're going to be placing your icicles, so hit <Command + F> (<Ctrl + F> in Windows) two or three more times or until your icicles are as long as you'd like them.
7. Rotate your canvas 90 degrees CCW to its original position.
8. Choose Filter -> Brush Strokes -> Accented Edges for the dialog box in Figure 8–36. Set the Edge Width to 2, the Edge Brightness to 39 and the Smoothness to 5.
9. Create a new Layer and, with the Airbrush Tool, brush randomly over the text, as shown in Figure 8–37. Make sure that you have white as your Foreground color, and choose a brush size around 35 pixels. When through, set the Layer Mode to overlay. Color Figure 48 shows the final image.

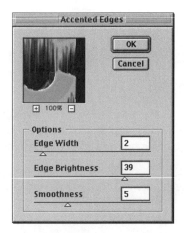

Figure 8–36: The Accented Edges dialog box.

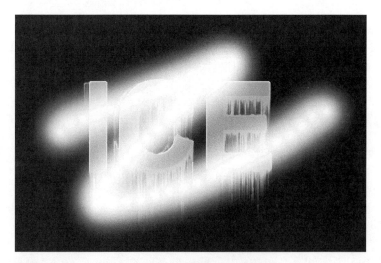

Figure 8–37: Airbrush white over the blue icy letters.

3D Moving Text—Forward and Backward

Making text look as though it has a 3D effect in Photoshop is hardly one of life's most difficult challenges. There are any number of ways to do it, and each has been done over and over again by designers looking to add a little dimension to their print and Web projects. This time, I've added a bit of a twist to the dimension, to give the illusion that the text is moving at full force—either forward or backward, depending on your need.

To create this effect, do the following:

1. Use a thick, bolded font to write your word. For the sake of this example, I'm just using the word *TEXT* in all caps.

2. The copy will appear in its own text Layer, so that you can go back and edit it later on in life. Great feature, but counterproductive for this effect. We'll need to play with filters, which don't work on text Layers. To fix this, render the Layer by choosing Layer -> Render -> Type. This will allow you to use filters, but your days of editing this particular copy are done, so make sure you spelled everything correctly.

3. Create a new Layer over the Layer you just rendered.

4. Make a selection of your text by <Command> (<Ctrl> in Windows) + clicking on the Layer that holds your text.

5. Expand the selection by choosing Select -> Modify -> Expand. Fill in a value that would bring your selection out just a bit without overdoing it (this value will change, depending on whether your canvas is hi-res or low-res).

6. With black as your foreground color, stroke your selection by choosing Edit -> Stroke. Fill in a Stroke value, again depending on the resolution of your canvas. Figure 8–38 shows my image at this point. I had stroked my selection with a width of 5 pixels (my canvas is 200 ppi).

7. Okay, here's where the filters come in. Make sure you have everything deselected, and, with your stroked outline Layer still active, choose Filter -> Blur -> Radial Blur. From the dialog box, choose Zoom, and set a relatively high Amount value. Figure 8–39 shows my image.

8. If you wanted to, you could stop at this point—it actually looks pretty good. But if we continue, we can make it look even better. Activate the original text Layer by clicking on it. Choose Filter -> Distort -> Spherize, and set the amount at 100%, the maximum value. Hit OK.

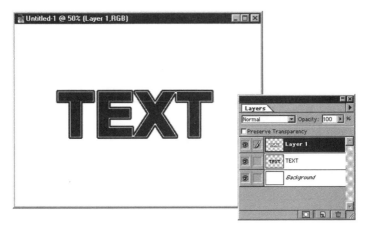

Figure 8–38: My stroke is on is own Layer, ready to manipulated.

Figure 8–39: The Radial Blur applied to my stroke Layer.

9. Activate the Layer with the stroked outline, and choose the same filter. To make the text look like it's coming forward, set the Spherize amount to 50%, half the amount of the actual text. Figure 8–40 shows what this looks like. To make the text look like it's moving backward, set the Spherize amount to 100%, the same as you did for the actual text. Then use Free Transform to make the results just a bit larger. Figure 8–41 shows the result.

Figure 8–40: The letters moving forward.

Figure 8–41: The letters moving backward.

Rock On, or Stoned Text

There is something about stone that can have a dramatic effect in art. It's not exactly the easiest effect to pull off, and as a challenge to myself I am in a perpetual state of trying to improve my rock effect on text whenever I have a free moment (I don't date very often…). I'll probably continue to try to perfect my graphic stone imagery, but the example I'll provide here is pretty good, I think.

1. Before you even lay out your text, open a new document. Keep the resolution low—this part of the effect works better with lower resolutions—but make the physical size large if you plan on creating your final image in hi-res.

2. Complete directions 1-3 in the section called "Rock or Paper Bag Texture (You Decide)," found earlier in this chapter.

3. With a new canvas, at whatever resolution you desire, set your text in a light gray color (to emulate stone). Again, for the sake of example, I'm using the word *TEXT* in all caps. I'd recommend using a serif font, since it tends to look better with stone textures.

4. Render the text Layer as we did in the last example so that we can use a filter on it.

5. Make some of the edges of the text rougher by choosing Filter -> Ripple. Set the Amount to a medium level and hit OK.

6. Ok, we're ready to add the preliminary stone texture. Choose Filter -> Texturize -> Texturizer and from the pull-down menu choose Load Texture. Find your *smoke.psd* file that you made earlier, and select that. Raise the Relief to a value of 47 or 48 in the Texturizer dialog box, and hit OK. If you can't see the stone texture on your letters like I have it in Figure 8–42, then go back and raise the relief to an even higher level.

Figure 8–42: The stone texture applied to my letters.

7. Give your words some perspective by using the Free Transform function. This part is not an absolute necessity—after all, you can certainly look at stone head on—but the perspective will help to provide an added dimension later that makes the effect look more realistic. I've just used a slight perspective and skew on my text, as shown in Figure 8–43.

Figure 8–43: Giving perspective will help add realism to your text later on.

8. The texture that you've placed should give you a good map of high and low areas. Use the Burn and Dodge Tools to give the effect of prominence in these areas. The Burn Tool will add shadows in some areas (they are sloping downward), and the Dodge Tool will add highlights to areas that should be higher up. You shouldn't have to go to heavy on this—just a touch here and there.

9. Add some more texture to the stone by using the most useless tool Photoshop has to offer—at least useless for its expressed purpose. The Sharpen Tool is a big waste of time—rarely does it have any positive effect when you are trying to sharpen an image. But it does a great job of adding extra stone texture to letters. Figure 8–44 shows an example close up of how the letters are affected by this tool being used in certain areas.

10. From the Layers Palette submenu, duplicate your text Layer, and, with the Move Tool, drag the stone text up a little (hold the <Shift> key while dragging to make sure you drag straight). Don't drag too far—just enough so that the text in the underlying Layer can be seen.

11. Make your original text Layer (the underlying Layer) active by clicking on it. Fill the text with a darker gray than the original shade you chose, and re-apply the stone texture, using the texturizer as we did earlier. By doing this, you're allowing the stone texture on this lower area to be straight up and down, rather than the perspective that we applied before. This is important in adding any kind of dimension.

Use the Burn and Dodge Tools to make the rock base on this Layer even darker and the paintbrush to touch up any spots that might need it. Add a drop shadow for even more realism, like my final image in Figure 8–45.

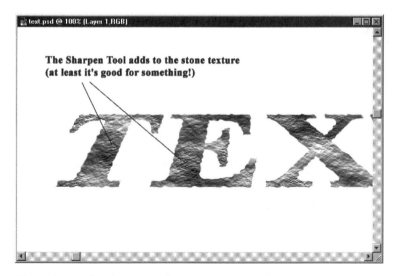

Figure 8–44: The Sharpen Tool can actually be useful!

Figure 8–45: My final stone letters.

CREATING A COLLAGE

Of course, creating collages is probably one of the reasons that you started using Photoshop in the first place. Making one image blend with another image can provide some of the greatest creative release that you'll have with Photoshop, so don't be afraid to pile on the pictures.

1. Open two images, such as the ones that I have open in Figure 8–46. For the sake of convenience, I've labeled them *Picture 1* and *Picture 2*.

Figure 8–46: The two pictures I'll use for my collage. The photo on the left will be called **Picture 1,** *while the photo on the right will be called* **Picture 2.**

2. Move Picture 2 onto Picture 1's canvas. It will be placed on its own Layer. Name this Layer *Picture 2*.

3. Depending on the size of your images, and what you want to do with the collage, you might want to resize your image a bit. In my example, I want to image of the eagle in Picture 2 to be significantly larger than it currently is. To resize the image upward, push <Command + T> (<Ctrl + T> in Windows) to access the Free Transform functions. You'll see the bounding box around Picture 2.

4. Drag one of the corner handle bars outward while holding the <Shift> key (for proportional constraint) to make the image larger. When through, press the <Return> key (<Enter> in Windows) to accept the transformation.

In Chapter 6, we learned that making things larger usually has a negative effect—you're asking Photoshop to provide pixel information that is not available, usually leaving your image blurry. But in this example, we went against that rule and made Picture 1 larger with the Free Transform function. The reason for that is that everything exists in moderation—while it's generally not advised as a rule to make things larger, you can usually get away with minor size increases without seeing any visible negative effects.

5. Drag the Layer marked *Picture 2 to* the Add Layer Mask button at the bottom of the Layers Palette.

6. As we learned in Chapter 5, while we are in Layer Mask Mode, the foreground and background revert to black and white, respectively, and the brush tools change their function. Choose the Gradient Tool, and make a straight gradient from white to black (hold the <Shift> key for gradient restraint). The effect, you'll notice, is

Figure 8–47: The final collage and its respective Layers Palette.

a different effect than what happened in Chapter 5, when we simply painted with either black or white. As Figure 8–47 and Color Figure 49 show, the image of the eagle in Picture 2 disappears gradually from the top to the bottom. I also moved the image and the mask up a bit, so that the Statue of Liberty could be seen better. Pretty majestic, huh?

This is because, by using the Gradient Tool, we are distributing the black pixels slowly over the course of the image. As we saw in Chapter 5, when we painted with black in a Layer Mask, we expanded the mask and hid the image. When we painted with white, we reduced the mask and exposed the image. When we use the Gradient tool, however, we're no longer working strictly 100% white or 100% black. Instead, by creating a gradient from black to white, we introduce shades of gray. As the gray gets darker along the gradient, the mask expands in that same amount. For example, toward the bottom of the mask, where there is 80% black and 20% white, there is an 80% mask, but 20% of the image is still visible.

As you can see by the final image, Layer Masks allow you to create collage effects in which one image fades into another. By creatively using Layers, multiple images, and Layer masks, you can create any number of interesting collages.

SUMMARY

While some purists will scoff at the idea of using filters in their work (apparently filters make design too easy), the truth is that for most of us, we're here to work, not just to play. And the bottom line is that filters make life not only easier and faster, but they make it better. And they can be fun to use! The hardest part is opening your imagination and just keep applying one filter after the next. There is never any end to the effects you can create, and a little trial and error with filters can go a long way!

appendix A

LAYER EFFECTS

As we saw in Chapter 4, there are a total of 10 individual Layer Effects that you can apply to any Layer of your image (except the Background—Layer Effects don't work on the Background Layer). This Appendix will review each effect one at a time, review ways that you can combine them together for added creativity, then discuss other important factoids about the effects that you'll need to know.

A DESCRIPTION OF EACH EFFECT

You create your effects through dialog boxes that you access either by clicking on the Layer Effects shortcut pop-up menu at the bottom of the Layers Palette or by choosing Layer -> Layer Style -> [desired effect]. From within any of the dialog boxes, you can easily access any other Layer Effect so that you can quickly apply more than one to your image. Figure A–1 shows the Drop Shadow dialog box to illustrate how you can apply multiple effects. On the far left of all effect dialog boxes is a list of all available Layer Effects, each with its own checkbox. Click the checkbox of another effect to apply the default settings for that effect to your image. Click the name of the effect to open the dialog box for that effect for more control in setting the variables.

The remainder of this section will concentrate on illustrating and explaining each Layer Effect. For illustrative purposes, we'll use the simple image in Figure A–2 for a base image to apply the setting to. The words *Layer Effects* exist in their own Layer, directly above the Background Layer, as you can see in the Layers Palette that accompanies the image in the figure.

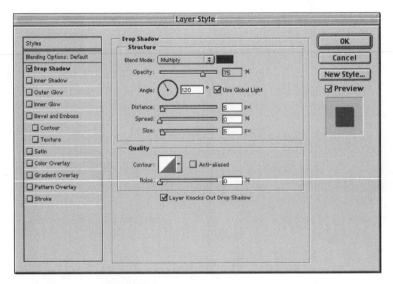

Figure A–1: Drop Shadow dialog box.

LAYER
EFFECTS

Figure A–2: Our base image.

 PLEASE READ THIS NOTE!!! Some of the values and setting areas in one dialog box appear in other dialog boxes. To save time and make this an efficient Appendix, I'll describe each value or setting only once—the first time that it appears. So it may be a good idea to read this particular area straight through, instead of jumping from one effect to another.

Drop Shadow and Inner Shadow

The Shadow Effects are two of the more useful Layer Effects. They let you quickly create shadows behind or inside any object on a Layer to give your image more depth.

The dialog boxes for both the Drop Shadow and Inner Shadow Effects look exactly the same, as is illustrated in Figure A–3. Even though the settings and value input areas are the same, the result is quite different.

The dialog boxes are fairly self-explanatory, each having the following setting and value areas:

Blend Mode

This is the same Blend Mode that we reviewed in Chapter 5. The Blend Mode you choose will change the way the Effect that you're placing interacts with any underlying color. The default Blend Mode is usually a pretty good choice, so unless you are seeking some type of special effect, there's rarely a need to change it.

Opacity

The Opacity slider and value area lets you select how opaque you wish your shadow to be. The higher the value, the more opaque—the lower the value, the more transparent.

Angle

The Angle value lets you set the direction of your light source. You can set it to the exact degree by filling in the value area manually, or you can drag the compass pointer for a more visual setting. For the maximum visual setting, move your cursor off the dialog box and onto the canvas. Click and drag to place the shadow in the desired location.

Use Global Light

One of the smartest features about Layer Effects is that they will keep the light sources consistent for you if you keep the Use Global Light box checked on. This means that if you set the light source for an object on Layer 1 (for example) at 130 degrees, so that the shadow is cast to the lower right, then any effect that you place on an object in Layer 2 will also be effected by that same light source, so that the effects are consistent. If you change the angle of light on Layer Two to -41 degrees, the shadow that was placed on Layer 1 will automatically adjust to these new settings.

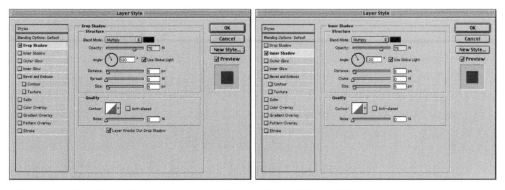

Figure A–3: The dialog boxes for Drop Shadow and Inner Shadow Effects..

Distance

You can decide how far away from your object a shadow will be cast by either manually entering the data or using the slider, or by just dragging the shadow, like we did when we set the Angle.

The further away your shadow is from your object, the lighter or more transparent it should be for a realistic effect. Make sure you appropriately adjust the opacity to work with the shadow distance. You might also consider increasing the size, which we'll read about in this section.

Spread (Drop Shadow) or Choke (Inner Shadow)

Setting higher values for both the spread and choke will create harder edges on your shadows, while simultaneously expanding the shadows outward. The expansion of ink in this way helps for setting traps when necessary a full discussion on traps can be found in *Digital Publishing To Go*.

Size

In older versions of Photoshop that had Layer Effects, the size was more appropriately named *Blur*. Set a higher value to make a blurrier shadow.

Quality

Check in and see how this works.

Figure A–4 gives a few samples of Drop Shadow and Inner Shadows, along with their relative settings.

Inner and Outer Glows

Eh. Better glow effects can be created manually. The Outer Glow effect typically works better and is more realistic when on a dark background. It's supposed to create a natural glow in and/or around your object, but they're really nothing to get excited about.

Figure A–5 shows the dialog boxes for both the Inner Glow and Outer Glow. As you can see, with the exception of one additional area within the Structure section for Inner Shadow, the dialog boxes are basically the same.

The Glow dialog boxes have the following settings:

In case you didn't read the important note earlier in this Appendix, let me repeat it now: Any settings that appear in these dialog boxes that also exist in the previous dialog boxes that we've already reviewed (the Drop Shadow and Inner Shadow) will not be repeated here.

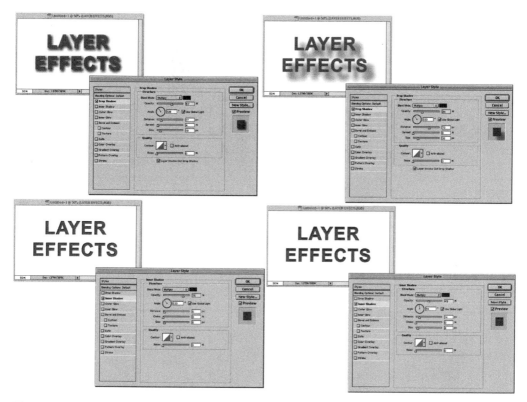

Figure A–4: Some samples of drop shadows with their respective settings.

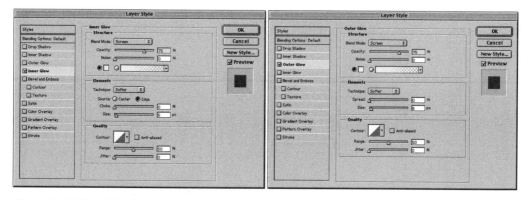

Figure A–5: The dialog boxes for Inner Glow and Outer Glow.

Noise

A handy little slide bar to include in the Layer Effects, this slider is a miniversion of the Noise Filter. Increasing the value will increase the amount of noise or grain that appear in your glows.

The Color Picker/Gradient Bar

Use the radio buttons to select whether you want your glow to be a solid color or to gradate out to transparency. Clicking on the color swatch will access the Color Picker so that you can choose whichever color you would like for your glow, while using the pull-down menu for the Gradient bar will allow you to manipulate the colors and extremities of your gradated glow.

Making a Better Outer Glow

Since the glows really kind of suck, I'm not going to bother making a sample to show but use some space instead for describing how to make a better glow manually. You can make a better glow than the one that you can create from the Outer Glow Layers effects. Dark backgrounds will still work best, however, as "glowing" kind of requires a contrast in color in order to be seen. But you can still gain more realism through alternate methods:

1. If you've been playing with different Layer Effects as you've been reading through this Appendix, clear them by choosing Layer -> Effects -> Clear Effects.
2. Make the Background Layer active by clicking on it.
3. Fill it with black so that the glow can be seen more distinctly.
4. Create a new Layer by pushing the New Layer button at the bottom of the Layers Palette.
5. With your new Layer active, create a selection of the type on the uppermost Layer. Use the method that was presented in the section "Making Selections from Layers," back in Chapter 5.
6. Choose Select -> Modify -> Expand. In the dialog box, fill in 5 in the value area and press OK.
7. Choose Select -> Feather and set the feather radius to 6. Press OK.
8. Fill your selection with a light color, preferably a white or yellow. Figure A–6 gives an example of what this looks like. You can manipulate the brightness of the glow by adjusting the Opacity of the Layer (see "Layer Properties" in Chapter 5). You can also use the Move Tool to place the glow off center if you wish.

Try making the words a darker color. It'll make the glow that much more powerful.

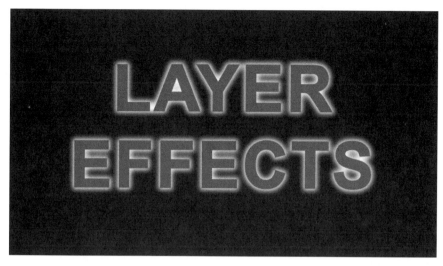

Figure A–6: You can create better outer glows yourself, without the Layer Effects.

Bevel and Emboss

Now THIS is a fun one—probably the most useful of all the Layer Effects. By giving you the option between four different types of bevel and emboss effects, you can use this feature to really add some dimension to your imagery. It does this by adding a highlight and shadow to the edges of your object. Figure A–7 shows the dialog box you'll use when creating a bevel and/or emboss effect.

There are several options that can be found in the Bevel and Emboss dialog box.

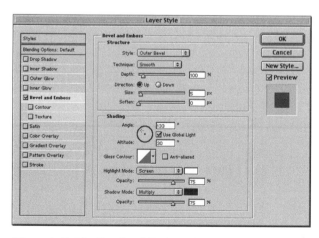

Figure A–7: The Bevel and Emboss dialog box.

Style

The drop-down menu lets you choose which type of bevel or emboss effect you want to use: Inner Bevel, Outer Bevel, Emboss or Pillow Emboss.

Technique

These three options give you some flexibility as to how the level or emboss is built.

Depth

Use this value area to determine how extreme your bevel or emboss effect will be. This is similar in nature to the Depth slider and value in previous versions of Photoshop, but with one major improvement: Earlier versions measured the bevel or emboss depth by pixels, with 20 pixels being the maximum setting. This didn't accomplish much for hi-res work. In this newer version, though, the depth is measured by percentage, and more extreme bevels and embosses can be created.

Use the drop-down menu next to the Depth slider to decide whether your bevel or emboss should be up (coming off your canvas) or down (going into your canvas). You can also do this by setting the angle of light, as we did with the Drop Shadow and Inner Shadow, to be coming from the lower right. Typically, when people see the darker bevels on the bottom and right, they perceive it as coming "up" off the canvas. When the darker bevels are on the top and left of the object, it's perceived to be pushing "down" into the canvas. Don't ask me why—I did as well in psych class as I did in accounting. Figure A–8 gives a few Bevel and Emboss examples.

NEW LAYER EFFECTS IN VERSION 6.0

Version 6.0 has come with a few new Layer Effects that weren't available in previous versions of the program. Although altogether an unremarkable set of new offerings, some of them may be at least a little beneficial to certain projects. Each of these can be accessed by using the Layer Effects button at the bottom of the Layers Palette.

Satin

As it sounds, this effect is meant to give the objects on a Layer a "satiny" feel by manipulating interior shadows, based on the shape of the objects. Figure A–9 provides a sample.

Color Overlay and Gradient Overlay

Both of these are so extraneous that I'm not going to even bother showing examples. Basically, the Color Overlay allows you to fill in the objects on your Layer with any color and set your Blend Mode from the same dialog box. The Gradient Overlay does pretty much the same thing, but with a gradient instead of a solid color. No big deal

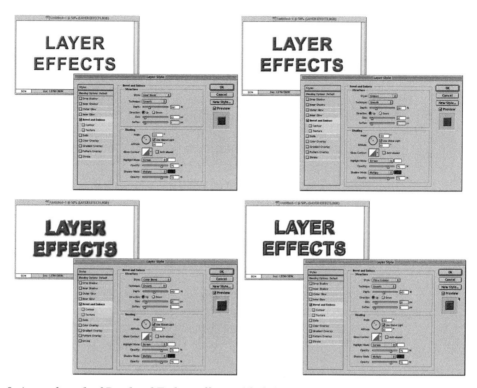

Figure A–8: A sample each of Bevel and Emboss effects, with their respective settings.

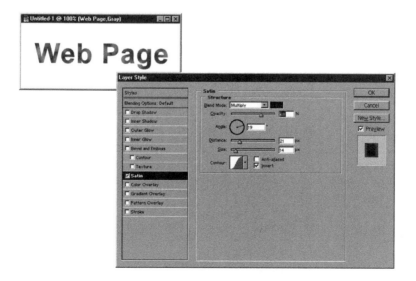

Figure A–9: Satin provides the objects on a Layer with a satiny feel.

here—just a bit of a time saver from how you might have otherwise filled in a color or a gradient without these features.

Pattern Overlay

The Pattern Overlay stands out mostly because of the preset patterns available and the ability to scale them instantly within the given objects. The dialog box shown in Figure A–10 shows a fairly simple number of options, with the main focus being on the Pattern drop-down menu, which allows you to choose from preset patterns or save your own custom pattern, and the Scale slider, which lets you adjust the pattern within the Layer objects.

Stroke

This one is actually really cool. The ordinary Stroke function, accessed by choosing Edit -> Stroke, allows you the bare minimum of control over any stroke you make. Besides the Blend Mode, you can pretty much just choose the color, pixel width and position of your stroke (inside, outside or center). But the Stroke Layer Effect gives you complete control over the strokes that you create.

You can use a slider to see how any particular stroke width will affect the Layer in question—a far cry from the Edit -> Stroke way, which lets you fill in one numeric value, hit OK and hope for the best. Better yet, the Fill Type drop-down menu lets you instantly access the Gradient Fill and the Pattern Fill and apply one or the other of them to the stroke itself. The example in Figure A–11 shows a stroke with a gradient fill applied to it.

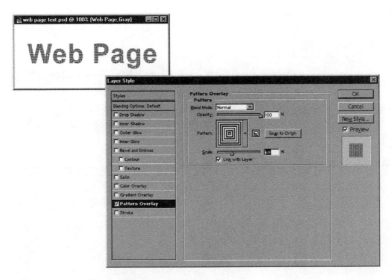

Figure A–10: The Pattern Overlay dialog box.

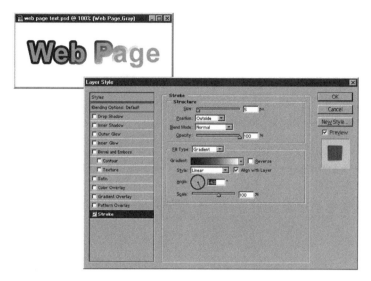

Figure A–11: The Stroke dialog box.

LAYER EFFECT FUNCTIONALITY

There is more to know about Layer Effects than the effects themselves. Photoshop provides you ways to make them easier to work with from a functionality and efficiency standpoint.

Working with Individual Effects

One of the better innovations in Photoshop 6.0 is the way the Layers Palette treats Layer Effects. Instead of just showing a small white "f" in a black circle on a Layer, Photoshop 6 provides each effect on its own individual sublayer. The sublayers are collapsible by clicking the small arrow next to the traditional "f" in a circle icon, and each effect can be thrown out or made invisible, independent of each other.

To change the settings for any particular effect, just double-click the effect's sublayer.

Separating Layer Effects

You'll notice as you work with Layer Effects that the effect takes place and resides on the same Layer as your object—in other words, the effect has become part of the Layer itself. This is unlike the result that would occur if you created the effect by hand.

The obvious benefit is that, when you create an effect such as a drop shadow manually, you have greater flexibility. You can manipulate it in ways that Layer Effects don't allow, such as skewing it, giving it perspective or masking it.

Well, nobody has ever accused those Photoshop developers of being anything less than brilliant. Because of the occasional need to work with the effect features, apart from the original object, they have provided the way to do that.

To separate the effects into individual Layers:

1. Activate a Layer that has a Layer Effect on it.
2. Choose Layer -> Effects -> Create Layers.

Or just right-click on the Effect Layer that you want to make into its own Layer, and choose the appropriate option from the pop-up menu.

Copying and Pasting Effects

Often, you'll want to use the same settings over and over again on different Layers. For example, let's say that we have a situation like the one we see on the left in Figure A–20. The square on Layer 1 has an inner bevel effect on it. We want the same exact effects— same settings and everything, to also apply to the circle on Layer 2 and the triangle on Layer 3.

It would be inefficient to activate each Layer individually and have to redo all of the settings for each object. Instead, just do the following:

1. Activate Layer 1.
2. Choose Layer -> Effects -> Copy Effects
3. Activate Layer 2.
4. Choose Layer -> Effects -> Paste Effects. You'll see that Layer 2 now has the same effects and settings as Layer 1.
5. Do the same for Layer 3. The right image in Figure A–12 shows the result.

Notice that the lower area of the Layer -> Effects menu also contains the option to Clear Effects, in case you decide that you no longer want to effects on any given Layer.

Pasting to Linked Layers

In the last example, we made life easier for ourselves by copying the effects from one Layer and pasting them onto each other Layer individually. In the case that we saw previously, we could have made life even easier, though, by instead doing the following:

1. Activate Layer 1.
2. Choose Layer -> Effects -> Copy Effects.

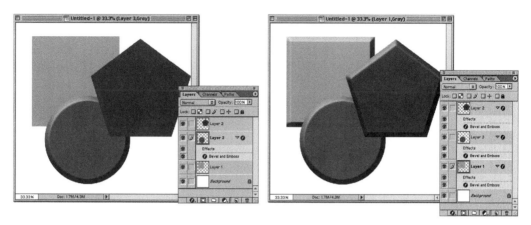

Figure A–12: Copying and Pasting Effects can make creating them multiple times quick and easy.

3. Link Layer 2 and 3 to Layer 1, as described in the "Linking Layers" section of Chapter 5.

4. Choose Layer -> Effects -> Paste Effects to Linked. The effects and settings paste onto each Layer in the link. Pretty convenient, huh?

Saving Styles

In older versions of Photoshop, if you had created a certain effect and wanted to save the variables that you had made to use again in the future, you'd pretty much have to resort to grabbing a paper and pen, and writing down the numeric values. With Photoshop 6.0, just click the Save Styles button on any of the Layer Effect dialog boxes, and provide your style with a name in the dialog box that appears. Very convenient!

SOME LAST, RAMBLING, GENERAL LAYER EFFECTS INFO

Even though that's really more on Layer Effects than I really had intended to provide, we've come this far, so we might as well finish it off. The following are just a few stray points that wouldn't be bad to keep in mind while working with Layer Effects:

◆ Once you merge a Layer that contains a Layer Effect with any other Layer, you will lose the ability to change the effect settings, copy the effects or clear the effects.

◆ The Layer Effects for all Layers work together in terms of lighting direction. If you have a drop shadow on one Layer that is cast down and to the right, it is assumed that there is a light source coming from the upper left that is needed to cast that particular shadow. Now, let's say that on another, completely independent Layer, we bevel an object and make the light source come from the lower right. Not only will that determine how that particular bevel is created, but it will also change the shadow that we were just talking about. That shadow will now be cast to the upper left, since the light source is coming from the lower right. Read that over again—you'll get it.

◆ If you want to change it so that the effects don't interact with one another, just click off the box marked *Use Global Settings* when you create your Layer Effect.

◆ Layer Effects are for the entire Layer, not just an individual object. That means that anything you put on or paint on a Layer with Layer Effects will also assume those same effects.

INDEX

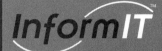